The Illusions of Egalitarianism

The Illusions of Egalitarianism

John Kekes

CORNELL UNIVERSITY PRESS

ITHACA AND LONDON

First published 2003 by Cornell University Press

Printed in the United States of America

Library of Congress Cataloging-in-Publication Data

Kekes, John.
    The illusions of egalitarianism / John Kekes.
        p. cm.
Includes bibliographical references and index.
    ISBN 0-8014-4190-0 (alk. paper)
    1. Equality.   2. Social justice.   3. Liberalism.   I. Title.
    HM821.K45 2003
    305--dc21   2003009503

Cornell University Press strives to use environmentally responsible suppliers and materials to the fullest extent possible in the publishing of its books. Such materials include vegetable-based, low-VOC inks and acid-free papers that are recycled, totally chlorine-free, or partly composed of nonwood fibers. For further information, visit our website at www.cornellpress.cornell.edu.

Cloth printing   10 9 8 7 6 5 4 3 2 1

for J. Y. K.
bis 120

Contents

Acknowledgments

A generous grant from the Earhart Foundation relieved me of teaching and administrative responsibilities for a whole year and made it possible to complete this book. I am very grateful to the officers of the Earhart Foundation for their past and present support of my work. I hope that this book will go some way to justify their confidence in me.

In the spring of 2002 I was Distinguished Visiting Lecturer at the University of Waterloo and presented an earlier version of chapters 1–5 in the form of lectures followed by extended discussion. I thank Jan Narveson for the invitation, for being my host, and for mixing the pleasures of music and philosophy. And I thank also the faculty and the students who attended, raised questions, and offered criticisms.

Nicholas Capaldi, Anthony O'Hear, James Ryan, and Lucas Swaine read the entire manuscript and offered helpful criticisms. I am indebted to them for interrupting their own work in order to help me do mine. I hasten to add that they bear no responsibility for the views I am defending and it should not be assumed that they agree with them.

My editor at Cornell University Press was once again Roger Haydon. His help, efficiency, encouragement, and good advice at every step along the way were more than I could hope for. It has been a pleasure to work with him over the years. He is all that an editor should be. I am deeply grateful to him.

In chapter 4 I use some material from chapter 6 of *Against Liberalism* (Ithaca: Cornell University Press, 1997). Chapter 8 has been published as an article in *Philosophy* 77 (2002): 503–17. Chapter 10 is a revised version of my contribution to *Morality, Reflection, and Ideology*, edited by E. R. F. Harcourt (Oxford: Oxford University Press, 2000).

Finally, in chapter 11 I borrow some ideas from chapter 8 of *A Case for Conservatism* (Ithaca: Cornell University Press, 1998).

I welcome communication from readers at jonkekes@nycap.rr.com.

J. K.

ITHAKA
Charlton, New York

The Politics of Illusions:
Introduction

Democratic nations are at all times fond of equality, but there are certain epochs at which the passion they entertain for it swells to the height of fury. . . . The passion . . . penetrates on every side into men's hearts, expands there, and fills them entirely. Tell them not that by this blind surrender of themselves to an exclusive passion, they risk their dearest interests; they are deaf. Show them not freedom escaping from their grasp, whilst they are looking another way: they are blind—or, rather, they can discern but one sole object to be desired in the universe.

ALEXIS DE TOCQUEVILLE, *Democracy in America*

1.1 The Illusions
This book is a criticism of the currently dominant version of liberalism. To distinguish it from other versions, we shall refer to it as *egalitarianism*, but its connection with liberalism is essential and it should be remembered. It should also be remembered that liberalism has non-egalitarian versions, although they will not be discussed here.

Perhaps the simplest statement of egalitarianism is that all human beings should be treated with equal consideration unless there are good reasons against it. This assumes that the initial presumption is in favor of equal consideration and it is departure from it that needs justification. It is a testimony to the current popularity of egalitarianism that many people regard this simple statement and the assumption on which it is based as truisms. But they are certainly not that, for a moment of thought gives rise to many serious questions about them.

Human beings differ in their characters, circumstances, talents and weaknesses, capacities and incapacities, virtues and vices; in their moral standing, political views, religious convictions, aesthetic preferences, and personal projects; in how reasonable or unreasonable they are, how well or badly they develop their native endowments,

1

how much they benefit or harm others, how hardworking or disciplined they were in the past and are likely to be in the future; and so forth. Given these manifold differences, why should the initial presumption favor equal, rather than unequal, treatment?

The questions mount when it is asked, as it must be, what are the respects in which equal consideration is assumed to be warranted? Clearly, parents should not treat their own and other people's children with equal consideration; people do not owe equal consideration to friends and strangers; governments betray their most elementary responsibility if they treat citizens and foreigners with equal consideration; a society would be self-destructive if it treated its moral and immoral, law-abiding and criminal, prudent and imprudent members with equal consideration. The questions grow in number and urgency when it is asked, as it must again be, what reasons are supposed to be good enough to justify unequal consideration? What differences among people would count against the initial presumption in favor of equal consideration? If differences in morality, reasonability, legality, and citizenship count, then very little remains of equal consideration, since there are great differences among people in these respects. And if these differences are not allowed to count, then how could it be justified to ignore them and treat people who differ in these respects with equal consideration?

These questions aim to show that the simple statement of egalitarianism is not the truism many people take it to be. If egalitarianism is to be defended, these questions, and others, must be answered. The criticisms of egalitarianism that will be advanced in this book aim to show that the answers that have been given by leading egalitarian thinkers are unacceptable. The truth is that egalitarianism is based on a cluster of overlapping illusions. They are comforting because if they were true, the world would be better, but they are nevertheless false. Believing them—even with as much passion as many egalitarians do—does not make them true, or our lives better. They falsify reality and prevent us from facing unpleasant and dangerous facts.

Here is a list of these illusions: more equality makes good lives more likely; responsibility holds only for intentional actions; justice requires the equalization of property; everyone ought to be treated with equal consideration; all human beings have equal moral worth; equal compassion for all is the basis of morality; it is immoral to have more than the basic necessities when others have less; equal freedom is the fundamental political value; political neutrality about the good should coexist with personal commitment to it; egalitarianism is the best defense of toleration; and the aim of political theory is to propound an ideal. By way of caution and explanation, it must be emphasized that this list is preliminary and will be refined; not all egalitarians hold all these illusions, although most hold most of them; some items on the list are inconsistent with others; the list is not meant to include all the illusions egalitarians may hold; and the aim of this book is to demonstrate, what is here merely asserted, that all these illusions are indeed false.

The world is a nasty place. War, disease, poverty, persecution, prejudice, torture, tyranny, lawlessness, terrorism, murder, theft, intolerance, ignorance, drug addiction, political and religious fanaticism, and other evils are frequent and recurrent. They poison lives not just in barbaric regions but also in moderately civilized and prosperous Western countries. It is in the West that Communists and Nazis murdered tens of millions of people who fell afoul of their irrational dogmas. It is here that two world wars and countless local and civil wars have massacred additional tens of millions of soldiers and civilians. It is here in America that murder and imprisonment rates are among the highest in the world; drug addiction is rampant; large numbers emerge from many years of schooling illiterate, innumerate, and ignorant of the most basic information about their country, let alone the world; a substantial percentage of the population exists outside of the political system because they live here illegally; many people feel they need guns to defend themselves and their homes against criminals; and it is here, if egalitarians are to be believed, that poverty, racism, sexism, homophobia, exploitation, and so forth create an unjust society.

How can egalitarians accept the illusions that the response to terrorism, crime, and drugs should be to guarantee equal freedom, rights, and resources to terrorists, criminals, drug pushers and to decent, law-abiding people; that evildoers and their victims have equal worth and deserve equal consideration; that the government should be neutral and tolerant in the face of the deep problems and external and internal enemies our society faces; or that justice requires taking from people what they have earned and giving it to those who have not earned it? The world of egalitarian illusions is not the world we live in. The gap between their illusions and our reality is huge. This is not a secret hidden from anyone. How can the moral and political obligations that might be appropriate if the illusions were true hold in our world in which the illusions are false?

Egalitarians acknowledge the existence of widespread evils but regard them as the predictable effects of deeper causes: injustice, discrimination, poverty, exploitation, and so forth. They corrupt people, egalitarians say, and that is why evil is widespread. The remedy is to make the bad political arrangements better. For that, however, it must be known what would be better, and that is what the illusions tell us. The aim of egalitarian thought is the formulation of a systematic account of what would be better. As its advocates put it, they are concerned with ideal theory. But this response is glaringly inadequate because the explanation of how bad political arrangements become bad is missing from it. Political arrangements are made by people. If they are bad, they reflect the badness of their makers. In that case, however, the explanation of widespread evils in terms of bad political arrangements falls far short of identifying their deeper causes, which must lie in human badness. But if that is the truth, then why would an ideal theory change the conduct of the many bad people who are responsible for widespread evil? Why would those who know what is good and bad aim in their actions to the good?

What is missing is the assumption that people are basically predisposed toward the good and against the bad. That is why an ideal theory could appeal to them and why bad political arrangements could be improved. The assumption, then, is that human beings are, if not basically good, at least inclined that way. This will be called *the optimistic faith*. It is held in a symbiotic relationship with the illusions; they are interdependent and strengthen each other. But the faith is no less false than the illusions it nourishes and which nourish it.

1.2 The Optimistic Faith

There is no shortage of explicit statements of the illusions, as we shall see in the chapters that follow, but statements of the faith are much rarer. It often appears only as a missing premise taken for granted by the faithful. There are, however, some forthright avowals of it by influential thinkers in the egalitarian tradition. According to Rousseau, "the fundamental principle of all morality, about which I have reasoned in all my works . . . is that man is a naturally good creature, who loves justice and order; that there is no original perversity in the human heart, and that the first movements of nature are always right."[1]

Kant agrees: man is "*not basically* corrupt (even as regards his original predisposition to good), but rather . . . still capable of improvement. . . . For man, therefore, who despite a corrupted heart yet possesses a good will, there remains a hope of a return to the good from which he has strayed." And again, "man (even the most wicked) does not, under any maxim whatsoever, repudiate the moral law in the manner of a rebel (renouncing obedience to it). The law, rather, forces itself upon him irresistibly by virtue of his moral predisposition."[2]

John Stuart Mill writes of the

leading department of our nature ... this powerful natural sentiment ... the social feelings of mankind—the desire to be in unity with our fellow creatures, which is already a powerful principle in human nature, and happily one of those which tend to become stronger, even without inculcation, from the influences of advancing civilization. ... Each individual [has] a stronger personal interest in practically consulting the welfare of others ... to identify his *feelings* more and more with their good. ... The good of others becomes to him a thing naturally and necessarily to be attended to. ... This mode of conceiving ourselves and human life ... is felt to be more and more natural. Every step in political improvement renders it more so.[3]

John Rawls, the preeminent egalitarian thinker of our own times, says that "the capacity for moral personality ... no race or recognized group of human beings ... lacks"[4] and that "moral personality is characterized by two capacities: one for a conception of the good, the other for a sense of justice." A conception of the good gives "a moral person ... a fundamental preference for ... a mode of life that expresses his nature as a free and equal rational being."[5] And "the sense of justice is continuous with the love of mankind ... the objects of these two sentiments are closely related, being defined in large part by the same conception of justice. If one of them seems natural ... so is the other."[6] And so "men's propensity to injustice is not a permanent aspect of community life: it is greater or less depending in large part on social institutions, and in particular on whether these are just or unjust."[7]

Thus, according to the optimistic faith, human beings are by nature inclined toward the good. Good political arrangements strengthen that inclination; bad ones corrupt it. Human beings do cause widespread evil; that, however, is an indication not of their true nature but of its corruption by bad political arrangements. Although this is a deeply and passionately held conviction, it is unreasonable because it ignores contrary considerations and it is closed to the possibility of criticism.

Some considerations ignored by the optimistic faith are the following. If bad political arrangements were alone responsible for widespread evil, then why do only some people who live under them become evildoers while many others do not, and why do many people become corrupt even though they benefit from the political arrangements that egalitarians regard as good? If American society is as bad because of injustice, discrimination, poverty, and exploitation as egalitarians say, then how could egalitarians themselves resist being corrupted by them? If resistance is possible, then people cannot be merely the passive subjects of political arrangements that unavoidably corrupt them. If egalitarians recognize that people differ in their predisposition to good and evil, then how can they blame evil merely on bad political arrangements? Why do we find the same familiar vices—cruelty, greed, selfishness, injustice, prejudice, irrationality, dishonesty, inhumanity—in all societies regardless of their political arrangements? Why does historical change affect only the forms but not the motives of evil actions?

John Maynard Keynes's comment on his circle's attachment to the optimistic faith is exactly right:

We repudiated all versions of the doctrine of original sin, of there being insane and irrational springs of wickedness in most men. We were not aware that civilisation was a thin precarious crust erected by the personality and the will of a very few, and only maintained by rules and conventions skillfully put across and guilefully preserved. . . . As a cause and consequence of our general state of mind we completely misunderstood human nature, including our own. The rationality which we attributed to it led to superficiality, not only of judgment, but also feeling. . . . I can see us as water-spiders, gracefully skimming . . . the surface of the stream without any contact with the eddies and the currents underneath.[8]

The reason why the optimistic faith is held contrary to the many facts that tell against it is that it is closed to criticism. It has a built-in stratagem for accommodating any fact that is inconsistent with it. Good actions, of course, are counted as confirmations of the basic human inclination toward the good. Bad actions are treated as evidence of the corrupting effects of bad political arrangements, and thus they too are taken to confirm the conviction that people are bad only because they have been corrupted. There is, therefore, nothing anyone could do that would be allowed to count as evidence against the optimistic faith. The ghastly facts of history, the hard realities of international affairs, the ubiquity of violence, fraud, and destructiveness within egalitarian societies can all be accommodated as reinforcements of the optimistic faith.

If the optimistic faith is indeed deeply flawed, why is it held by many people who pride themselves on being reasonable, and who are certainly well educated and highly intelligent? Because the faith is based on a feeling, not on reason, intelligence, or education. The feeling is a mixture of the wish to make the world a better place, pity for human suffering, and hope for a future better than the past. These sentiments do credit to those who have them. But they have been allowed to get out of hand. They have grown into a moral passion that falsifies reality and demonizes critics.

The wish focuses on human virtues and ignores human vices. The pity sentimentalizes sufferers and fails to recognize that their own immorality, imprudence, and character defects are often responsible for their plight. The hope ignores that the same human vices that caused the past to be in need of improvement will continue to jeopardize the future. Contrary to impassioned egalitarian rhetoric, critics of the optimistic faith who point out these falsifications need not be stupid, inhumane, or selfish; they may just be more realistic about the facts of life. Nor need the critics who deny that there is only a basic human predisposition to the good embrace the equally unreasonable view that human beings are basically wicked. They may just hold that human beings are basically ambivalent.

The time has come, therefore, to add the optimistic faith to that odd collection of historically influential but false beliefs which includes, among others, the divine right of kings, classless society, superiority of the white race, damnation outside the church, planned economy, and an idyllic prehistoric society from which civilization has caused us to fall farther and farther. Perhaps these beliefs are merely the adolescent fantasies of humanity, and now that the passage of time and the vicissitudes of history have caused us to mature somewhat, reason and realism will slowly replace them. Perhaps.

1.3 The Argument

The foregoing remarks were intended to indicate the direction of the argument, but they are, of course, not the argument itself. The argument is given in the chapters that follow. Each chapter examines one of the illusions that is symbiotically connected with the optimistic faith. It considers the reasons that have been given in support of the illusion by an egalitarian thinker whose work has been generally recognized as influential, shows the inadequacies of these reasons, and proposes a more realistic alternative to the illusion.

The primary purpose of the argument is critical: to show that the illusions are false and the optimistic faith untenable. The constructive part is there mainly to show that a reasonable alternative is available. A systematic development of this alternative may be found elsewhere.[9]

2/

The Inconsistency of Aims

It is one of the commonest beliefs of the day that the human race collectively has before it splendid destinies of various kinds, and that the road to them is to be found in the removal of all restraint on human conduct, in the recognition of a substantial equality between all human creatures, and in fraternity or general love. These doctrines . . . are regarded not merely as truths, but as truths for which those who believe in them are ready to do battle. . . . Such, stated in the most general terms, is the religion of which I take "Liberty, Equality, Fraternity" to be the creed. I do not believe it.

JAMES FITZJAMES STEPHEN, *Liberty, Equality, Fraternity*

2.1 The Illusion

Egalitarian liberalism has many versions and there is no definition that would cover all of them. This is acknowledged by its defenders themselves.[1] Yet these versions must have something in common, otherwise there would be no reason to regard them as different versions of the same political outlook. The place of a definition may then be taken by the identification of some common elements. One approach is to begin with some policies egalitarian liberals typically advocate in the contemporary American context: the legal enforcement of greater racial, sexual, and economic equality; proportional taxation; antipoverty programs; affirmative action; publicly financed education, health care, and abortion; decreased funding for defense; increased funding for foreign aid; food stamps for those who need them; Medicare; greater government regulation of businesses, especially of large corporations; and high income and inheritance taxes to pay for these policies.

The reason egalitarians typically favor these policies rather than some of the countless other available ones is that they are thought to reflect equality—the value they regard as basic and interpret as requiring equal freedom, rights, and resources. Although egalitarians disagree with one another about the precise interpretation and the respective importance of freedom, rights, and resources, they share the commitment to policies that aim to equalize them, and they think that equality should override such other values as peace, prosperity, order, security, civility, happiness, or patriotism when they conflict. If we ask why equality should be overriding, we reach the deepest egalitarian assumption, which is a moral view about the form good human lives should take. This view animates egalitarianism. It attributes to people the sentiment that "I wish my life and decisions to depend on myself, not on external forces of whatever kind. I wish to be an instrument of my own, not of other men's, acts of will. I wish to be a doer . . . deciding, not being decided for, self-directed, and not acted on by external nature."[2] According to egalitarians, living in this manner depends on equal freedom, rights, and resources, which are jointly thought by them to be the key to good lives. All undamaged human beings have the capacity to live in this way. This is the most fundamental respect in which they are equal. The development and exercise of this capacity requires the continuous transformation of society in order to enable ever more people to live such lives through the steady increase of equality. This may be called the constructive aim of egalitarianism.

The achievement of this aim, according to egalitarians, is frustrated by the widespread evils of our society: poverty, exploitation, crime, the abuse of military and police power, racism, sexism, and other forms of discrimination. *Evil* is the most severe term of condemnation our vocabulary affords. Evil is not just bad but extremely bad: serious undeserved harm that human beings inflict on others. It is *serious* because it injures the capacity for normal functioning; *undeserved* because there is no excusing or extenuating reason for its infliction; and it is caused by *human beings*, not natural disasters or other calamities. There are people motivated by cruelty, greed, fanaticism, envy, selfishness, and so forth who inflict evil on others habitually and predictably. These character traits are *vices*, and people in whose characters vices dominate are *evildoers*. Thus *evil* refers to actions, *vice* to character traits, and *evildoer* to people. Egalitarians must be committed to decreasing the widespread evils that stand in the way of achieving their constructive aim. This may be called the corrective aim of egalitarianism.

The illusion that concerns us in this chapter is that by combining the pursuit of the corrective aim of decreasing evil and the constructive aim of providing more equal freedom, rights, and resources the conditions of good lives will be secured.[3] This is an illusion because the two aims are inconsistent.

2.2 The Problem of Fully Intentional Evil

Evil is caused by either intentional or nonintentional actions. Actions are intentional if they are chosen on the basis of adequate understanding and evaluation. Actions that meet these conditions are fully intentional. Actions are not fully intentional if they are based on choices among alternatives forced on people, such as being burned alive or jumping out of a skyscraper; or if they are based on more or less deficient understanding and evaluation, such as ignorance of relevant facts or indoctrination in an unreasonable ideology. Actions that are not fully intentional are nonintentional. It will become crucially important in the next chapter to distinguish between nonintentional actions that are partly intentional and those that are totally unintentional, but this complication will be ignored for the moment. We shall proceed here by classifying all actions as either fully intentional or nonintentional.

Suppose that the main causes of widespread evil are fully intentional actions. This means that there must be many people who frequently cause serious undeserved harm to others, and mean to do just that. What could lead people to act in this way? One possibility is that they are moral monsters: mass murderers, torturers, dictators, terrorists, and similar malefactors who intentionally injure their victims. They make it a policy for themselves to treat others in evil ways. The psychological springs of their actions may be violent hatred, passionate indignation, thirst for power, self-loathing projected outward, cynicism, destructiveness, and so forth. These vices may be traced to real or imagined evil they themselves have suffered, keenly felt personal shortcomings, long-term brutalization, or extreme selfishness.

Moral monsters, however, are rare, probably rarer than moral saints. Monsters not only have to have as clear vision, great strength of character, and exceptionally strong sense of purpose as saints, but must also hide from others their true nature, since public opinion is generally disposed to pay at least lip service to the good. Being a moral monster is very difficult, and so few people can be supposed to become and continue to be monstrous. It is implausible, therefore, to attribute widespread evil to them.

Another possibility is that evil actions are performed fully intentionally by people who systematically subordinate moral to personal, ideological, religious, or aesthetic values. If such values require them to perform evil actions, they knowingly and deliberately choose to do so. Their justification is that they believe that their values are more important than the evil they inflict on others. They are self-centered, fanatical, or they see themselves as the instruments of their gods, or they are aesthetes who have grown cruel in their indifference to humanity. In one way, they are like moral monsters because they do evil intentionally, but in another way they are unlike them because moral monsters do it for its own sake, whereas these people do it for some other reason.

One possible egalitarian view, then, is that such people are the main causes of widespread evil. What must be done to make evil less widespread is to stop them from subordinating moral to other considerations. This cannot be a matter of merely making clear to them that they have made a mistake because these people will deny that they have done so. They are familiar with the relevant facts, they know about the requirements of morality, but they have decided that some personal, ideological, religious, or aesthetic value justifies their evil actions. If egalitarians are committed to decreasing widespread evil and if it is the result of fully intentional actions, then they must be in favor of curbing the actions of fully intentional evildoers.

This policy, however, is not one that egalitarians could follow while remaining faithful to their basic values. For if widespread evil were the result of fully intentional actions, it could be decreased only by preventing people from performing evil actions. Since these actions are, by hypothesis, fully intentional, decreasing evil requires that evildoers should have less freedom, rights, and resources than others because they make evil actions possible. The restrictions would have to be considerable, since the fully intentional actions from which widespread evil is supposed to result must be numerous to account for evil's being widespread.

If widespread evil were in the main fully intentional, then the corrective aim of egalitarianism of decreasing evil and its constructive aim of ever more equal freedom, rights, and resources would be inconsistent. A society committed to decreasing evil could not then be egalitarian. And a society committed to increasing the equality of freedom, rights, and resources would make evil more widespread.

2.3   The Problem of Nonintentional Evil

Egalitarians are better served by attributing widespread evil mainly to nonintentional actions, which, it should be remembered, range from partly intentional to totally unintentional. Our present concern is with showing why egalitarian policies cannot decrease evil if it is nonintentional. Actions are nonintentional if they are forced or if the people who perform them do not understand or evaluate correctly their significance. When nonintentional actions are evil, their agents do not see them *as* evil. They see them under some other description, and their misperceptions are symptomatic of a cognitive or moral failure. They are cruel, but they see themselves as treating their victims as they deserve; they are fanatical, but they believe themselves to be principled; they are greedy, but it seems to them as taking their fair share; they are prejudiced, but they appear to themselves as objective. They are, therefore, not morally monstrous but morally deficient.

The attractions of this answer for egalitarians are numerous. It is psychologically plausible; it explains how unexceptional people, like countless Nazi and Communist functionaries, can come to cause horrendous evil; and it avoids the inconsistency between the corrective and constructive aims which arises if widespread evil is attributed mainly to fully intentional actions. The most pertinent feature of this answer, however, is the explanation that is supposed to follow from it about how the increase of equality would decrease evil. If widespread evil is the result mainly of nonintentional actions, then, egalitarians may suppose, making actions fully intentional will make them less evil. If much evil is done because people lack freedom to choose or because they are unable to understand and evaluate reasonably their alternatives, then, it is supposed, greater freedom and better understanding and evaluation will correct their misperceptions and stop them from mistaking evil for something else. If this is right, the constructive aim of egalitarianism is not inconsistent with but a necessary requirement of realizing the corrective aim.

There are two reasons, however, why this answer, like the preceding one, fails. The first is that it does not follow from widespread evil being caused mainly by nonintentional actions that if more actions were made fully intentional, then evil would become less widespread. It is perfectly possible that if nonintentional evildoers come to understand and evaluate their actions accurately, and thus stop misperceiving their true nature, then they would continue to act the same way as before. Their reaction to the realization that they are cruel (not just), fanatical (not principled), greedy (not fair), prejudiced (not objective) may just be to embrace these vices and the actions that follow from them. They have developed their vices because some preexisting experience, feeling, desire, belief, hope, or fear created receptivity to them. The newly acquired knowledge that their character traits are vices, not virtues as they previously believed, will not by itself motivate them to change themselves. They may just shrug and say: that is the way I am. And even if they do not just shrug, because they are motivated by their new knowledge to try to change themselves, the force of that motive may not be strong enough to defeat the contrary forces of the preexisting motives that made them receptive to their vices in the first place; especially not, since their vices are by their very nature habitual. Making nonintentional actions fully intentional, therefore, may leave evil as widespread as it was before.

To make this answer plausible, egalitarians must further suppose that fully intentional actions tend to be good. Only if this supposition were true would making nonintentional actions fully intentional decrease evil. But why should it be supposed that fully intentional actions tend to be good and that evil ones are in the main nonintentional? The reason egalitarians give is that if people were allowed to make choices without the corrupting influences of unequal political arrangements, without having their choices, understandings, and evaluations clouded by poverty, discrimination, crime, and exploitation, if they were not brutalized, indoctrinated, or enraged, if they had time and opportunity to think about their lives and actions, then they would do good, not evil. To increase their freedom, rights, and resources is to decrease their vulnerability to unequal political arrangements. It is because evil is the product of these arrangements that reforming them in accordance with the requirements of equality will decrease evil. Egalitarians who give this answer are thus committed to the belief that people are naturally inclined toward the good and they do evil because of the corrupting influences of unequal political arrangements. This belief is the optimistic faith in the propensity for the good to be a dominant motive, and the success of the attempt to reconcile the constructive and corrective aims of egalitarianism depends on it.

Egalitarians attribute the fact that evil is widespread in all societies, regardless of their political arrangements, to the failure to implement the egalitarian values. As Rawls puts it, "Men's propensity to injustice is not a permanent aspect of community life; it is greater or less depending in large part on social institutions, and in particular on whether they are just or unjust."[4] He says that the view of human nature that underlies egalitarianism is "the high point of the contractarian tradition in Kant and Rousseau." According to this tradition, "a person is acting autonomously when the principles of his action are chosen by him as the most adequate possible expressions of his nature as a free and equal rational being."[5] At the core of the optimistic faith in the propensity for the good to be a dominant motive is thus the view that human beings are by their nature free, equal, rational, and just. When they act fully intentionally, they express their nature, and when they do evil, they act contrary to their nature because they have been corrupted by unequal political arrangements.

The optimistic faith, however, is indefensible for reasons introduced earlier (in 1.2) and now elaborated. First, it is held in such a way as to make it impossible to adduce evidence against it. Both good and evil actions are regarded as confirmations of the faith. If actions are good, it is because the propensity for the good dominates; and if actions are evil, people still have a dominant propensity for the good, although they have been corrupted by unequal political arrangements. Egalitarians who hold this faith are in a position strikingly similar to that of many Christians. As Christians believe that bad human beings, not God, are responsible for evil, so egalitarians believe that bad political arrangements, not human beings, are responsible for widespread evil. As Christians base their beliefs on what they take to be the nature of God, so egalitarians base their beliefs on what they take to be human nature. And as Christians have to contend with the problem of evil, so egalitarians have to contend with its secular equivalent.

Second, the assumption that widespread evil is attributable mainly to bad political arrangements ignores the obvious question of how political arrangements become bad. Political arrangements are human creations; whether or not they are bad depends on the people who create and perpetuate them. If human beings have a dominant propensity for the good, how could the arrangements they make be bad? If the moral status of actions depends on preexisting political arrangements, how could these arrangements be improved or new arrangements free of defects be established? If people are as much at the mercy of political arrangements as these egalitarians suppose, how could egalitarians themselves have escaped from the influence of the prevailing bad arrangements to an extent sufficient to diagnose their badness? If it is possible to escape the corrupting influences of bad arrangements, how could continued adherence to them not have something to do with the preexisting propensities of the participating people for evil? And were *those* preexisting propensities for evil also the products of bad arrangements? And if they were, how did *those* arrangements become bad?

Third, the faith in the basic human propensity for the good is not merely unsupported by the available facts but inconsistent with them. The facts are that evil is widespread in all human societies; the vices of selfishness, greed, envy, aggression, prejudice, cruelty, and so forth motivate people as much as the contrary virtues do; virtues and vices may be intentionally or nonintentionally formed; and both may be natural and basic or the products of external influences. It would be as implausible to infer from these facts that the propensity for good is dominant as that the propensity for evil is dominant. If the facts warrant any inference, it is that human beings are morally ambivalent. The faith in the dominance of the propensity for the good flatters humanity by painting a rosy picture of wonderful possibilities while neglecting the hard facts that it cannot accommodate. It is a sentimental falsification that substitutes illusion for reality. It cannot therefore provide the justification that egalitarians need for decreasing evil by making freedom, rights, and resources more equal.

Egalitarians may deny that they are committed to this faith. They may claim that they can be as hardheaded about evil as anyone else. In that case, however, they owe a reason for supposing that by increasing equality they will succeed in decreasing evil. If evil actions were in the main fully intentional, then making the freedom, rights, and resources of evildoers more equal would make evil actions more widespread, so this cannot be the reason that egalitarians need to provide. If, on the other hand, evil actions were mainly nonintentional, then egalitarians must still explain why the increase of equality would decrease evil. The old explanation was the faith in the propensity for the good to be dominant, but if egalitarians disavow it, if they believe that motives are mixed and that the propensity for both good and evil is variable, then they cannot suppose that more freedom, rights, and resources would give greater scope to good actions and smaller scope to evil ones. If they really do not hold the optimistic faith, then they ought to believe that more equal freedom, rights, and resources would make evil more widespread.

Egalitarians are thus left with a choice between two alternatives, both unacceptable to them: they can maintain their commitment to increasing equality, with or without the optimistic faith. This will result in the frustration of their corrective aim of decreasing evil. Or they can acknowledge that the freedom, rights, and resources of evildoers must be decreased in order to decrease evil. This will frustrate their constructive aim of increasing equality. In either case, the egalitarian aim of decreasing evil by increasing equality remains inconsistent.

2.4 Spreading Evil

Suppose, however, that this objection can somehow be met. Perhaps the optimistic faith is not indefensible. There would still be a reason for rejecting the policy of increasing equality. Take a society in which evil is widespread because many people living in it nonintentionally cause it under the influence of unequal political arrangements. The egalitarian approach to improving the status quo is to make nonintentionally evil actions fully intentional. This requires putting people who act in these ways in a position in which they can improve their choices, understandings, and evaluations. The egalitarian policy that aims to accomplish this is to increase the extent to which freedom, rights, and resources are equally available for everyone. Suppose this was done. What would happen in that society?

Before the egalitarian policy was put in place, evil was widespread. Then the policy is implemented and people—who must be numerous if evil is widespread—are given more freedom, rights, and resources. Is it not obvious that the result would be that evil becomes more widespread? The egalitarian policy involves weakening the existing curbs on evil actions. How could this not lead to giving greater scope to them? Admittedly, the curbs could not have been particularly effective before, but surely, weakening them further will not alter the vices of the people which lead them to act in evil ways. The egalitarian policy will make it easier for them to do evil.

This criticism egalitarians will indignantly reject. They will say that no reasonable egalitarian ever supposed that equality should be promoted without qualification. They will point out that the egalitarian tradition has always been centrally concerned with protecting potential victims of the misuse of freedom, rights, and resources. Increasing equality is not meant to be a license to do whatever anyone pleases, but is intended to provide an opportunity to pursue a reasonable conception of a good life in a way that does not hinder others from doing likewise.

That this has been and is an aim of egalitarianism is of course true. But it has not been properly appreciated by egalitarians that widespread evil makes the achievement of this aim impossible. If evil is acknowledged to be widespread, and if the faith in the dominance of the propensity for the good is not held, then in an egalitarian society there will be a moral minority whose actions are good and for whom freedom, rights, and resources are guaranteed, whereas for the remaining immoral majority, whose actions cause widespread evil, there will be less freedom, rights, and resources to prevent them from acting in evil ways. Such a society of course is radically at odds with the constructive aim of egalitarianism.

If egalitarians took widespread evil seriously, they would have to stop advocating policies that weaken rather than strengthen existing curbs on evildoers. In fact, however, egalitarians continue to advocate their policies as if evil were not widespread. The fundamental reason for this is that they fail to see the inconsistency between their corrective and constructive aims. It is true that egalitarians are committed to both these aims, but their inconsistency makes their joint achievement impossible.

2.5 Actual Responses
It is a remarkable feature of the voluminous literature that evil is simply not discussed in the many books and articles that are regarded as important statements of egalitarianism. Ronald Dworkin's much-cited and anthologized "Liberalism" makes no mention of it, nor does his recent book, *Sovereign Virtue*.[6] The articles on liberalism by Mau-

rice Cranston in *The Encyclopedia of Philosophy*, Richard Flathman in *The Encyclopedia of Ethics*, Alan Ryan in *A Companion to Contemporary Political Philosophy*, and Jeremy Waldron in the *Philosophical Quarterly* have nothing to say about it.[7] Thomas Nagel in his various books and articles ignores it completely.[8] John Rawls in the six hundred pages of *A Theory of Justice* devotes a single paragraph to it, only to distinguish among different sorts of moral worth or lack of it.[9] Joseph Raz recognizes that evil is widespread but says nothing about the obstacle it presents to well-being or about how to cope with it.[10]

One is prompted to ask why egalitarians proceed in this way. Stuart Hampshire (about whom more will be said shortly), writing as an avowed egalitarian liberal, says, "The notion of evil is the idea of a force . . . not merely contrary to all that is praiseworthy and admirable and desirable in human life, but a force which is actively working against all that is praiseworthy and admirable." And he goes on: "The known successes of the Nazi movement in Germany and elsewhere ought to have destroyed forever . . . an innocence in moral philosophy."[11] "If one follows the liberal tradition of Mill, Sidgwick, G. E. Moore, and John Rawls, one is liable to think of great public evils as a falling away from the pursuit of . . . the good."[12] "They wrote as if it were sufficient to establish some truths about the great goods for mankind and then deduce from these truths the necessary . . . social policies. It is not sufficient."[13] This is exactly right. Egalitarians affirm what they take to be the good as if that were an antidote to evil. But it could be an antidote only if the optimistic faith were correct, only if evil occurred because people were ignorant of the good. As Hampshire forcefully says, however, evil is not just ignorance of the good but an active force that motivates people in a contrary direction. Egalitarians ignore this at their peril. They must contend with the fact that cruelty, aggression, greed, selfishness, and envy actively motivate people and compete with the motives of kindness, altruism, decency, and justice.

There are a few egalitarians who do endeavor to face evil. One of them is Annette Baier.[14] She asks why it would be reasonable to act morally well in a society where evil is widespread. She reflects on Hume's memorable observation that "I shou'd be the cully of my integrity if I alone shou'd impose on myself a severe restraint amidst the licentiousness of others."[15] She then asks, "Is justice then an ideal which is committed to a perhaps groundless liberal faith?" and adds, "I shall proceed within the limits of the comforting liberal faith," but a "faith, for rational persons, must appear reasonable." What makes it reasonable "is the great unreasonableness of any alternative to it." She adds that "the best one can say for the reasonableness of willing to believe in the value of (possibly) unilateral moral action is that the alternative . . . must lead eventually to an outcome disastrous for all."[16] She concludes that the "just man *now*, in an unjust world, has no certainty, only faith and hope, that there really can and will be a just society."[17]

There are two problems with this view. One is that there is nothing in it that would support egalitarianism. The defender of any faith in the eventual victory of any view of justice or the good can appeal to this faith. There is no reason why Nazis, Communists, or terrorists could not say that they are acting justly in an unjust world in the faith and hope that the good will prevail. So even if everything Baier said were true, she would not have succeeded in showing that egalitarians have a way of coping with evil. The other problem is that Baier is mistaken in claiming that any alternative to the optimistic faith is disastrous for all. A perfectly reasonable alternative is to recognize the human propensity for evil and enforce political arrangements that curb evil actions. This, as we have seen, would be contrary to the constructive aim of egalitarianism, and perhaps that is the reason why Baier does not consider it a reasonable alternative.

Another egalitarian response to evil is Jonathan Glover's.[18] He does indeed face evil as he relentlessly catalogs some of the most horrible instances of it in the twentieth century. Reflecting on recent history, Glover says that "the psychology of the human species can be seen as having a strong propensity both for getting trapped into conflict and also for cruelty and mass killing. Twentieth-century wars, massacres, and genocides come from combining this psychology with modern technology. . . . The psychology so visible in the twentieth century is a recurring one. . . . Inhumanity can be seen . . . stretching from our own time back to the eighteenth century. Of course it goes further back. It goes as far back as we know" (413). Having acknowledged all this horror, Glover nevertheless aims "to defend the Enlightenment hope . . . that by understanding more about ourselves we can do something to create a world with less misery. I have qualified optimism that this hope is well founded. . . . We need to look hard and clearly at some monsters inside us. But this is part of the project of caging and taming them" (7).

What, then, is the foundation of Glover's qualified optimism and hope? He identifies the causes of widespread evil as "political and social" and "ethical and psychological." The measures he recommends to cope with the political and social causes include "proper policing of the world," "legitimate and properly backed international authority to keep the peace and to protect human rights," and the "need to avoid large-scale utopian projects" (401). This plan calls for two comments.

First, the implementation of these measures requires restricting the freedom of evildoers, depriving them of the resources to perpetrate atrocities, and curbing their rights to do as they please. These requirements serve well the corrective aim of egalitarianism, but they are inconsistent with its constructive aim. By recommending these measures, Glover has in fact relinquished the central claim of egalitarianism, namely, to be able simultaneously to decrease widespread evil and increase equality.

Second, the political and social causes of widespread evil operate through the actions of human beings. If evil occurs, it is because human beings cause it. Political and social influences on people's actions are influences exerted by other people. In the last analysis, therefore, political and social causes have psychological roots. It is always people who commit atrocities, and they do so either because of the monsters inside them or because of the monsters inside those who influence them. The quiddity of the causes of evil, therefore, is psychological. Glover would probably agree. He says that "to avoid further disasters, we need political restraints on a world scale. But politics is not the whole story. We have experienced the results of technology in the service of the destructive side of human psychology. Something needs to be done about this fatal combination. . . . It is too late to stop the technology. It is to psychology that we should now turn" (414).

Glover's recommendation of what should be done if we turn to psychology is to develop a "sense of moral identity and the human responses" (406). He explains: "This sense of identity has a moral charge when it is not a matter of style or personality but is of deeper character. . . . The question of the sort of person you want to be is central . . . [it] can lead us to a clearer understanding of our deepest desires and values. . . . Those who gain this self-knowledge see that their happiness depends on psychological integration, or wholeness" (26–27). What makes responses human is sympathy and moral imagination. They make "vivid the victims and the human reality of what will be done to them" (409). At the same time, Glover recognizes that "the sense of moral identity does not always hold people back from doing terrible things" (402), that "sympathy can also fail as a restraint" (407), that "there are common psychological patterns . . . [in which] human responses are overwhelmed, weakened, narrowed or eliminated in ways which recur" (408). But, he says, "the best hope . . . is to work with the grain of human nature, making use of the resources of moral identity and the human responses" (409).

This final remark makes obvious the groundlessness of Glover's hope and the inconsistency of his position. For he assumes that "the grain of human nature" is good. He assumes this despite his earlier recognition that "the psychology of the human species can be seen as having a strong propensity . . . for cruelty and mass killing. . . . Inhumanity . . . goes as far back as we know" (409), that "moral identity does not always hold people back from doing terrible things" (402), and that the failure of human responses is a common psychological pattern (408). In fact, what we encounter in Glover's hope is the commitment to the optimistic faith in the fundamental goodness of human beings. The remarkable feature of it in the present case is that Glover holds the faith in the face of the overwhelming evidence that he himself has adduced against it.

A third egalitarian who faces evil is Stuart Hampshire. He avows his "socialist sympathies, and loyalty to the political Left,"[19] but he is also realistic about the danger evil presents. His reflections have been provoked by encounters with some of the most prominent Nazis, whom he interrogated after World War II. He writes: "Unmitigated evil and nastiness are as natural . . . in educated human beings as generosity and sympathy: no more, and no less, natural. . . . High culture and good education are not significantly correlated with elementary moral decency."[20] He goes on: "There is nothing mysterious or 'subjective' or culture-bound in the great evils of human experience . . . : murder and the destruction of life, imprisonment, enslavement, starvation, poverty, physical pain and torture. . . . They are evil without qualification, if nothing can be said about consequences which might palliate the evil."[21] And he adds: "In so far as the great evils are manmade . . . they are so far great moral evils, although the Communist leader, or the Grand Inquisitor, will refer to his own conception of the good as redeeming the evil."[22]

These thoughts, taken together, imply that causing evil is natural to human beings (as is causing good). Hampshire accepts that this is so, and asks what can be done about it. His answer is "that there is a recognisable level of common decency, which I have tried to analyse with the notion of minimum procedural justice, and that evil . . . consists in the uncompensated violation of this basic justice. . . . In weighing in politics conflicting moral claims and competing conceptions of the good, this minimum justice plays the role of scales."[23] Hampshire's eloquent and moving words about common decency and minimum justice are certainly true. They are requirements of civilized life, and when they are violated, barbarism follows. The question, however, remains: what reason is there for supposing that egalitarianism can protect these indispensable requirements?

Why would not the natural tendency to "unmitigated evil and nastiness" result in the violation of common decency and minimum justice? Why would people act on their good, rather than evil, dispositions if "high culture and good education are not significantly correlated with elementary moral decency"? Why would it not lead to making evil more, rather than less, widespread to implement the egalitarian policies and provide more freedom, rights, and resources for potential evildoers? Why does Hampshire not apply to himself what he so rightly says about other egalitarians: they write "as if it were sufficient to establish some truths about the great goods of mankind and then deduce from these truths the necessary . . . social policies. It is not sufficient." Hampshire leaves these questions unanswered. His diagnosis of the problem, like Glover's, is accurate; his prescription of decency and justice as remedies is correct; but he leaves a gaping hole between his diagnosis and the remedy he proposes. If the diagnosis is correct, and there is a natural human tendency to cause evil, then the remedy requires other measures than the egalitarian policies that encourage people to follow their natural tendencies.

Judith Shklar is another egalitarian liberal who has taken evil seriously. She says that "liberalism has only one overriding aim: to secure the political conditions that are necessary for the exercise of personal freedom. Every adult should be able to make as many effective decisions without fear or favor about as many aspects of her or his life as is compatible with the like freedom of every other adult. That belief is the original and only defensible meaning of liberalism." She calls this view "the liberalism of fear." Freedom can be threatened in many ways, but she thinks that "the fear and favor that have always inhibited freedom are overwhelmingly generated by governments." Among all the sources of social oppression, "none has the deadly effect of those who, as agents of the modern state, have unique resources of physical might and persuasion at their disposal."[24] According to the liberalism of fear, "there is a *summum malum*, which all of us know and would avoid if only we could. That evil is cruelty and the fear it inspires, and the very fear of fear itself." And she claims that "what liberalism requires is the possibility of making the evil of cruelty and fear the basic norm of its political practices and prescriptions."[25]

Shklar says many impassioned things on this topic, but none of it helps avoid the superficiality of the liberalism of fear. Governments cannot generate fear, threaten freedom, or be cruel; only people acting on behalf of governments can do that. The question is why people do this and what would stop them. The answer must be that people do it because they have a propensity to cause evil. And what would stop them is the restriction of their freedom, rights, and resources to act on their propensity. If evil and the fear of it are widespread, then the restrictions must be correspondingly widespread. Consequently, a society in which the liberalism of fear rules may have very little freedom, rights, and resources. This is precisely the opposite of what is promised by "the original and only defensible . . . liberalism."

The merit of Baier, Glover, Hampshire, and Shklar is that they recognize the need to cope with the widespread evil that threatens civilized life. This is certainly better than ignoring evil, as is done by all the influential egalitarian liberals cited earlier.[26] But it is still not good enough because the only way of coping with widespread evil is to institute policies that are contrary to increasing equality. Facing evil does not remove the inconsistency between the constructive and corrective aims of egalitarianism; it merely makes it harder for egalitarians to avoid acknowledging it.

2.6 Possible Responses

One possible response egalitarians may offer, in addition to the actual ones just considered, is to acknowledge that there is evil but deny that in egalitarian societies it is widespread. They may point at the highly favorable contrast between such evils as exist in egalitarian democracies and in various unsavory left- and right-wing regimes in power elsewhere. Egalitarian democracies are not perfect, its defenders may say, but they are considerably less imperfect than, say, China, Iran, Iraq, or Saudi Arabia, not to mention the Stalinist Soviet Union or Nazi Germany.

This, of course, is true. Any reasonable critic must admit that egalitarian societies are better than many others. But this does not help avoid the dilemma that egalitarians face. It is either true or false that in egalitarian societies there is widespread evil in the forms of such inequalities as poverty, exploitation, crime, abuse of military and police power, racism, sexism, and so on. If true, then the egalitarian policies aiming to decrease evil have a point, but as we have seen, their success depends on providing unequal freedom, rights, and resources for the many people who are responsible for widespread evil. These policies go against the constructive aim of egalitarianism, which is to increase equality. If false, then the egalitarian policies—aiming at greater racial, sexual, and economic equality, antipoverty programs, affirmative action, food stamps, and so forth—are unnecessary and pointless because the evil they aim to decrease is not widespread enough to warrant them. Depending on whether egalitarians acknowledge widespread evil in egalitarian societies, their policies are doomed to be either unsuccessful or pointless.

Another possible response is to acknowledge that there is widespread evil even in egalitarian societies and that decreasing it requires unequal freedom, rights, and resources, but to insist that this is not a defect of egalitarianism, just an unavoidable feature of political life. Values often conflict, and politics is just the process of trying to balance their respective claims. Because of widespread evil, equality cannot be as extensive as egalitarians wish, but they may argue that their policies represent the best attempt to have as much equality and as little evil as political realities permit.

There is something at once right and wrong with this response. The view of politics as the process that balances the conflicting claims of values is right. What is wrong is the failure to see that balancing the conflicting aims of increasing equality and decreasing evil in effect results either in decreasing equality or in increasing evil. Two considerations make this evident. Egalitarians promise that an egalitarian society will come ever closer to having equal freedom, rights, and resources, and that this will make more lives better than any other approach could do. But if evil is widespread, and if decreasing it depends on decreasing equality, then the promise of egalitarianism must remain unfulfilled.

The other consideration vitiating this response is that the promise of egalitarianism is not merely that it will increase equality and decrease evil, but that it will do so *by* making freedom, rights, and resources more equal. The promise thus includes not merely the approximation of a valuable aim but also the way that aim is approximated. This is an essential feature of the promise because without it there would be nothing specifically egalitarian about it. Even dictatorial regimes can be defended by saying that they aim to make freedom, rights, and resources more equal and decrease evil insofar as possible in some particular context. That was just the rhetoric of communists and fellow travelers. The egalitarian promise is that in egalitarian societies there will be a steady equalization of freedom, rights, and resources. But if decreasing evil depends on decreasing these admittedly valuable things, as this response to the criticism concedes, then the promise of egalitarianism cannot be fulfilled.

Yet another response egalitarians may offer is to concede that widespread evil presents a serious problem for their position but to argue that their opponents have the same problem. They may say that all reasonable ideologies have the corrective aim of decreasing evil and the constructive aim of transforming society in accordance with whatever happen to be their basic values. And all ideologies must face the fact that their corrective and constructive aims conflict, so that they could decrease evil only by decreasing the extent to which their basic values prevail. If this were right, it would be unfair to criticize egalitarianism for having a problem that all ideologies have.

The trouble with this response is that it rests on a false supposition. The problem is equally serious only for ideologies whose constructive aim includes weakening restrictions on human conduct. It is only because egalitarianism has that as part of its constructive aim that it is open to the charge that it makes evil more rather than less widespread. There are political views that have no faith in the propensity for the good to be dominant, that recognize that motives are naturally mixed, that people are no more or less prone to develop virtues than vices, and that political arrangements reflect moral imperfections. Such views will not favor weakening the curbs on human conduct; on the contrary, they will aim to strengthen them. They will not commit themselves to the suicidal policy of aiming at equal freedom, rights, and resources for all people without asking whether or not they habitually act in evil ways. For such political views, widespread evil will not present as serious a problem as it does for egalitarianism, whose defenders proceed in a contrary way. And because egalitarians do proceed in a contrary way, it is not unfair to blame them for their consequent inability to cope with widespread evil.

The failure of these responses strengthens the claim that the corrective and constructive aims of egalitarianism are inconsistent: decreasing evil is incompatible with equalizing freedom, rights, and resources. There is, therefore, an illusion at the very core of egalitarianism. It obscures the fact that decreasing evil is possible only by curtailing the conduct of evildoers.

3/

The Denial of Responsibility

[It] must be allowed, that *sentiments* are every day experienced of blame and praise, which have objects beyond the dominion of will and choice, and of which it behoves us ... to give some satisfactory theory.

DAVID HUME, *An Enquiry Concerning the Principles of Morals*

3.1 The Illusion

One reason for the failure of egalitarians to recognize the inconsistency between their constructive and corrective aims is the indefensible optimistic faith. Egalitarians correctly suppose that widespread evil is the result mainly of nonintentional actions, but they go on to suppose incorrectly that if nonintentional actions were replaced by fully intentional ones, then evil would become less widespread. We have seen in the preceding chapter why this supposition is wrong. But there is another reason why egalitarians fail to see the inconsistency at the core of their position: the illusion that people are not responsible for their nonintentionally evil actions. Such actions are acknowledged to be evil, but they are not allowed to reflect on the evildoers because the actions were not chosen by them or because they were unable to understand or evaluate correctly their significance. According to egalitarians, only fully intentional actions redound to the discredit of those who perform them. If this were true, egalitarians could consistently acknowledge that evil is widespread, that it is the result mainly of nonintentional actions, and deny that making evil less widespread requires decreasing the freedom, rights, and resources of nonintentional evildoers. Treating nonintentional evildoers unequally would be to hold them responsible for actions they did not choose or whose significance they were unable to recognize as a result of some deficiency in their understandings or evaluations. And that, egalitarians claim, would be wrong. The aim of this chapter is to show that this is an illusion and that people often *are* responsible for their nonintentionally evil actions.

Let us begin with the initial understanding that responsibility is liability to condemnation and punishment, and concentrate on responsibility for evil actions. There is responsibility also for good actions, which may merit praise and reward, but they will not be dealt with here. Evil actions, it will be remembered, cause serious undeserved harm to others. Our present concern, however, is not with evil actions themselves but with how evil actions reflect on the people who perform them. Responsibility has to do with judging people, not actions.

In simple cases, people perform fully intentional evil actions and are held responsible because of them. They are liable to be condemned and punished for them, but they need not be. There may be exempting or extenuating considerations that make it reasonable to hold people responsible but not to condemn them, or to condemn but not to punish them, and each of these forms of disapprobation allows for various degrees of severity. To understand responsibility as liability to condemnation and punishment, therefore, does not mean that if responsibility is justifiably ascribed, then condemnation and punishment become automatically appropriate. It means rather that the question of their appropriateness arises. A good society must protect its members from evil, and condemnation and punishment are important ways of doing so. But they can be misused, and so a standard is needed for their justified use. That standard is responsibility.

3.2 Three Cases

Consider now three people who perform nonintentionally evil actions. The first is a janitor in a school. His pay is low, his life is boring and empty, he is barely literate, and he has no prospects of a better future. If he were articulate, which he is not, he would describe his life as hopeless. He takes drugs to alleviate his condition and becomes addicted. To support his habit, he acts as a pusher. The children at the school where he works present an eager market, and he regularly sells them drugs. Many of the children become addicted, and they, in turn, also act as pushers. There can be no doubt that the janitor regularly performs evil actions. He causes great undeserved harm to children. But he does so nonintentionally. He has drifted into addiction as an unconsidered response to the hopelessness of his life. And since he is semiliterate and unreflective, he does not understand the significance of what he is doing. If he thinks about it at all, he tells himself that he is doing what many others around him are doing, that if he were not supplying the children with drugs someone else would, and that he needs the relief in his life that being a pusher enables him to have. Yet he causes the ruin of many children.

The second is a prostitute. She has been raised by her mother, who is herself a prostitute. Her childhood has been loveless. From an early age she has been prostituted by her mother. She is now a young woman with practically no education and no knowledge of the world outside the neighborhood where she plies her trade. In order to tolerate her life, she shuts off her feelings. This is the cost of protecting herself from the bad feelings that would be the natural reactions to her past and present. She ekes out her life in this manner and then gets AIDS. She knows it because a routine examination, forced on her during one of her periodic arrests, has revealed it. She knows that it will kill her, but she has no feelings even about that. She goes on as before, and she infects hundreds of her clients. She simply does not think about what she is doing or about the consequences of her actions. She has no interest in her clients beyond their brief transactions. She has few real choices because most of her alternatives are forced on her; she does not really understand or evaluate what she is doing because she cannot bear to think about it. Yet her nonintentionally evil actions inflict serious undeserved harm on many people.

The third is a terrorist. From early childhood he has been indoctrinated by his parents, teachers, and community to follow a violent white supremacist ideology. It is believed by everyone around him that there is a conspiracy against the white race and that the only way to oppose it is through violent acts of protest directed against atheists, blacks, and Jews. The terrorist grows up to believe that morality requires violent actions against these conspirators. Killing or maiming them is regarded as a justified act of self-protection and the means of putting an end to the conspiracy. Such doubts as he may occasionally have at the sight of the mayhem he is causing are put to rest by those he recognizes as authorities. He is reassured, praised, and respected for killing and maiming people who have caused him or his people no harm. He is misled by people who, probably, have been misled themselves. In any case, in the terrorist's life there is a pattern of evil actions, but they are nonintentional because the choices the terrorist believes himself to make are between false alternatives and he does not understand the true nature of his acts because he has been deceived all his life. All the same, he murders and maims many innocent people.

These three people share certain features that centrally affect the appropriateness of the ascription of responsibility for nonintentionally evil actions. The evil actions of the pusher, the prostitute, and the terrorist are not isolated episodes but part of a pattern. These people do what they do habitually and predictably; their actions follow from and reflect their characters. The pusher is amoral, the prostitute is inhuman, and the terrorist is fanatical. These are vices, they have a prominent place in the characters of these people, and their evil actions flow from their vices. Once their characters have been formed, it is extremely difficult for them to act contrary to them because it is virtually impossible for them to regard alternatives to what they are doing as live options; their understandings of their circumstances and actions follow from their history and experiences; and the evaluations of their lives and conduct suffer from the poor understanding and few choices that their characters and circumstances afford. Their evil actions, therefore, are not the fully intentional results of their choices, understandings, and evaluations but the nonintentional consequences of their characters and circumstances. Moreover, these people had no significant control over the formation of their characters either. They became amoral, inhuman, and fanatical as the readily understandable consequences of the circumstances in which they found themselves. They did not choose to become vicious; they became vicious as a result of hopelessness, abuse, and indoctrination. Bearing these common features in mind, let us ask, is it appropriate to hold people responsible for their characteristic patterns of evil actions if neither their actions nor their characters are fully intentional?

3.3 The Answer

Albert Hofstadter says that "the moral man subjects his essential individuality to the authority of what he is convinced is right. . . . He is not compelled by anything outside . . . to perform his action. The force that determines the performance is the force of his own self."[1] Against this background, he claims that in "true moral evil the actor is convinced that the norm he violates is morally right. He is convinced that he is setting himself against what he ought to do, intentionally doing what he ought not to do. Evil cannot exist . . . save in and through his active opposition to what is perceived as good and right." He goes on to say that "this perversity of will is the essential form of evil" and that this "is pure wickedness." The implication is that "he who acts against the good, not realizing that it is the good he acts against, is not evil," because such a person is not "an evil man acting malevolently but . . . a good man assailed by a maleficent principle that has lodged in . . . part of him."[2]

It follows that the pusher, the prostitute, and the terrorist are really good people who happened not to realize that they were acting against the good, so they should not be held responsible for their evil actions. Hofstadter regards the presence of full intention as an essential condition for the ascription of responsibility. Since the pusher, the prostitute, and the terrorist were not acting fully intentionally, it is inappropriate to hold them responsible for their evil actions.

Stanley Benn says, "By 'wickedness' I mean whatever it is about someone that warrants our calling him a wicked person. It is therefore a different notion from what makes an action an evil deed, for an evil deed may be done by someone who is not wicked but only weak or misguided."[3] Wickedness presupposes full intention because "wickedness in a person requires that he adopt an evil maxim." Benn thinks that "a psychopathic personality may not count as wickedness at all." Such a person does evil, but "he does not see it as evil, except, perhaps, in a conventional sense: This is something that I know most people do not like being done, so I had better conceal the body. But the kind of considerations that might justify and rationalize conventional disapproval can get no purchase on his understanding. . . . Such a person cannot be wicked."[4] Like Hofstadter, Benn assumes that full intention is necessary for responsibility. Benn does not think, therefore, that people who habitually and predictably perform evil actions, like the pusher, the prostitute, and the terrorist, should be held responsible since they do not "act on principles" that they have arrived at fully intentionally. Like Hofstadter, Benn does not say why this is so. Why is it inappropriate to hold people responsible who nonintentionally, but regularly, cause evil?

Gary Watson discusses Robert Harris, a particularly callous multiple murderer. He provides a harrowing description of Harris's murder of two boys. He then describes, equally harrowingly, the brutalized childhood of the murderer. And then Watson agonizes: the murderer "both satisfies and violates the criteria of victimhood. His childhood abuse was a misfortune inflicted upon him against his will. But at the same time . . . he unambivalently endorses suffering, death, and destruction, and that is what (one form of) evil is. . . . [Our] ambivalence results from the fact that an overall view simultaneously demands and precludes regarding him as a victim."[5] Watson hesitates to hold Harris responsible because the evil he did was in some sense traceable to the evil that was done to him. Harris's unfortunate personal history interrupts the progression from condemning his actions to condemning him.

But why is the evil that was done to him a reason for not condemning him and holding him responsible? Watson answers: "The fact that [Harris's] . . . cruelty is an intelligible response to his circumstances gives a foothold not only for sympathy, but for the thought that if *I* had been subjected to such circumstances, I might have become as vile. . . . This thought induces not only an ontological shudder, but a sense of equality with the other: I too am a potential sinner. . . . Admittedly, it is hard to know what to do with this conclusion."[6]

It is a noteworthy feature of Watson's discussion that his attention is concentrated on the murderer. He shows great subtlety in probing for the right response. But he says nothing, after the murders are recounted, about the evil the murderer caused. Two boys were brutally murdered; their future was taken away from them; their families had to endure the loss, the gory details of the crime, and their own feelings of grief, rage, and helplessness. Such things often happen, and they may happen to those we love and to ourselves. Watson, in agreement with many egalitarians, agonizes over the criminal and glosses over the crime. Surely, there is something seriously askew here.

Perhaps the purest expression of the egalitarian attitude is Susan Wolf's. She asks her readers to consider

the case of the victim of a deprived childhood . . . a man who embezzled some money, fully aware of what he was doing. . . . Yet it seems he ought not to be blamed for committing his crime, for, from his point of view, one cannot reasonably expect him to see anything wrong with his action. We may suppose that in his childhood he was given no love—he was beaten by his father, neglected by his mother. And the people to whom he was exposed when he was growing up gave him examples only of evil and selfishness. From his point of view, it is natural to conclude that respecting other people's property would be foolish. For presumably no one had ever respected his. . . . In light of this, it seems that this man shouldn't be blamed for an action we know to be wrong. For if we had his childhood, we would not have known either. . . . It is because he couldn't have had reason that this agent should not be blamed.[7]

At another place Wolf says:

Responsibility depends on the ability to act in accordance with the True and the Good. If one is psychologically determined to do the right thing for the right reason, this is compatible with having the requisite ability. . . . But if one is psychologically determined to do the wrong thing, for whatever reason, this seems to constitute a denial of that ability. . . . Being psychologically determined to perform good actions is compatible with deserving praise for them, but . . . being psychologically determined to perform bad actions is not compatible with blame.[8]

Just like Hofstadter, Benn, and Watson, Wolf assumes that the appropriate ascription of responsibility depends on the intentions of the evildoers, not on their habitual and predictable evil actions. All of them deny the appropriateness of the ascription of responsibility, if the evil actions are not fully intentional. But why should full intention be required for responsibility? The egalitarian answer leads to a view about responsibility that is one of the deepest sources of egalitarianism. We can get at this view by way of considering the distinction between causal and moral responsibility.[9] If there is no doubt that people have performed some particular actions, then they can be said to be responsible for them. But this may mean simply that they were the pivotal links in the causal chain that led to the action, as the recent earthquake is for the collapse of a house, or that they are morally accountable for the action, as Stalin is for the show trials in the 1930s. The first is causal responsibility, the second is moral responsibility.

Moral responsibility differs from causal responsibility in making it appropriate to condemn people for their evil actions. What makes condemnation appropriate in one case but not in the other is supposed to be that fully intentional actions involve free choice and adequate understanding and evaluation of what is chosen. This distinction may then be enlisted to defend the denial of moral responsibility of those who habitually and predictably do nonintentional evil. Such people are supposed by egalitarians to be only causally responsible. It is inappropriate to hold them morally responsible.

This view glosses over two fundamental difficulties. The first is that the denial of responsibility for patterns of nonintentional actions contradicts reasonable moral judgments held by virtually everyone. Consider the moral standing of the pusher, the prostitute, and the terrorist. They are not to be condemned, according to the egalitarian view, because they are only causally and not morally responsible for their actions. Now consider their counterparts on the opposite end of the moral spectrum: people who are decent, altruistic, and reasonable, but they too are acting nonintentionally, perhaps because they have been indoctrinated by a benign creed.

The implication of the egalitarian view is that people who perform these good and evil actions have exactly the same moral standing: none, because they are only causal, not moral, agents. Neither are morally responsible because neither are acting fully intentionally. But this is absurd. How could it be reasonably denied that it is morally better to be decent, altruistic, and reasonable than amoral, inhuman, and fanatical? To be sure, it is better still to possess and exercise virtues intentionally than nonintentionally, but is it not obvious that, fully intentional or not, virtues and good actions are morally better than vices and evil actions? Yet the denial of moral responsibility for patterns of nonintentional actions commits egalitarians to the absurdity of rejecting this obvious moral judgment.

The second difficulty is that moral and causal responsibility cannot be distinguished as clearly as the egalitarian view requires. If people ought to be held morally responsible only for their fully intentional actions, then it is crucial to realize that people ultimately have no control over their characters and circumstances on which intentions depend. For people can influence their political, social, or economic circumstances, if at all, only in insignificant ways, and characters are contingent on genetic endowments, upbringing, and later conditions of life. Acting fully intentionally thus ultimately depends on the kind of character people have, but that is ultimately the product of conditions and circumstances over which they can exercise no intentional control. As a result, people have ultimately only causal responsibility for their moral responsibility. If it were inappropriate to ascribe moral responsibility to people who habitually and predictably cause nonintentional evil, then it would be also inappropriate to ascribe it to people whose actions are fully intentional, since fully intentional actions ultimately depend on nonintentional factors. If this argument were correct, the ascription of moral responsibility could never be appropriate.

This difficulty is not one of the hoary problems raised by determinism but that, whatever the truth is about determinism, the egalitarian view is inconsistent. For the refusal to ascribe moral responsibility for nonintentional actions and the willingness to ascribe it only for fully intentional ones are incompatible, since fully intentional actions depend on nonintentional factors. To avoid these difficulties, we need an argument to show why full intention is necessary for moral responsibility.

The argument is that the ascription of moral responsibility is appropriate only for those who possess the capacity to meet their responsibility. Material objects, plants, animals, infants, and the insane are exempted from moral responsibility because they lack the capacity to meet it, whereas adults who have the capacity are subject to it. And the capacity, of course, is to perform fully intentional actions, that is, actions based on reasonable choice, understanding, and evaluation. The pusher, the prostitute, and the terrorist are deficient in that capacity, and that is why it is inappropriate to hold them morally responsible for their patterns of nonintentionally evil actions.

3.4 The Conditions of Moral Responsibility
The response to this argument requires getting clearer about the conditions that warrant the ascription of moral responsibility and then determining whether the egalitarian denial of it is reasonable. This will leave open the question of when condemnation and punishment are in order, but we shall return to that later. The ascription of moral responsibility depends on four conditions: the *characters* and *intentions* of the evildoers, and the *contexts* and *consequences* of their ac-

tions. The first two are internal conditions, having to do with the psychological states or processes antecedent to evil actions. The second two are external conditions, concerning social influences on what people do and the effects of their actions on others. We shall assume that the people in question are causally responsible for evil actions. The remaining question is whether they are also morally responsible.

Character has an obvious bearing on moral responsibility because it makes a difference whether people's evil actions are habitual and predictable or uncharacteristic episodes. If people have vices, then their actions reflect them in appropriate circumstances. Cruel people tend to act cruelly, selfish ones selfishly, and so forth. Normally, there is a presumption in favor of holding people morally responsible for their characteristic evil actions. The presumption may be defeated by exempting or extenuating considerations, but otherwise it holds. If, on the other hand, actions are uncharacteristic departures from usual patterns, then it needs to be explained why people have acted that way. It may have been an accident; a response to great provocation, temptation, or emergency; they may have been sick, drunk, grief-stricken, or under great stress. Moral responsibility for uncharacteristic evil actions is contingent on the explanation of why people have acted that way.

Consequences have a similarly obvious relevance to the ascription of moral responsibility. People are normally responsible for the serious undeserved harm they cause. That is the consequence that must be taken into account. It is because of it that they are liable to condemnation and punishment. Actions, of course, often have unforeseeable consequences, which make it inappropriate to hold people morally responsible for all the consequences of their actions. But it is not inappropriate to do so for readily foreseeable ones. If people fail to foresee consequences that others in their position would normally foresee, then the causes of their failure need to be understood. If they were permanently or temporarily handicapped, that is one thing; if they were inattentive, negligent, or uncaring, that is another. The presumption, therefore, is to hold people morally responsible for the foreseeable consequences of their actions unless there are exempting or extenuating circumstances.

The context of actions also matters, especially the moral standards of the surrounding society. Evil actions may violate the prevailing standards. It would be extraordinary if evildoers were ignorant of them, since at least the most important moral standards of a society must be as familiar to its members as the language they speak. In our society, for instance, no one could plausibly claim ignorance of the moral standards prohibiting murder or armed robbery. But people may do evil even when they act in conformity to the prevailing moral standards because the standards may be morally unacceptable, even though the society accepts them. It makes a difference to people's moral responsibility whether their evil actions follow accepted practices. People may do evil but not think that it is evil because they have been led to believe otherwise by their moral education and moral authorities. The presumption is in favor of holding people morally responsible for their evil actions that violate the moral standards of their society. If their evil actions conform to the prevailing standards, that may be a reason for exemption or extenuation. How strong a reason it is depends on whether they could be reasonably expected to call into question the prevailing standards.

This brings us to intention, which clearly has a bearing on moral responsibility. The discussion has so far proceeded on the assumption that actions are either fully intentional or nonintentional. This, however, is too simple because actions can be nonintentional for two very different reasons. One is that people may altogether lack the capacity to choose, understand, or evaluate their actions, or they may have the capacity but their circumstances make it impossible to exercise it; they may be insane or incapacitated by exceptional stress. The actions of such people are unintentional. The other reason is that although people have both the capacity and the opportunity to exercise it, they do so only to a limited extent; they choose without awareness of the alternatives or without a serious attempt to understand or evaluate them. Their actions are only partly intentional. The result is that the distinction between intentional and nonintentional actions should be replaced with the distinction between fully intentional, partly intentional, and unintentional actions. This has important consequences for the ascription of moral responsibility.

Actions are fully intentional if they are based on unforced choice between alternatives whose significance is adequately understood and evaluated. People routinely perform fully intentional actions, but doing so need not be a conscious, articulate, or laborious process. It may simply be the continuation of an approved and successful pattern of past actions, such as making oneself get up in the morning to go to work or picking a dish from the menu. Fully intentional actions require neither high intelligence nor much reflection.

It is normally appropriate to hold people morally responsible for their fully intentional evil actions. They chose such an action, they knew what they were doing, so they are accountable for it. But even in such cases exemptions or extenuations may be justified. The action may have been the only way of avoiding a greater evil, or people made an understandable mistake in thinking that the action was not evil. We may say, then, that people are morally responsible for their fully intentional actions unless there are exempting or extenuating considerations.

Actions are unintentional if they are done by people who lack or cannot exercise the capacity to choose, understand, or evaluate their alternatives. It is normally inappropriate to ascribe moral responsibility for unintentional actions. Exceptions, however, must be recognized. For people may be morally responsible for putting themselves in circumstances that make it impossible for them to exercise their capacity, such as getting drunk.

Actions are partly intentional if the people who perform them have the capacity to choose, understand, and evaluate their alternatives but do not exercise it. The ascription of moral responsibility depends on why they fail to do so. The reason may be difficult external circumstances or some internal weakness or failure. It is often unclear how large a part intention plays in an action because it is unclear just exactly how difficult are the circumstances, how much stress, pressure, or temptation makes choices forced, how well people need to understand the available alternatives, or how reasonable should be their evaluations. The ascription of the right degree of moral responsibility depends on resolving these unclarities. If the action was only partly intentional because of difficult circumstances, moral responsibility is extenuated; if it was because of some personal defect, the degree of moral responsibility is greater.

In the light of these conditions, it is possible to specify when the ascription of *full* moral responsibility is justified. People have full moral responsibility if their actions are characteristic, cause serious undeserved harm, violate prevailing moral standards, and are fully intentional. If these conditions are met, there are no exempting or extenuating circumstances. It is then appropriate both to condemn without qualification the people for performing such actions and to punish them severely, as in the cases of yet another murder committed by a contract killer, yet another innocent person made to suffer by a torturer, yet another group of citizens maimed by a terrorist's bomb.

Moral responsibility, however, may be *partial* rather than full because there are extenuating circumstances. There is a great variety of such circumstances and it is impossible to specify them in advance, but illustrative examples are readily found. If the evil action is uncharacteristic (murder in response to great provocation), if it conforms to the prevailing standards of a morally flawed society (mutilating criminals), if it is partly intentional (conscripts fighting in an unjust war), then the moral responsibility of evildoers is only partial. In these cases, condemnation is still warranted, but it needs to be qualified, and whether punishment is appropriate depends on the strength of the extenuating circumstances. It may also happen that the ascription of moral responsibility for an evil action is entirely inappropriate, for it may be the result of insanity, subnormal intelligence, or the breakdown of morality in extreme situations. Condemnation of the action is then still appropriate, but not of the person who performed it. And that, of course, also makes punishment unwarranted.

We can now ask about the moral responsibility of the pusher, the prostitute, and the terrorist. Their evil actions form habitual and predictable patterns, so they meet the condition of being characteristic. They also meet the condition of causing serious undeserved harm: to the children enticed into addiction by the pusher, to the people infected with AIDS by the prostitute, and to the people killed or maimed by the terrorist. Nor is there any doubt that they violate prevailing moral standards and that these evildoers cannot but know what these standards are. The last condition, however, is not met, because their actions are not fully intentional. In each case, the evildoers' understanding of the significance of their actions is clouded by their circumstances. But they are not totally without understanding, and they are of normal intelligence. It is reasonable, therefore, to recognize that their moral responsibility is not full. Their imperfect understanding of the significance of what they are doing is an extenuating circumstance. It would perhaps be too demanding to say that even if they lack the understanding, they ought to have it. For that may require too much of them. The reasonable judgment is that their moral responsibility is partial because they meet only three of the four conditions of full moral responsibility.

Ascribing partial moral responsibility to these people, however, is a requirement of morality. A central concern of morality is to protect the conditions in which good lives can be lived. One of these conditions is to protect people from evil. No one committed to morality can fail to regard that as important. The pusher, the prostitute, and the terrorist regularly cause evil. They do not do it accidentally or rarely. They are the kind of people who tend to do that, who tend to violate prevailing and reasonable moral standards of which they cannot be ignorant. Since their actions follow from and reflect their characters, their characters must also be matters of moral concern. This concern must manifest itself in regarding their characters as morally bad, in believing that the world would be a better place if there were no people like them, in teaching children not to be like them, and in doing whatever is warranted by reason and morality to prevent them from acting in their evil ways. The ascription of partial moral responsibility to them signifies that their moral standing is lowered because they violate the conditions that make good lives possible.

The ascription of partial moral responsibility, however, leaves it open what specific action should follow. Whether they should be condemned, and if so, how severely, whether the condemnation should lead to punishment, and if so, how serious it should be are questions that remain to be answered. But the questions arise because the ascription of partial moral responsibility is appropriate. Perhaps the pusher, the prostitute, and the terrorist should not be condemned or punished as severely as those whose identical actions are fully intentional. These possibilities, however, do not touch the more fundamental claim that morality makes it appropriate to ascribe partial moral responsibility to them.

3.5 The Mistake

Egalitarians who think like Hofstadter, Benn, Watson, and Wolf are committed to denying that the pusher, the prostitute, and the terrorist are anything more than causally responsible for their evil actions. We can now see their mistake. They are correct in thinking that these people's moral responsibility is not full, but they are incorrect in concluding that they have no moral responsibility at all. Their mistake is to fail to appreciate the complexities involved in the ascription of moral responsibility. If they recognized that its ascription is usually a matter of degree and that several conditions have a bearing on the degree to which it holds, then they would not conclude that the absence of full responsibility means no responsibility or that only one of four conditions is relevant to its ascription.

Egalitarians have been led to this mistake by concentrating on one of the internal conditions of moral responsibility at the expense of both the external conditions and the other internal condition. They think that moral responsibility depends exclusively on whether the evildoers' actions are fully intentional. That this is a mistake becomes obvious once it is realized that it leaves out absolutely crucial facts: namely, the evil done and the damages caused, the violation of reasonable moral standards, and the evildoers' past patterns of habitual and predictable evil actions.

Reflection on morality reinforces this criticism. Morality must be committed to decreasing evil because it is an obstacle to whatever goal morality is reasonably thought to have. It is a matter of great importance, therefore, to influence people's characters so as to dispose them toward the good and against evil. Doing so certainly requires influencing their intentions. The reason for that requirement, and for endowing it with moral significance, however, is the effect of people's actions on others. Intentions matter from the moral point of view because of the moral quality of subsequent actions. By focusing on intentions, egalitarians lose sight of the reason why intentions matter. Egalitarians agonize over the extent to which people are able to choose, understand, and evaluate their actions, but they forget about the reason why doing so is morally important.

In making this mistake, egalitarians are acting under the influence of the Kantian approach to morality that focuses on what motivates actions and largely ignores their consequences. In avoiding this mistake, we must not fall into the opposite, consequentialist, error of insisting that only consequences matter. Stressing the external conditions of moral responsibility at the expense of internal conditions is as mistaken as the reverse. Reasonable judgments about moral responsibility will recognize the relevance of both external and internal conditions.

The mistaken egalitarian denial of moral responsibility for partly intentional actions would not be important if only fully intentional actions were evil. But egalitarians agree that this is not so: fully and partly intentional and unintentional actions can all be evil, and widespread evil is caused mainly by not fully intentional actions. Since morality must aim to decrease evil, it must be concerned with all actions that cause it, not just with fully intentional ones. The egalitarian argument, however, places partly intentional and unintentional actions outside moral concern, thus exempting numerous evildoers from moral responsibility. Whatever restraint morality can then exercise is thereby removed from their conduct. This is why the egalitarian approach to moral responsibility makes evil more widespread. The result is that it is impossible for egalitarians to pursue successfully their corrective aim of decreasing evil and to remove the most serious obstacle to the achievement of their constructive aim of increasing equality.

These criticisms appear to be so obvious that the appeal of the egalitarian denial of moral responsibility cries out for an explanation. The explanation is that its appeal is based on the fear that if people are held responsible for less than fully intentional actions, then it would be impossible to recognize exempting or extenuating circumstances. This would be a morally unacceptable regression to the barbaric practice of strict liability that recognizes no difference between the moral responsibility of insane and normal people. This fear, however, is groundless. The recognition of the four conditions of moral responsibility provides the moral resources for drawing the appropriate distinctions.

3.6 Condemnation and Punishment

The egalitarian fear will be laid to rest if the question of whether people should be held morally responsible is distinguished from the question of how much moral responsibility should be ascribed to them. The first question is whether they should be held liable to condemnation and punishment at all. The second question arises only if the first is answered affirmatively, and it is about the appropriate degree of condemnation and punishment.

The answer to the first question is that normally people should be held liable to condemnation and punishment for the readily foreseeable consequences of their actions. The reason for this is that normally people have the capacity to benefit and harm others and to take this into consideration when they act. This capacity is part of human nature. If people fail to use this capacity, or use it badly, then they are normally liable to condemnation and punishment. This is an essential part of morality.

It must, of course, be recognized that there may be exceptional circumstances in which normalcy does not hold. The four conditions of moral responsibility make it possible to identify such circumstances and to distinguish among full, partial, and no moral responsibility. They guide us in what to look for that would show why circumstances are not normal. An evil action may have been uncharacteristic, partly intentional, or unintentional, or prompted by a prevailing but bad moral standard. We then have to look further to see why the action was uncharacteristic, just why it fell short of being fully intentional, or whether the questioning of the prevailing standard could have been expected. If these complications occur, the ascription of moral responsibility becomes a matter of judgment. But by appealing to the conditions, we can tell how the judgment should be made and what is relevant to making it.

The answer to the first question is, then, that the pusher, the prostitute, and the terrorist have partial moral responsibility, and they are liable to some degree of condemnation and punishment. Condemning them expresses the judgment that they are morally bad people because they made children addicted to drugs, infected people with AIDS, and murdered and maimed innocent people. It is to blame them for these actions, stigmatize them publicly, shun them privately, hold them up as examples to avoid, teach children not to be like them, warn others not to associate with them, expect them to feel guilt and shame, and condemn them even more if they are devoid of these feelings.

If this seems unduly harsh, the suffering they have caused should be remembered. The reluctance to accept the appropriateness of condemnation would dissipate if the concrete details of the lives of drug-addicted children, of people slowly dying of AIDS, of people maimed by a bomb were made vivid to oneself and if it were brought home to one that the suffering thus imagined must be multiplied by the large number of people whom these evildoers doomed. It should also be remembered that the condemnation is warranted by morality, which commits one to judging evil adversely. The condemnation, therefore, reflects not a hard heart but the seriousness of the evil toward which it is directed.

The appropriate degree of condemnation, however, is not as severe as it might be because the circumstances of the lives of the pusher, the prostitute, and the terrorist had much to do with their becoming evildoers. They have come to act in evil ways not because they have set out to cause evil but because they have become unable to act fully intentionally. Something has intervened between their actions and their choices, understandings, and evaluations. This extenuates the degree of condemnation that is appropriate but does not exempt the evildoers. For they do evil habitually and predictably, and by knowingly violating reasonable moral standards they cause serious undeserved harm to many people. They are properly condemned, although it would be a mistake to condemn them as severely as if their evil actions were fully intentional.

Moral responsibility, condemnation, and punishment form a continuum along which the divisions are blurred. Moral responsibility shades into condemnation, which shades into punishment. The justified ascription of moral responsibility does not merely create liability to condemnation but recognizes its appropriateness, and that is already a condemnation. Similarly, the more severe condemnation gets, the more it takes the form of punishment. Publicly expressed adverse moral judgment, social ostracism, being held up as a bad example are mild forms of punishment. Punishment, like moral responsibility and condemnation, allows for various degrees of severity, ranging from severe condemnation to long-term imprisonment and execution. To say, therefore, that evildoers deserve punishment leaves it open how severe the punishment ought to be.

The pusher, the prostitute, and the terrorist deserve severe punishment because they have committed felonies. Selling drugs to children, knowingly spreading AIDS, committing murder and mayhem are serious crimes. The criminal justice system has procedures for determining the appropriate punishment for them, which is likely to be long-term imprisonment. But our interest is not in the legal aspect of punishment. Legal punishment may be morally unacceptable if the criminal justice system is immoral, as it was in the Soviet Union and

Nazi Germany. So the question is whether the punishment of these evildoers would be morally justified.

The moral justification of punishment is a controversial matter, and this is not the place to debate the merits of various justifications. Perhaps it will suffice to make clear instead what is assumed to be the appropriate justification. Punishment is a response to evildoing. It consists in treating evildoers as they deserve to be treated. They deserve to suffer harm because they caused undeserved harm to others. The harm punishment inflicts should be proportional to the harm that has been caused. Punishment, of course, may accomplish more than treating evildoers as they deserve. It may protect people, deter potential evildoers, reform the criminal, restore the victim's confidence, enhance social stability, express indignation, and so forth. But its justification is that it metes out to evildoers what they deserve. Given this view, the punishment of the pusher, the prostitute, and the terrorist is not only legally but also morally justified. They deserve to be punished because they have caused much serious undeserved harm to many people. How severely they should be punished can be determined by the procedures of the criminal justice system. These procedures will take into account the extenuating circumstance that none of the three has acted as a fully intentional agent.

We may conclude, then, that egalitarians are committed to an illusion in thinking that evildoers should be held morally responsible and be liable to condemnation and punishment only if their actions are fully intentional. Unintentional and partly intentional actions extenuate the deserved degree of moral responsibility, condemnation, and punishment, but they do not exempt evildoers from these forms of moral disapprobation. This illusion has the serious consequence of preventing egalitarians from coping with the main source of widespread evil, namely, with less than fully intentional actions. As a result, egalitarians cannot successfully pursue the corrective aim of decreasing evil, and since evil is an obstacle to good lives, they cannot succeed in their constructive aim either.

4/

The Corruption of Justice

It is just . . . to render to each his due.

PLATO, *The Republic*

4.1 The Illusion

The case for holding evildoers responsible for their evil actions even if they are not fully intentional and the egalitarian denial of the appropriateness of doing so both derive from a deeper assumption about justice. The case for responsibility may be described as resting on the claim that evildoers *deserve* to be held responsible for regularly causing serious undeserved harm to others regardless of whether they cause it fully intentionally. Their actions are unjust, and holding them responsible is just. The assumption underlying this claim is that justice requires that people should get what they deserve and should not get what they do not deserve.

The denial of responsibility in such cases may be interpreted in two ways. One agrees that justice requires that people should get what they deserve but denies that being held responsible for other than fully intentional actions is deserved. Reasons against this have been given in the preceding chapter. The other denies that the connection between justice and desert is as close as some anti-egalitarians claim. The first reflects agreement about what justice is and disagreement about its application. The second reflects a far more basic disagreement about the very nature of justice. The topic of this chapter is the second disagreement.

This disagreement turns on the question, at the center of contemporary political thought, of what the connection is between justice and desert. Discussion of the question is dominated by Rawls's theory of justice, which is widely regarded as having already achieved the status of a classic, even though fundamental objections to it have not been met.[1] This consensus about Rawls's theory, however, rests on the illusion that justice requires depriving people of their legally acquired property in order to benefit others regardless of whether they deserve it. The prevailing consensus is based not on the merits of the theory but on its success in articulating the shared illusion of egalitarians.

The basic mistake of Rawls's view is that it supposes that what people deserve depends on the principles of justice, when in fact the justice of principles depends on whether they secure for people what they deserve. Desert is as primary as justice itself because desert is a necessary constituent of justice. A view of justice cannot be acceptable if it fails to recognize the essential connection between justice and desert and if it fails to evaluate principles of justice on the basis of their propensity to ensure that people get what they deserve. A view of justice that does not recognize the centrality of desert is like a view of competition that does not recognize the centrality of winning and losing.

The argument will begin with a sketch of the reasons for regarding the connection between justice and desert as essential; go on to consider Rawls's denial of the essential nature of their connection and raise some fundamental questions about Rawls's whole approach; and then provide a more detailed account of the view of justice as desert. This account will strengthen the conclusion about responsibility reached at the end of the preceding chapter and thereby reinforce the criticism that the corrective and constructive aims of egalitarianism are inconsistent.

4.2 The Ideal of Justice

The motivation behind the view of justice as desert may be understood by reflecting on the failure of Plato's account of justice in *The Republic*. Plato thought that justice as a virtue of individuals consists in the control of their wants and emotions (appetites and passions, as it is usually translated) by their reason. By analogy, justice as a virtue of societies consists in the rule of those who are motivated by reason over those who are motivated by wants and emotions. Plato thought this because he thought that reason provides knowledge of the good. If individuals and societies are motivated by that knowledge, life will go well for them, both morally and politically. The explanation of why many individuals and societies are bad is that uncontrolled wants and emotions divert them from the reasonable pursuit of the good.

Plato's view assumes that the good exists in a supersensible world; that it can be known, but only by those few who have the necessary talents and education to comprehend the supersensible world; that the good is independent of human wants and emotions; that those who know the good cannot but be motivated by it; and that the lives of individuals and societies are good to the extent to which they are motivated by knowledge of the good. It is a consequence of these assumptions that people necessarily end up with what they deserve because the goodness or badness of their lives is proportional to the extent to which they conform to the good. This necessity is guaranteed by what may be called cosmic justice.

Plato's assumptions have been extensively criticized on the grounds that there is no reason to believe that there is a supersensible world because any evidence accessible to human beings must come from the sensible world; that even if there were a supersensible world, it could not be known by human beings; that those who have claimed to have knowledge of the good have given many conflicting accounts of it; that the good cannot be independent of human wants and emotions because human beings are the ultimate judges of the goodness of their lives and they must judge at least partly on the basis of the satisfaction of their wants and their emotional attitudes toward their lives; that knowledge of the good often fails to motivate those who are morally bad or weak; and that human experience testifies against *the* good because individuals and societies can be good in many different ways. The cumulative effect of these and other criticisms is strong enough to warrant the conclusion that Plato's account of justice fails.

These criticisms, however, do not justify the rejection of Plato's view of justice as an ideal. The conviction is widely shared that the world ought to be such that people motivated by reason and goodness have good lives and that bad lives result from unreasonable or immoral motivation. Whatever may be the ultimate truth about cosmic justice, virtually no one believes that in life, as we know it in the sensible world, cosmic justice guarantees that people get what they deserve. The world is inundated with contingency. Good people often come to undeserved harm, and bad people often enjoy undeserved benefits, even in the long run. Although it is generally acknowledged that this is so, it is generally wished that it were otherwise. The wish may take forms that range from moral outrage to a resigned lament, but it is a wish that hardly any reflective person is without. This, of course, is consistent with the fact that reflective people also have other wishes about how the world should be, and those wishes may conflict with the one for cosmic justice. The point is merely that the wish for cosmic justice is generally felt by those who think about such matters. This is enough to show that Plato's ideal of justice lives, even if his account of justice is dead.

The motivation behind justice as desert can now be seen as the endeavor to approximate the ideal of justice—that the benefits people enjoy and the harms they suffer should be proportional to the goodness and badness of their lives—as closely as the contingencies of life allow. Aristotle shared this ideal, as well as many of the doubts about Plato's account of justice, and he took a significant step toward clarifying it. It is possible to extract from his *Nicomachean Ethics* the formula that justice consists in treating equals equally and unequals unequally.[2]

This formula, however, is much too vague to be useful as it stands. It is a condition of the application of any principle in any context that the like cases that come under its purview should be treated alike and different cases differently. This is as true of classifying fauna, diagnosing illness, adding numbers, and so forth as it is of justice. The Aristotelian formula, therefore, is insufficiently informative about why some principles are principles of justice. Furthermore, it is clear that for any two things it is always possible to find respects in which they are alike and respects in which they are different. The Aristotelian formula is incomplete because it does not specify what considerations are relevant to judging whether two things are equal or unequal. It may, then, be said that the Aristotelian formula correctly identifies consistency as a necessary condition of justice, but it is clearly not a sufficient condition.

The additional condition, however, is readily derivable from the ideal of justice that benefits and harms should be proportional to the goodness and badness of their recipients. This condition is desert. Justice should be understood in terms of consistency and desert: equals should be treated equally and unequals unequally in respect to desert. The reason why some principles are principles of justice is that they are concerned with people getting what they deserve. And the respects in which people are equal or unequal are the goodness or badness of their lives and the benefits and harms they enjoy or suffer. Consistency and desert are, then, individually necessary and jointly sufficient conditions of justice.

Desert is a noun that refers to the object that is deserved. The *OED* (1961) gives as the pertinent definition of the verb *to deserve:* "2. to have acquired, and thus to have, a rightful claim to; to be entitled to, in return for services or meritorious actions, or sometimes for ill deeds and qualities; to be worthy to have." And *The Unabridged Random House Dictionary* (1987) defines *to deserve* as "1. to merit, be qualified for, or have a claim to (reward, assistance, punishment, etc.) because of actions, qualities, or situations. . . . 2. to be worthy of, qualified for, or have a claim to reward, punishment, recompense, etc." Let us for the moment understand desert in the light of these definitions. A more analytical account will follow later on.

4.3 Rawls on Justice

Rawls denies that it is a requirement of justice that people should get what they deserve: "There is a tendency for common sense to suppose that income and wealth, and the good things in life generally, should be distributed according to moral desert. . . . Justice as fairness [Rawls's theory] rejects this conception."[3] And he adds: "The principles of justice . . . do not mention moral desert, and there is no tendency for distributive shares to correspond to it" (311). Rawls's denial of the essential connection between justice and desert is contrary to common sense and the traditional way of thinking about justice that has prevailed from the times of the Old Testament to our own, but he believes that there is a good reason for it. This reason is that what people come to deserve depends on their innate capacities and the circumstances of their lives, but "the initial endowments of natural assets and the contingencies of their growth and nurture in early life are arbitrary from the moral point of view" (311). To treat people justly is thus not to treat them as they deserve because they have no control over their capacities and circumstances that determine what they deserve. "No one deserves his place in the distribution of natural assets any more than he deserves his initial starting place in society" (311).

The obvious objection to this is that although people have no control over their native capacities and early circumstances in life, they do have control over what they make of their capacities and circumstances. What they deserve depends on their efforts in developing their capacities and responding to their circumstances. Rawls, however, rejects this. "The effort a person is willing to make is influenced by his natural abilities and skills and the alternatives open to him. The better endowed are more likely, other things equal, to strive conscientiously, and there seems to be no way to discount for their greater good fortune. The idea of rewarding desert is impracticable" (311–12). According to this view, what people deserve is a matter of luck, and justice should not reward or punish people for being lucky or unlucky.

The acceptance of this view would require the fundamental alteration of morality, law, and politics. They all rest on the belief that people are normally responsible for their actions and that it is reasonable to praise or blame, reward or punish them accordingly. But if Rawls's view were accepted, this would be unjust. If people have no control over their actions because what they do depends on their "natural abilities and skills and alternatives open to [them]," then what actions they perform is a matter of luck. If Rawls were right, no one would be responsible for anything. It would then be unjust to hold people responsible even for their fully intentional actions because whether they could act intentionally is also a matter of luck. Benefiting or harming others, having virtues or vices, being morally good or bad would all be matters of luck, and people should not be held accountable for any of it. These implications threaten the foundation of civilized life, and it is well to bear in mind that this is part of the cost of accepting what Rawls calls justice. This is a cost that even some of Rawls's fellow egalitarians are unwilling to pay because he "prescinds from any consideration of individual responsibility."[4]

As unacceptable as the costs are of following Rawls in denying the essential connection between justice and desert, worse yet are the consequences of following him in how he proposes to fill the lacuna in justice left by the exclusion of desert. He says that justice requires the recognition "that undeserved inequalities call for redress; and since inequalities of birth and natural endowments are undeserved, these inequalities are to be somehow compensated for. . . . In order to treat all persons equally . . . society must give more attention to those with fewer native assets and to those born into less favorable social positions. The idea is to redress the bias of contingencies in the direction of equality" (100–101). Rawls explains how this is to be done: it should be agreed "to regard the distribution of natural talents as a common asset. . . . Those who have been favored by nature . . . may gain from their good fortune only in terms that improve the situation of those who have lost out" (101). Society should be "arranged so that these contingencies work for the good of the least fortunate" (102).

The implication of this view is that justice requires that if people gain from being, say, attractive, witty, smart, or energetic, then some of their property should be taken from them to compensate those who are ugly, boring, dull, or sluggish. It is a further implication of what Rawls calls justice that Nobel Prize winners should compensate members of the Flat Earth Society, successful inventors should compensate cranks, great artists should compensate producers of kitsch "in order . . . to redress the bias of contingencies in the direction of equality." People's achievements redound to their credit as little as failures count toward their discredit. Since no one is responsible for anything, success and failure are matters of luck, and justice requires spreading it out evenly. This is to be done by the difference principle, which is one of Rawls's two principles of justice.

The difference principle is that "social and economic inequalities are to be arranged so that they are both (a) to the greatest benefit of the least advantaged, and (b) attached to positions open to all under conditions of fair equality of opportunity" (83). According to it, justice requires that a society should set up a perpetual equalizing machinery that works to redistribute property from those who have more to those who have the least. It is essential to understanding the significance of this principle that the redistribution of property is to go on independently of how those who have more came to have it and why those who are among the least advantaged are in that position. It makes no difference, given the oddly named difference principle, if people have more property because they have worked hard and well and earned it by legitimate means. Nor does the principle take into account if people are among the least advantaged as a result of their criminality, imprudence, deliberate renunciation of wealth, addiction, bankruptcy, gambling, and so on. The principle deems the mere fact of being among the least advantaged a sufficient reason to deprive those who have more of legally acquired property in order to give it to those who, for whatever reason, are among the least advantaged. This is to be done not once or twice but perpetually, and it is to be done in the name of what Rawls calls justice.

Consider in concrete terms the morally unacceptable consequences of this principle. Think of the pusher, the prostitute, and the terrorist (discussed in 3.2 on), but let us change their situations and suppose that they are among the economically least advantaged members of society. Now compare them with decent people in the same economic situation: the pusher with another janitor in the same school who had spurned drugs; the prostitute with her sister who has also been abused but who works as a nurse's aide; and the terrorist with a classmate who had resisted indoctrination and makes a poor living as a dirt farmer. According to the difference principle, the pusher and the janitor, the AIDS-spreading prostitute and the nurse's aide, the terrorist and the dirt farmer are entitled to the same distributive shares. Their bad economic situation is said to be due to contingencies that are arbitrary from the moral point of view. The pusher's enticement of young children to addiction, the prostitute's indifference to infecting hundreds of people with AIDS, and the terrorist's murder and injury of many innocent people make no morally relevant difference. Justice requires, in Rawls's view, that they should benefit equally from the redistribution of property.

Let us now change the scenario a little. The pusher, the prostitute, and the terrorist continue as before, but the janitor, the nurse's aide, and the dirt farmer have succeeded in improving somewhat their economic position. They have worked harder, saved more, spent less, and as a result they are no longer among the least disadvantaged. They are by no means affluent, but they are not poor either. According to the difference principle, the contingencies of life, among which are counted the efforts of the janitor, the nurse's aide, and the dirt farmer, are to be redressed in the direction of equality. And that means, on Rawls's view of justice, that some of the property of the janitor, the nurse's aide, and the dirt farmer should be taken from them and given to the pusher, the prostitute, and the terrorist.

These outrageous consequences follow because the difference principle takes for granted that justice requires disregarding the responsibility of individuals for their economic situation and not asking whether people deserve to have or to lack property. "The principles of justice . . . do not mention moral desert, and there is no tendency for distributive shares to correspond to it" (311). The difference principle holds it to be a requirement of justice to ignore the differences between those who made an effort and succeeded, who made an effort and failed, who could have made an effort but did not, who could not have made an effort, and who made a much weaker effort than they could have.

It is an odd sociological phenomenon that numerous highly intelligent people who have been trained to think critically and analytically have shown themselves positively eager to fall in with this Orwellian maneuver of calling blatant injustice just. The explanation that suggests itself is that Rawls and his followers are hell-bent on opposing economic inequality and they do not hesitate to expropriate a word with favorable connotations to put in a better light what they are doing. It would have been forthright for Rawls to call his book plainly *A Theory of Economic Equality,* and for his followers to welcome it for that reason, rather than to disguise it under the false label of justice.

The difference principle is Rawls's second principle of justice. The first is "the equal liberty principle," which says that "each person is to have an equal right to the most extensive total system of equal basic liberties compatible with a similar system of liberty for all" (250). A just society, according to Rawls, first guarantees equal basic liberties for everyone and then permits only those inequalities to result from people's exercise of their liberties which benefit most the least advantaged. The two principles jointly constitute what Rawls calls justice. The question is, of course, what reason there is for accepting these principles. Rawls's answer leads to the deepest level of his theory.

Rawls derives the principles from a hypothetical situation he invents, called the original position. He imagines rational and self-interested people coming together to legislate for all times the principles under which they will live. They are likely to choose principles that will favor them. Rawls stipulates, however, that the principles would have to be acceptable to all of them. In order to achieve the required unanimity, Rawls invents another hypothetical device, the veil of ignorance, behind which are supposed to be the legislators in the original position. They know nothing about their own characters, circumstances, and positions in the society for which they are legislating, so they do not know what principles would favor them. They will, therefore, choose principles that would render tolerable even the worst position that they may end up having in the imagined society. Rawls claims that his two principles of justice are the principles the legislators would choose. He says that

> since everyone's well-being depends upon a scheme of cooperation without which no one could have a satisfactory life, the division of advantages should be such as to draw forth the willing cooperation of everyone taking part in it, including those less well situated. Yet this can be expected only if reasonable terms are proposed. The two principles . . . seem to be fair agreement on the basis of which the better endowed, or more fortunate in their social position, neither of which we can be said to deserve, could expect the willing cooperation of others. . . . Once we decide to look for a conception of justice that nullifies the accidents of natural endowment and the contingencies of social circumstance . . . we are led to these principles. (15)

Rawls's claim that people in the original position and behind the veil of ignorance would choose his two principles of justice has been put to experimental test in several different ways by different experimenters. Their findings have been helpfully summarized by David Miller, and the remarks that follow are indebted to him.[5] Miller's conclusion is that "the evidence surveyed . . . highlights popular attachment to desert as a major criterion for income distribution, and suggests that a distribution centered on this criterion is potentially more stable than one that aims to raise the position of the worst-off group regardless of considerations of desert and need."[6]

One series of experiments supporting Miller's conclusion involved randomly selected subjects who were asked to rank four principles for distributing income they will receive as a group without any of them knowing what their share of the income might be.[7] These principles were Rawls's difference principle, which involved maximizing the minimum income; maximizing the average income; maximizing the average income but with a minimum level below which no one's income would fall; and maximizing average income but restricting the gap that could exist between top and bottom income. Participants ranked the four principles both individually and in groups of five in which they had to agree on the ranking. The difference principle was *never* selected by any group. By far the most popular choice was to maximize the average income but with a minimum level. Two-thirds of the individual participants and more than three-quarters of the groups selected this principle. This outcome makes obvious that Rawls is simply mistaken in his claim.

Suppose, however, that there is some reason for disregarding this result and the numerous other experimental refutations of Rawls's claim. Let us do as Rawls asks and imagine ourselves into the hypothetical situation he has invented. What principles would it be reasonable to want our future society to be guided by? One would certainly want the society to maintain peace and avoid war; be as prosperous as possible; guarantee the security of citizens and their property against criminals; protect the environment from pollution; keep the infrastructure in safe working order; provide an education that makes its citizens literate, numerate, and informed about their society and environment; and so forth. Of all the principles one might want, Rawls picks two and ignores the rest. He gives no reason for it.

That, however, does not stop him from claiming, "Justice is the first virtue of social institutions . . . laws and institutions . . . must be reformed or abolished if they are unjust" (3). But he does not say why justice is the first virtue rather than peace, prosperity, order, security, healthy environment, educated citizenry, and so forth. The point is not that it is not justice but something else that is the first virtue of social institutions. The point is that many virtues are necessary for having decent and workable social institutions, and justice is only one of them. Why is having a fine system of justice more important than not having the population decimated and the country occupied by a vicious enemy, or not having a subsistence economy, or not having rampant crime that endangers the survival of the society, or not having an unacceptably high level of pollution, or not having sufficiently well educated citizens to cope with the workings of a complex industrial society? Rawls does not say.

The principles of justice reasonable for a society to have must take into account other principles that are also reasonable to have. These other principles guide conduct in concrete, historically conditioned circumstances, making it necessary to know against what potential enemies is peace to be maintained and at what cost; what is the best way to achieve prosperity, given the available resources, workforce, and trading partners; how to protect order and against what kind of threats; how serious is the pollution and what would be the consequences of reducing it for employment, prosperity, security, and so forth. These and countless other concrete questions must be faced and answered in order to have decent and workable social institutions. Rawls's procedure, however, makes that impossible. For it assumes that there is a first virtue of social institutions to which other things must be subordinated no matter what happens; that the first virtue is justice; and that its principles can be formulated in abstract and general terms by a thinker who regards it as a mark of excellence to ignore the concrete circumstances of the society about which he is moralizing.

What Rawls calls justice, therefore, denies that people should get what they deserve, ignores their responsibility for their actions and economic condition, discounts their efforts, ascribes principles to people that experimental evidence shows they would not hold, rests on abstractions that deliberately ignore the concrete realities to which they are meant to apply, and holds it to be a requirement of justice to systematically deprive people of their legitimately earned income in order to give it those who have not earned it.

Rawls claims for this corruption of justice that "each person possesses an inviolability founded on justice that even the welfare of society as a whole cannot override. For this reason justice denies that the loss of freedom for some is made right by a greater good shared by others. It does not allow that the sacrifices imposed on the few are outweighed by the larger sum of advantages enjoyed by many" (3–4). And the author who writes these fine words regards the talents of allegedly inviolable persons as common assets, and permits people to use their talents only for the improvement of others, even if the others are criminal, imprudent, immoral, or do not wish to be improved. Nor does the author of these lines hesitate to impose on a few the sacrifice of their legitimately acquired property on the grounds that their sacrifice is made right by the greater good of those who have less. It is hard to know whether the corruption of justice or the concomitant invasion of freedom is worse.

4.4 The Nature of Desert

The defense of justice as desert must do more than show that Rawls's attempt to sever their connection is untenable. It must explain what desert is and why it is a matter of justice that people should get what they deserve and should not get what they do not deserve. Let us, then, turn to a detailed account of desert itself, an account that begins with the dictionary definitions (given at the end of 4.2).[8]

If people deserve some benefit or harm, it is because of some fact about them. This fact is the *basis* of desert, and that they are entitled to some benefit or harm on that basis creates a *claim* of desert. Desert is thus relative to people because its basis is a fact about them and the claim is for some benefits or harms that they ought to have. The fact that forms the basis of desert may be a character trait, such as a virtue or a vice, an excellence or a fault, a skill or a deficiency; or it may be a relation, for instance being a taxpayer, a competitor, a child of, or an employee; or it may be an explicit or implicit agreement, like having made a promise, got married, or enrolled as a student; or it may be an action that was kind or cruel, thoughtful or unthinking, fair or unfair. The basis of desert, then, is some characteristic, relation, agreement, or action of some person. Each of these bases allows for considerable variety within it. Desert, therefore, does not have a unitary basis; it is a pluralistic notion.

The claim of desert is that the person in question ought to enjoy some benefit or suffer some harm on the relevant basis. The claim need not be made by the person concerned; indeed, it is not often that people lay claim to some deserved harm. Nor need there be any other person or institution that makes the claim on behalf of the person. The claim should be understood in the very general sense that someone has a certain benefit or harm coming and that it would be good, right, proper, fitting for the person to receive it. The claim sometimes could and should be enforced, but it need not be. It need not even be enforceable because there are perfectly legitimate claims of desert that are not directed toward any person or institution, such as that evildoers do not deserve to live happily until they die of old age or that good people do not deserve the misfortune that befalls them.

The ascription of desert is partly backward- and partly forward-looking. It looks backward toward its basis, and it looks forward from there to lay claim to the appropriate benefit or harm. The ascription of desert thus always requires a particular type of reason, and the claim it creates always requires a particular type of justification. Both requirements are met by the basis of desert. It may thus be said that hard and intelligent work deserves success, employees deserve wages from their employers, children deserve a decent upbringing from their parents, acts of kindness deserve gratitude from their recipients, just as hypocrites deserve to be exposed, incompetent physicians deserve to lose their licenses, and criminals deserve punishment. The justification of these claims is to point at the relevant characteristic, relation, agreement, or action that provides the basis for claiming that the person to whom it is attached deserves the appropriate benefits or harms.

The basis for justified claims of desert, however, has a further requirement because not just any characteristic, relation, agreement, or action provides the required reason. To serve as a reason, the basis must be something that warrants the benefits or harms consequent upon it. There must be an explanation of what makes it fitting that the person concerned should receive some benefit or harm. The appropriate explanation, then, strengthens the reason that can be derived from the basis of desert by pointing at the feature that makes a characteristic, relation, agreement, or action a fitting basis for some benefit or harm. The required explanation therefore must point at some excellence or fault, achievement or failure, compliance or noncompliance, commission or omission that provides the basis for claiming that a particular person deserves some particular benefits or harms. Punishment is deserved because its recipient is a criminal; loyalty is deserved because it is owed to a friend; the repayment of a loan is deserved because one promised it; admiration is deserved because the action was courageous.

From this follow several ways in which the ascription of desert may be mistaken. One is a factual mistake about the basis of desert. The person who was thought to be a burglar really is not, so punishment is inappropriate. Another is a mistake in thinking that the basis of desert warrants the benefits or harms that it is thought to warrant. This may result from a mistaken evaluation of the basis, such as thinking of chastity as a virtue. Or it may involve a correct evaluation that is mistakenly applied, for instance thinking correctly that modesty is a virtue but mistaking humility for it. A further mistake is one of proportion. The person in question does indeed deserve benefits or harms on the basis that is rightly supposed to warrant them, but the benefits or harms received exceed what is appropriate. The burglar deserves imprisonment but not for life; the novelist deserves good reviews but not a Nobel Prize. The last is the logical mistake of ascribing desert without regard for its basis. The mistake is not that there is thought to be a basis when there is none; rather, the ascription of desert occurs in disregard of whether it has an appropriate basis. In this way, benefits or harms may be distributed not on the basis of some properly evaluated characteristic, relation, agreement, or action but for some other reason.

The significance of this last kind of mistake is considerable. Just as a person cannot be held to a promise if none has been made, or be guilty of a crime if none has been committed, so desert cannot be ascribed unless it has a basis. The reason for this is that without a basis the benefits and harms received cannot—logically cannot—be deserved. Benefits and harms may be received for reasons of want, love, prudence, generosity, paternalism, religious belief, political expediency, and so forth. But they can be deserved only if there is a specific reason for receiving them. And that reason must be that their recipients are entitled to them because of some characteristic, relation, agreement, or action of theirs which makes it fitting that they should enjoy or suffer those particular benefits or harms.

It is just this element of fittingness that Rawls's view of justice lacks. To say that everybody deserves the same benefits is to ignore the fact that people differ in respect to their characteristics, relations, agreements, or actions, and thus in respect to the bases on which desert can reasonably be ascribed to them. The charge Rawls famously leveled against utilitarianism also applies, as Robert Nozick points out, to egalitarianism: it "does not take seriously the distinction between persons."[9]

To reply to this by saying that there may be some respects in which all normal people are alike, such as their capacity for moral personality, as Rawls claims,[10] and that is why they all deserve the same benefits, is to make the logical mistake about the basis on which desert can be reasonably ascribed. For it is not enough for the ascription of desert that people be alike in some way; it must also be explained why that likeness creates a basis for desert. The basis must be something that warrants the claim to some particular benefit or harm. The capacity for moral personality fails these conditions. For there are obvious differences among the characteristics, relations, agreements, and actions of people who are alike in possessing the capacity for moral personality: the capacity may or may not be used; if used, it may be for good or evil; if used for good, it may or may not be successful. All these, and other considerations, affect whether the capacity for moral personality provides a basis for desert and what the desert is.

The force of this argument is not diminished by substituting for the capacity for moral personality the capacity for rationality, or feeling pleasure or pain, or happiness, or something else. The fact that people are alike in some respect is not enough to create a basis for desert. It must also be shown why that likeness creates a basis for desert-claims. Why would the mere possession of a capacity be a fitting basis for enjoying the same benefits or suffering the same harms, especially since the capacity is used in different degrees and ways by different people?

4.5 The Imperfections of Justice

It is a consequence of the view of justice as desert that any adequate account of justice must have at least two aspects. The first is the distribution of benefits and harms. Justice as desert is the view that their distribution should be based on the characteristics, relations, agreements, and actions of the recipients. The second aspect is the rectification of the injustice that is bound to occur in the distribution of benefit and harms. The standard to which just distribution and rectification should aim to conform is the ideal that benefits and harms should be proportional to the goodness or badness of their recipients. And their goodness and badness are to be understood in terms of conforming to or violating the requirements set by the characteristic, relations, agreements, and actions that constitute the bases of desert. These bases make concrete what cosmic justice would come to in the context of a particular society.

Justice in general requires that people should get what they deserve. Justice in particular, however, varies from society to society because the characteristics, relations, agreements, and actions that define desert vary. These variations reflect the different circumstances, conceptions of a good life, traditions, and customs that have emerged and endured in the history of different societies. This is why different societies can accept the concept of justice as desert and yet subscribe to different conceptions of justice. They can all regard cosmic justice as their ideal and simultaneously interpret its requirements differently.

The fact remains, however, that the ideal of cosmic justice is unattainable regardless of how it is interpreted. What stands in the way is the human condition. The ideal is a regulative ideal that guides, not a goal that is to be achieved. The reason for this is that there are unavoidable limitations that always stand in the way of having as just a system of distribution and rectification as the ideal of cosmic justice requires. The most obvious way in which scarcity limits just distribution is through the insufficiency of the available resources. No matter how strong is the commitment to implementing a particular conception of justice, if there is not enough money, food, medicine, prison space, police protection, or hospital care available, then people cannot have what they deserve.

Rectification is concerned with correcting unjust distribution. Its purpose is to make benefits and harms proportional to desert. This endeavor, however, is limited by the disproportionality that is an insurmountable obstacle to rectification. Some forms of unjust harm cannot be rectified. Nothing could compensate people who sacrificed their lives for a noble cause, who were blinded or disfigured in an accident for which they were not responsible, who were forced to spend the best years of their lives in concentration camps on trumped-up charges, or who contracted AIDS through blood transfusion. Nor is there a proportional punishment for mass murderers, torturers, or fanatics who destroy great works of art. Nothing could redress such imbalances because no benefit or harm could be commensurate with what created them. Disproportionality, therefore, unavoidably limits efforts at rectification.

The practical significance of the limits on the distributive and rectificatory aspects of justice is that efforts to make life more just must be directed largely toward alleviating injustice. Injustice, however, is always a specific offense against specific individuals who suffer specific unjust harms in specific contexts. Injustice is alleviated to the extent to which specific remedies are found for specific injuries. It is useless, therefore, to approach the question of how life can be made more just by attempting to construct abstract principles of justice. Even if such principles were to succeed in commanding the assent of reasonable people, they could not be used to overcome the limits of justice because the principles would lack the essential concrete detail. The efforts to construct a system of justice as a substitute for cosmic justice must be seen, therefore, as possible only within limits imposed by external conditions. These limits are unavoidable because scarcity and disproportionality cannot be eliminated from human lives.

Part of the reason for stressing these aspects and limitations of justice is to call attention to two significant differences between Rawls's conception of justice and the view of justice as desert. First, Rawls thinks that the achievement of justice depends on having the basic structure of a society reflect the right principles of justice. Justice is thus a result of the right institutional arrangements. The view of justice as desert certainly acknowledges the necessity and importance of having the right institutional arrangements, but it denies that having them is sufficient for justice. For scarcity and disproportionality present obstacles that not even the right institutional arrangements can overcome. The significance of this is that Rawls's conception nurtures, whereas the view of justice as desert repudiates, the egalitarian illusion that a society will be just if it has the right institutional arrangements.

Second, the view of justice as desert implies that justice is presupposed rather than, as Rawls claims, created by institutional arrangements. Justice is an objective ideal that is not relative to any institutional arrangements; it exists in its own right, and institutional arrangements merely approximate it more or less closely. The objectivity of the ideal of justice does not mean that it has independent existence. It means that it is an ideal that reasonable and reflective people will accept, even if they also accept other, possibly conflicting, ideals, and even if they try to achieve the ideal of justice in different ways.

The recognition of these differences between Rawls's conception and the view of justice as desert may lead to the thought that the two sides are talking past each other. They have quite different concerns, which each side pursues under the label *justice*, but this, it may be thought, is merely a verbal disagreement. Rawls is concerned with the fair distribution of economic benefits. Justice as desert is concerned with making benefits and harms proportional to the goodness or badness of their recipients. What matters is not whether their respective theories are called theories of justice but whether they are supported by good reasons. This attempt at pacification, however, does not work. When Rawls claims that distribution based on desert is unjust and when defenders of desert say that distribution that ignores desert is unjust, they are not having a verbal disagreement. Each finds the policies that follow from the other's theory morally objectionable. Their disagreement, therefore, is moral, not merely verbal.

It must now be asked, what reason can be given in support of the prima facie claim that people should get what they deserve? Why should benefits and harms be proportional to the goodness or badness of their recipients? The answer is that people should get what they deserve because it follows from the nature of goal-directed action. Consider typical patterns of human conduct. People have various *wants:* physiological and psychological, personal and social, self-interested and altruistic, important and trivial, long-term and temporary, and so forth. They follow *policies* aimed at satisfying or not satisfying their particular wants. These policies may be the conscious and articulate results of reflection and deliberate choice, or they may be the unreflective and inarticulate outcomes of custom, habit, personal defects, or training. In either case, their aim is both short-term concerning a particular want and long-term reflecting their more distant *goals*, such as living a certain kind of life, being a certain kind of person, serving a certain cause, and so forth. The conjunction of wants, policies, and goals leads people to perform some *action* that follows their policy and aims to bridge the gap between their wants and goals. The pattern of wants, policies, goals, and actions is permeated with beliefs about what wants to satisfy, what policies to follow, what goals to have, what actions to perform, and how to coordinate their relevant activities with the similar activities of others. These beliefs may be reasonable or unreasonable. Mistakes may occur at each step along the way, not just because reasonable beliefs may turn out to be false but also because there are numerous internal obstacles to forming reasonable beliefs.

Suppose people hold and act on reasonable beliefs. The expectation is that they will then succeed in achieving their goals. Yet they may still fail through no fault of their own because other people who are guided by unreasonable beliefs may prevent them or because the contingencies of life may place obstacles in their way. If this happens, and the expectation is disappointed, it gives rise to the belief that since they have done everything they reasonably could, they ought to have succeeded. This expectation and belief are the sources of the claim that people should get what they deserve. The lamentable fact remains, however, that people often fail to get what they deserve, even though they have done all they could. That is part of the reason for having a system of justice, which is the device societies have evolved to get people what they deserve. This system is inspired by the ideal of cosmic justice, the substitute for the belief in the existence of cosmic justice. The contingencies of life, however, often prevent people from getting what they deserve. The aim and the justification of a system of justice is to bridge this unfortunate gap between what people deserve and what they have. Bridging it depends on specifying the bases of legitimate claims of desert. Different societies specify them differently as a result of differences in their histories and circumstances. So different societies have different systems of justice, but they are systems of justice if, and only if, they aim to close the gap between what people deserve and what they have. Although complete success will elude all systems, the unavoidable imperfections of justice ought to act as a spur to close the gap as much as possible.

4.6 Justice as Desert

Let us now consider two objections to the view of justice as desert. The first is that the distribution of benefits and harms on the basis of desert is practically impossible. Rawls says, "The idea of rewarding desert is impracticable" (312), and Friedrich Hayek, who is no egalitarian, objects on the same ground.[11] The idea behind the objection is that in contemporary Western societies there is no agreement about what a good life is. There are many conceptions of a good life, what people are thought to deserve depends at least partly on which conception is accepted, and so there is bound to be much disagreement about what people deserve. The problem is exacerbated by the fact that what people deserve partly depends on their beliefs and efforts, and these are not open to observation. It is unrealistic to suppose that political decisions about the distribution of benefits and harms and about the rectification of unjust distribution could take such subjective factors into account.

This objection rests on two assumptions that have led to misunderstanding the view of justice as desert. The first is that what people deserve depends on their personal excellences, and the second is that the distribution of deserved benefits and harms is the responsibility of the government. Both these assumptions are mistaken, but neither is totally mistaken. Personal excellences are among the bases of desert, but they are merely one among many. The government does have responsibility for the distribution of some deserved benefits and harms, but many others are distributed by civic institutions that function independently of the government.

The bases of desert are the characteristics, relations, agreements, and actions of the recipients, and personal excellences are among their characteristics. Even if it were true that there are great practical difficulties in ascertaining what personal excellences people have, this would not invalidate desert-claims based on their relations, agreements, and actions. These bases of desert are open to public observation, and there is no greater practical difficulty in identifying them than there is in identifying countless other features that people have.

It adds to the implausibility of this objection that it is often possible to identify personal excellences, even though they have a subjective dimension. What, according to this objection, runs into great practical difficulty is routinely done by families, teachers, coaches, selection committees, employers, musicians, and countless other people who are charged with making judgments about the personal excellences of some people. These judgments, of course, can be good or bad. If they are good, the alleged practical difficulties have been overcome. If they are bad, it need not be because practical difficulties stand in the way.

This last rejoinder, however, will be regarded as irrelevant because of the second mistaken assumption on which the objection rests. If the distribution of deserved benefits and harms were the responsibility of the government, then the success of individuals in identifying personal excellences would be irrelevant. The question then is whether governments, not individuals, can succeed in formulating policies about the distribution of benefits and harms based on personal excellences. The answer to this question is twofold. First, the distribution of deserved benefits and harms is based not just on personal excellences but also on the relations, agreements, and actions of the recipients. Second, their distribution is not the exclusive prerogative of the government, for civic institutions play a very large role in it.

The civic institutions are families, schools, universities, corporations, athletic competitions, small businesses, orchestras, museums, quiz shows, honor societies, foundations, committees that award prizes, parole boards, neighborhood groups, arbitration panels, and many other more or less formal associations of people that stand between the private concerns of individuals and the political responsibilities of the government. These civic institutions distribute money, honors, status, prestige; they distinguish among excellence, mediocrity, and deficiency; they set standards and evaluate performance by them; they assign rewards and mete out punishments; they have ways of rectifying violations of their procedures and standards; and they continually face and resolve disputes among their members about these matters. These civic institutions routinely identify personal excellences relevant to their concerns, and, of course, they do the same with the relevant relations, agreements, and actions of their members.

Even if it were true, therefore, that practical difficulties prevent the government from knowing what the deserved distribution of benefits and harms is, the same would not be true of civic institutions. But, of course, it is not true that practical difficulties prevent the government from doing what civic institutions do. The government encounters no great practical difficulty in identifying some requirements of relations, such as marriage, parenthood, or citizenship; of agreements, such as taking out a mortgage, enlisting in the army, buying a car, or being a patient in a hospital; and of actions, such as driving a car, having a fight, or appealing a verdict. All these cases constitute bases for the distribution of benefits and harms, which may or may not be received. For all these cases there exist avenues for rectification if the distribution goes wrong. And there are proper forums for settling conflicts regarding distribution and rectification. There is, therefore, no good reason to suppose, as the first objection does, that distribution based on desert is vitiated by great practical difficulties.

The second objection is that the view of justice as desert takes for granted that the characteristics, relations, agreements, and actions that form the bases of desert-claims in a particular society are themselves just. But, of course, they may not be just, and so justice as desert may perpetuate existing injustice rather than change it. Justice as desert is a conservative view that defends prevailing arrangements instead of reforming defective ones.

This objection rests on the mistaken assumption that the view of justice as desert is committed to the uncritical acceptance of the prevailing bases of desert. Of course there are deplorable, coercive, exploitative, unfair, ignorant, stupid, and prejudice-ridden bases for distributing benefits and harms. Of course justice requires reforming them. The crucial question is, what makes these bases objectionable from the point of view of justice? And the answer is that they are objectionable because they stand in the way of people getting what they deserve.

The objection, however, will be pressed. If justice requires that people should get what they deserve on the basis of their characteristics, relations, agreements, and actions, then how can the justice of the bases themselves be determined? On what ground could the prevailing arrangements of a particular society be criticized on the view of justice as desert? The answer is obvious. They could be criticized on the ground that they rest on some mistake in fact, evaluation, proportion, or logic that prevents people getting what they deserve. Being born into the nobility does not warrant special privileges because it has no more than an accidental connection with good characteristics. Master-slave relations are prejudice-ridden because they wrongly suppose that the slaves are inferior to the masters. Marriage contracts in which the husband acquires ownership of the wife's property are unfair agreements because they falsely deny the wife's capacity to make reasonable decisions. The punishment of theft by cutting off an arm is a deplorable action because of its disproportionality. In all these cases, the arrangements that have prevailed led to people getting more benefits or harms than they deserve, and that shows that the arrangements are unjust. The bases of that judgment are the mistakes on which the arrangements rest. What justice as desert requires, therefore, is not that people should get what they deserve according to the prevailing bases of desert, but that they should get it on the basis of those prevailing bases that are free of mistakes in fact, evaluation, proportionality, and logic. That mistake-free arrangements for distributing benefits and harms should be perpetuated may be a conservative view, but it is also one that all reasonable people will share. It must be acknowledged, of course, that there may be serious disagreements about whether a particular basis of desert is free of mistakes. These disagreements, however, concern the question of what is deserved. They are regarded as important precisely because the disagreeing parties accept that, whatever it is, justice requires that people should get what they deserve.

It is now possible to sum up the argument for the view of justice as desert. Consistency and desert are individually necessary and jointly sufficient conditions of justice. Consistency requires treating equals equally and unequals unequally. Desert specifies that the treatment should be in respect to the distribution of benefits and harms and the rectification of miscarried distribution. Claims of desert are based on the characteristics, relations, agreements, and actions of the recipients which are generally recognized in the recipients' society as warranting specific benefits and harms. General recognition, however, may be faulty because it may involve mistakes in fact, evaluation, proportion, and logic. The appropriate bases of desert, consequently, are only those characteristics, relations, agreements, and actions that are reasonably believed to be free of such mistakes. Desert-claims made on such bases are legitimate. There is a presumption in favor of meeting them, but the presumption may be defeated by considerations that make it reasonable that people should get fewer or more benefits and harms than they deserve. Those who think that this would be justified in a particular case acquire the burden of showing why some consideration is more important than the claim of desert. Legitimate and un-

defeated desert-claims ought to be met, but scarcity and disproportionality may still present insurmountable obstacles to meeting them.
The human condition renders all systems of justice imperfect.

The preceding is intended as a summary of the account of the concept of justice. There are many different and reasonable conceptions
of justice because the characteristics, relations, agreements, and actions that are thought to be the bases of legitimate desert-claims reflect the different histories and circumstances of different societies
and their civic institutions. Such differences, however, concern the
different bases of desert, but they presuppose that there is a prima
facie reason to meet legitimate claims of desert. Meeting them is the
aim of justice.

It follows from the view of justice as desert that Rawls's view of
justice is radically mistaken. It recommends taking property from
people who have more and giving it to those who have less, without
asking whether the first deserve to lose it and second deserve to receive it. Whatever reasons may be given in favor of this recommendation, justice cannot be among them because desert is an essential constituent of justice and Rawls's view fails to recognize it. Rawls's view,
therefore, is not of justice but of the equal distribution of property. It
would clarify current disputes about economic egalitarianism if this
were acknowledged. In any case, Rawls's view rests on the illusion
that justice requires the equalization of property regardless of
whether its present owners or future recipients deserve it. The truth is
that justice requires that people should have or get what they deserve
insofar as the contingencies of life permit.

The Groundlessness of Egalitarianism

What we have to deal with in the case of "social justice" is simply a quasi-religious superstition of the kind which we should respectfully leave in peace so long as it merely makes those happy who hold it, but which we must fight when it becomes a pretext of coercing other men. And the prevailing belief in "social justice" is at present probably the greatest threat to most other values of a free civilization.

FRIEDRICH VON HAYEK, *Law, Legislation, and Liberty*

5.1 The Illusion

The aim of this chapter and the next is to consider the egalitarian argument for equality. The central claim is that equality is the most basic value and it requires that everyone should be treated as an equal. This is taken to be a moral requirement, and it is supposed that the key to it is the redistribution of property. We have seen in the preceding chapter the failure of Rawls's attempt to defend economic equality as a requirement of justice. The egalitarians we shall discuss in this chapter attempt to defend it as a requirement of morality. According to them, morality requires systematically depriving a large majority of a sizable portion of their legally owned property in order to benefit a much smaller minority. This view is merely the latest instance of a lamentable historical tendency that was traditionally defended by the supposed excellences of those who were privileged at the expense of others. Egalitarianism is different because its attempted defense appeals to the deficiencies of those whom it favors. The claim is that the fact that some people own less property than others makes it a moral requirement to equalize the difference between them.

The justification proposed for this claim is the illusion that a society ought to treat everyone with equal consideration.[1] As a rough measure, let us say that in our society the large majority being deprived of legally owned property consists of those who live above the poverty level and the much smaller minority consists of those who live below it. The majority includes approximately 87 percent of the citizens, and the minority constitutes about 13 percent.[2] The illusion leads egalitarians to discriminate systematically in favor of 13 percent of the population at the expense of 87 percent on the grounds that equal consideration requires it.[3] Some having more than others makes it morally obligatory to take it from the former and give it to the latter, regardless of how those who have more came to have it and how those who have less came to have less.

It is easy to be lulled into acquiescence by the relentless egalitarian rhetoric that appeals to this supposed obligation. But it should be recognized that egalitarianism requires the equalization of the ownership of property between, for example, muggers and muggees, burglars and homeowners, rapists and their victims, illegal immigrants and blue-collar workers, welfare cheats and taxpayers, spendthrifts who did not save for retirement and prudent ones who did, risk takers who lost and cautious investors who gained, and so forth. The supposed obligation laid on our society by egalitarians is to treat good and bad, prudent and imprudent, law-abiding and criminal people with equal consideration. If the consequences of being bad, imprudent, and criminal catch up with people and they find themselves below the poverty level, then it becomes the obligation of the government to deprive good, prudent, and law-abiding people above the poverty level of a considerable portion of their property in order to give it to those below it. For morality requires the government to treat everyone with equal consideration, which in turn requires the equalization of unequally owned property.

5.2 Arbitrary Claims

It may be thought that so implausible a view cannot be widely held, but we have the assurance of well-known egalitarian thinkers that it is: "No government is legitimate that does not show equal concern for the fate of all those citizens over whom it claims dominion and from whom it claims allegiance"; "the fundamental argument is not whether to accept equality, but how best to interpret it"; "the principle that all humans are equal is now part of the prevailing political and ethical orthodoxy"; the explanation of "our code" is that "in all cases where human beings are capable of enjoying the same goods, we feel that the intrinsic value of their enjoyment is the same"; and "we believe . . . that in some sense every citizen, indeed every human being . . . deserves equal consideration. . . . We know that most people in the past have not shared [this belief]. . . . But for us, it is simply there."[4]

Perhaps it will not be regarded as unduly mistrustful to ask who the "we" are that subscribe to this amazing obligation of equal consideration. Do "we" include Chinese peasants? the castes of India? Indonesians murdering each other over religious and ethnic differences? the Japanese who make it very hard for people of other races to live among them? murderous African tribes? all those men who, according to some egalitarians, are sexist? all those whites who, according to some egalitarians, are racist? Do Shiites regard infidels with equal consideration? Arabs the Jews, Serbians the Bosnians, and vice versa? all those capitalists whom egalitarians blame for so many of our ills? Are they perhaps Republicans who keep electing presidents, senators, and congressmen who explicitly repudiate the view that "we" hold?

These questions will no doubt be decried as unfair. What egalitarians mean by "we," it will be said, are those whose business it is to think about political matters. But this cannot be, because there are numerous such thinkers who are highly critical of egalitarianism, even if egalitarians do not take the trouble to respond to their criticisms.[5] It is beginning to look as if "we" included only a small number of egalitarian thinkers and those whom they manage to influence. In effect, "we" refers to the left wing of the Democratic party in America and to the democratic and not so democratic socialists in Europe. The membership in this "we" is therefore insufficiently numerous to place egalitarianism beyond questioning. If, then, it is questioned, what response do egalitarians offer?

It is regrettable that one of their responses is to abuse their critics. They say things such as: "All humans have an equal basic moral status. They possess the same fundamental rights, and the comparable interests of each person should count the same in calculations that determine social policy. . . . These platitudes are virtually universally affirmed. A white supremacist or an admirer of Adolf Hitler who denies them is rightly regarded as beyond the pale of civilized dialogue."[6] Having placed beyond the pale of civilized dialogue the critics of egalitarianism, it becomes unnecessary to meet the objections of all these white supremacists and Nazis. "We cannot reject the egalitarian principle outright, because it is . . . immoral that [the government] should show more concern for the lives of some than of others."[7] And "a distribution of wealth that dooms some citizens to a less fulfilling life than others, no matter what choices they make, is unacceptable, and the neglect of equality in contemporary politics is therefore shameful."[8] That makes it immoral and shameful not to equalize the property of good, prudent, law-abiding and bad, imprudent, and criminal people. Or they say, "Some theories, like Nazism, deny that each person matters equally. But such theories do not merit serious consideration."[9] So that the critics listed in note 5—Charvet, Flew, Frankfurt, Hayek, Kekes, Lucas, MacIntyre, Matson, Narveson, Pojman, Raz, and Sher—are, or are like, Nazis. Or again, "Any political theory that aspires to moral decency must try to devise and justify a form of institutional life which answers to the real strength of impersonal values," and "impersonal values" commit one to "egalitarian impartiality."[10] All critics of egalitarianism, then, fail in moral decency. Just imagine the wave of indignation that would descend on someone who would dare to say such things about defenders of egalitarianism.

Egalitarians, however, offer another response, which, in its own way, is even more remarkable than the preceding ad hominem one. Here are some examples of it. Richard Arneson concedes that "non-utilitarian moralities with robust substantive equality ideals cannot be made coherent."[11] He nevertheless regards disagreement with them as beyond the pale of civilized dialogue.

Brian Barry says, "The justification of the claim of fundamental equality has been held to be impossible because it is a rock-bottom ethical premise and so cannot be derived from anything else."[12] This is a mealy-mouthed admission that egalitarianism rests on an unjustifiable assumption.

Isaiah Berlin tells us: "Equality is one of the oldest and deepest elements in liberal thought and it is neither more nor less 'natural' or 'rational' than any other constituent in them [sic]. Like all human ends it cannot be defended or justified, for it is itself which justifies other acts."[13] So egalitarianism is based on a rationally indefensible article of faith.

Joel Feinberg, discussing the attitude behind egalitarianism, declares that it "is not grounded on anything more ultimate than itself, and it is not demonstrably justifiable. It can be argued further against skeptics that a world with equal human rights is a *more just* world . . . a less *dangerous* world . . . and one with a *more elevated and civilized* tone. If none of this convinces the skeptic, we should turn our back on him and examine more important problems."[14] One wonders whether egalitarians would be satisfied with such a response if they occupied the position of the skeptic regarding conservative or religious attitudes.

Will Kymlicka writes, "Every plausible political theory has the same ultimate source, which is equality. . . . A theory is egalitarian . . . if it accepts that the interests of each member of the community matter, and matter equally. . . . If a theory claimed that some people were not entitled to equal consideration from the government, if it claimed that certain kinds of people just do not matter as much as others, then most people in the modern world would reject that theory immediately."[15] So we are invited to believe as an obvious truth that most people would immediately reject the view that torturers and their victims, or the scourges and benefactors of humanity do not matter equally. Kymlicka gives no reasons for this breathtaking claim: it is the assumption from which he proceeds.

Thomas Nagel says that he is going to explore a "type of argument that I think is likely to succeed. It would provide a moral basis for the kind of liberal egalitarianism that seems to me plausible. I do not have such an argument."[16] This does not stop him, however, from claiming that "moral equality, [the] attempt to give equal weight, in essential respects, to each person's point of view . . . might even be described as the mark of an enlightened ethic."[17] Years later he says, "My claim is that the problem of designing institutions that do justice to the equal importance of all persons, without unacceptable demands on individuals, has not been solved," but he nevertheless "present[s] a case for wishing to extend the reach of equality beyond what is customary in modern welfare states."[18] Although Nagel explicitly acknowledges the lack of justification, he does not hesitate to advocate as the mark of an enlightened ethic that people should be deprived of their legally owned property. Imagine claiming that although one can offer no justification for it, one nevertheless regards it as the mark of an enlightened ethic that blacks should be deprived of their freedom.

Rawls concludes his discussion of "The Basis of Equality" by saying that "essential equality is . . . equality of consideration," and goes on, "Of course none of this is literally an argument. I have not set out the premises from which this conclusion follows."[19] So once again the absurd policy of equal consideration for good and bad, prudent and imprudent, law-abiding and criminal people is put forward with the explicit acknowledgment that the premises from which it is supposed to follow have not been provided.

Larry Temkin describes his book as offering "a coherent, systematic, non–ad hoc method for accommodating, explaining, and ultimately guiding our egalitarian judgments. . . . Although I think most of the arguments that have been offered against equality can be refuted, let me emphasize that this book is neither a defense, nor an attack on, the ideal of equality. I do not address the question of whether one *should* care about inequality."[20] Apparently, "our egalitarian judgments" may be taken for granted—all we need is a method for guiding them.

Not far below the surface of this flaunted indifference to making a reasoned case for egalitarianism, which, it should be remembered, makes it obligatory to deprive people of their legally owned property, is the widely shared prejudice that the rejection of egalitarianism is immoral. The labels of Nazi, racist, white supremacist, sexist, Social Darwinist, reactionary, egoist, and so forth readily spring to the lips of many egalitarians by way of maligning their opponents and making the justification of egalitarianism unnecessary. If their opponents avowed analogous prejudices instead of defending their position, egalitarians would rightly charge them with substituting groundless moral self-righteousness for reasoned arguments. Egalitarians should take to heart Mill's words: "The worst offense . . . which can be committed by a polemic is to stigmatize those who hold contrary opinions as bad and immoral."[21]

It cries out for an explanation how egalitarians could feel justified in proceeding in this supercilious manner. One possible explanation is that they regard the simplest statement of egalitarianism (discussed in 1.1) as a truism. That statement is that all human beings should be treated with equal consideration unless there are good reasons against it. If this were indeed a truism, egalitarians would not need to worry about justifying it. They could then merely take it for granted and argue among themselves about questions of detail, such as what policies best express equal consideration and what constitutes a good enough reason to warrant unequal treatment.

The simple statement, however, is not a truism but a highly questionable claim that ignores the enormous differences among human beings. How could it be reasonable to treat everyone with equal consideration in light of the great human variety of intellectual, emotional, and moral capacities and performances; of strengths and weaknesses; of excellences and deficiencies; of religious, moral, and aesthetic views; of personal projects, ideals, and relationships; and so forth? These differences are numerous and important. They concern dimensions of life that people rightly regard as essential to their well-being. Treating people with equal consideration unjustifiably ignores these differences. But if these and other differences were recognized as good reasons that warrant unequal treatment, then the presumption in favor of equal treatment would collapse under the weight of the frequency and the importance of the exceptions that have to be made to it. No doubt, there are respects and circumstances in which people should be treated with equal consideration. But egalitarianism goes far beyond this to claim that there is always a presumption for equal treatment, that it is always exceptions to it that have to be justified.

That claim, however, must be supported by arguments that egalitarians, as we have seen, have disdained to provide and probably cannot provide. This makes their abuse of critics even more objectionable.

5.3 Dworkin on Equality

Against this dismal background comes Ronald Dworkin's new book, *Sovereign Virtue: The Theory and Practice of Equality.* One turns to it with the expectation that it will provide a reason for accepting the pronouncement on page 1: "No government is legitimate that does not show equal concern for the fate of all those citizens over whom it claims dominion and from whom it claims allegiance. Equal concern is the sovereign virtue of political community—without it government is only tyranny—and when a nation's wealth is unequally distributed, as the wealth of even very prosperous nations now is, then its equal concern is suspect." Dworkin recognizes that equal concern is open to various interpretations. He accepts one of them, which claims that equal concern is best understood in terms of equality of resources.

It should be said at once that the argument supporting this pronouncement is not to be found in this book. That this is so is made clear by Dworkin himself. "I have tried to show the appeal of equality of resources, as interpreted here, only by making plainer its motivation and defending its coherence and practical force. I have not tried to defend it in what might be considered a more direct way, by deducing it from more general and abstract political principles. So the question arises whether the sort of defense could be provided. . . . I hope it is clear that I have not presented any such argument here."[22] And a little further on he writes: "My arguments are constructed against the background of assumptions about what equality requires in principle. . . . My arguments enforce rather than construct a basic design of justice, and that design must find support, if at all, elsewhere than in these arguments" (118).

Egalitarians may find this admission disarming. But if it is remembered that on the basis of this admittedly undefended and unsupported theory Dworkin urges depriving people of their legally owned property and condemns opposition to it as immoral and shameful, then a less indulgent judgment will seem to be warranted. That judgment is that Dworkin's theory rests on specious moralizing instead of reasoned argument. Its readers should not be cowed into believing that his book of five hundred dense pages sprinkled with moral fervor rests on a more solid foundation than Dworkin's unjustified sentiments.

The core of these many pages is an account of equality of resources as the correct interpretation of equal concern. This account bears a striking resemblance to an argument, but it is in fact a tedious elaboration of what Dworkin himself calls an egalitarian fantasy concerning the ideal distribution of resources (162–63). Such distribution must meet "the envy test," which asks whether people are satisfied with the resources they have and do not prefer someone else's resources instead of their own. It should not escape notice how extraordinary it is to make envy the test of ideal distribution. Envy is the vice of resenting the advantages of another person. It is a vice because it tends to lead to action that deprives people of advantages they have earned by legal and moral means. The envy test does not ask whether people are entitled to their advantages; it asks whether those who lack them would like to have them. And of course the answer will be, given the human propensity for envy, that they would like to have them, that they are not satisfied with what they have. Dworkin, counting on this, claims that the ideal distribution would be one that removes this dissatisfaction. It would distribute advantages so evenly that no one could be envious of anyone else's. Instead of recognizing that envy is wrong, Dworkin elevates it into a moral standard.

Having based his egalitarian fantasy on a vice, Dworkin proceeds to explain how it would work as a test for imaginary people in an imaginary situation. People on a desert island participate in an auction. They bid for miraculously available resources by the use of clamshells, which they possess in equal numbers. Through their bids, they express their preferences, and because all start with the same number of clamshells, no one can have an advantage that others could envy. The auction keeps going until all the people have used up their clamshells. Dworkin thinks that the auction will not, by itself, eliminate unacceptable inequalities because post-auction lives will be affected by luck. He distinguishes between brute and option luck. The contingencies of life that no one can control are brute luck. How people's deliberate and calculated choices, expressed by their bids, turn out is option luck. Dworkin then adds to the imagined auction the fantasy of a compulsory insurance market in which people must purchase protection against the risk of bad luck. If life goes badly, insurance payments will compensate for it. People, therefore, will not suffer from the brute luck of having been born with handicaps. Dworkin says that "this imaginary auction [and, one may add, insurance scheme] can serve as a rough model in designing political and economic institutions for the real world in search of as much equality of resources as can be found" (14). Dworkin then fills more than one hundred pages imagining how the imaginary bidders and insurers in this imaginary situation are likely to proceed.

Reactions to this sustained exercise in fantasy are likely to range from admiration to exasperation. Be that as it may, the question needs to be asked how this egalitarian fantasy relates to the real world. How should individuals act if they apply the model of the auction and the insurance scheme to the allegedly immoral society in which they live? And why should it be supposed that if the model were applied, the inequalities Dworkin finds immoral and shameful would be lessened? Dworkin's answer to the first question is that "it is a complex and perhaps unanswerable question what equality of resources asks of us, as individuals, in our own society" (281). But since the fantasy was meant to help us answer that very question, and it seems that it will not do that, what is its point? Dworkin's answer to the second question is that "it is, of course, impossible to say in advance just what the consequences of any profound change in an economic system would be, and who would gain or lose in the long run" (105). So that if a society were crazy enough to change its economic system to reflect Dworkin's model of auction and insurance scheme, the inequalities that are anathema to Dworkin may just increase as a result. Dworkin's theory thus rests on an unargued assumption and gives no reason to suppose that its goal could be achieved by the means it provides. The remarkable thing is that both the groundlessness of the theory and the impossibility of telling whether it would lead to its goal are explicitly acknowledged by Dworkin.

5.4 Some Problems of Egalitarianism

Although the considerations just presented show that no good reason has been given for accepting Dworkin's egalitarianism, it is worthwhile to consider it further because it illustrates problems that most versions of egalitarianism have. One of these problems concerns the egalitarian attitude to individual responsibility. Dworkin says that "someone who is born with serious handicaps faces his life with what we concede to be fewer resources, just on that account, than others do. This circumstance justifies compensation, under a scheme devoted to equality of resources" (81). But people may have fewer resources as a result of contingencies that make it impossible for them to satisfy their preferences or realize their ambitions. "The latter," Dworkin says, "will also affect welfare, but they are not matters for compensation under our scheme" (81). The difference is between brute and option luck. The idea is that if life goes badly for people because of circumstances over which they have no control, they should be compensated; if it goes badly because they have chosen a way of life that is more vulnerable to luck than another they might have chosen, they should not be compensated. This may seem like a sensible idea until it is asked what counts as brute as opposed to option luck.

This question splits the egalitarian ranks. Dworkin agrees with Rawls that "the initial endowment of natural assets and the contingencies of their growth and nurture in early life are arbitrary from the moral point of view."[23] But he disagrees when Rawls goes on to say that "the effort a person is willing to make is influenced by his natural abilities and skills and alternatives open to him. The better endowed are more likely, other things equal, to strive conscientiously, and there seems to be no way to discount for their greater fortune."[24] Dworkin rejects this because Rawls "prescinds from any consideration of individual responsibility," whereas "the hypothetical insurance approach . . . makes as much turn on such responsibility as possible" (5). Dworkin believes that "though we must recognize the equal objective importance of the success of a human life, one person has a special and final responsibility for that success—the person whose life it is" (5). Rawls thinks that whether inequalities are morally objectionable must be decided independently of individual responsibility; Dworkin thinks that only those inequalities are morally objectionable for which people with less property cannot be held responsible. In this disagreement, both kinds of egalitarians have a decisive objection to the other. Dworkin is right and Rawls is wrong: any acceptable approach to politics must take into account people's responsibility for having or lacking property. Rawls is right and Dworkin is wrong: the choices people make and the property they have partly depend on their natural assets and circumstances, for which they cannot be held responsible.

What follows is a dilemma that egalitarians cannot resolve. If they acknowledge that people are partly responsible for the property they have, then they must agree with the anti-egalitarian claim that it is morally unacceptable to equalize the property of responsible and irresponsible people. If egalitarians insist that individual responsibility makes no difference in deciding what property people should have, then they are committed to the morally unacceptable policy of depriving good, prudent, and law-abiding people of their legally owned property in order to give it to others even if they are bad, imprudent, and criminal.

Dworkin opts for the first alternative, and so he must answer the question of how to distinguish between brute luck, which he thinks is incompatible with the assignment of responsibility, and option luck, which, according to him, is compatible with responsibility. His answer is: "Equality of resources assumes a fundamental distinction between a person, understood to include features of personality like convictions, ambitions, tastes, and preferences, and that person's circumstances, which include the resources, talents, and capacities he commands. . . . Equality of resources aims to make circumstances . . . equal" (14). Thus, according to Dworkin, brute luck affects people's property, talents, and capacities, and for them people are not responsible. Option luck affects people's convictions, ambitions, tastes, and preferences, and for them they are responsible. The fact that some people have less in the way of property, talents, and capacities "justifies compensation . . . equality of resources . . . seeks to remedy . . . the resulting unfairness" (81).

It follows that if people are unimaginative, lethargic, or gloomy, if they have poor memory or a displeasing physical appearance, if they lack a sense of humor or manual dexterity, and if this affects their success in life, as it is all too likely, then they should be compensated by depriving others of their legally owned property. No reasonable person can accept this absurdity. But if some did, they would still have to contend with Rawls's point that people's convictions, ambitions, tastes, and preferences, for which, according to Dworkin, they are responsible, are decisively influenced by their property, talents, and capacities, for which they are not supposed to be responsible. So the distinction between option and brute luck collapses.

Dworkin, therefore, must choose: he can give up the idea of making equality of property depend on individual responsibility or he can accept the idea that the distribution of property should depend on individual responsibility. The first alternative commits him to Rawls's version of egalitarianism, which he has good reason to reject. The second alternative commits him to the anti-egalitarian position against which he so self-righteously and without good reasons inveighs.

The second problem concerns the egalitarian attitude toward the plurality of political values. Egalitarianism is an ideology, and its fundamental substantive claim is that the government's obligation to treat all citizens with equal consideration is a political value that overrides any other political value that may conflict with it. Dworkin makes clear that this is his position: "Equal concern is the sovereign value of political community—without it the government is only tyranny. . . . Equal concern is a precondition of political legitimacy—a precondition of the majority's right to enforce its laws against those who think them unwise or even unjust" (1–2). Dworkin is not alone in positing an overriding value. Rawls, for instance, says, "Justice is the first virtue of social institutions . . . laws and institutions no matter how efficient and well-arranged must be reformed or abolished if they are unjust. Each person possesses an inviolability founded on justice that even the welfare of the society as a whole cannot override."[25] But if egalitarians are committed to there being an overriding political value, then they cannot also be committed to pluralism, which denies that there is any political value that ought always to override any political value that conflicts with it. Egalitarians cannot be pluralists, and pluralists cannot be egalitarians.

Dworkin is clear on this point. He says that his book is "contrary in spirit to . . . the value pluralism of Isaiah Berlin . . . [who] insisted that important political values are in dramatic conflict—he particularly emphasized the conflict between liberty and equality." Dworkin, by contrast, "strive[s] to dissipate such conflicts and to integrate these values" (5). He defends the view that "if we accept equal resources as the best conception of distributional equality, liberty becomes an aspect of equality rather than, as it is often thought to be, an independent political ideal potentially in conflict with it" (121). If we then ask just how the supposed conflict between equal property and liberty is to be dissipated and how the two values are to be integrated, we get Dworkin's reply: "Any genuine contest between liberty and equality is a contest liberty must lose. . . . Anyone who thinks liberty and equality really do conflict on some occasion must think that protecting liberty means acting in some way that does not show equal concern for all citizens. I doubt that many of us would think, after reflection, that this could ever be justified" (128). This calls for several comments.

First, that "many of us" do think, after reflection, that on occasion liberty may override equal resources is obvious and its denial is absurd. The "many of us" include all those liberals, like Berlin, who are genuine pluralists; all those conservatives and Republicans who oppose policies that involve depriving people of their legally owned property in order to give them to those who own less; and all those political thinkers (listed in note 5) who offer reasoned arguments against egalitarianism. Dworkin's claim is no more than inflated rhetoric familiar from political speechifying but out of place in what purports to be reasoned argument.

Second, Dworkin's "solution" to dissipating the conflict between liberty and equality and to integrating the two values is to subordinate liberty to equality. If that is a solution, it is one that is available to all parties to all conflicts among values. Dworkin, however, denies that. He says: "We might be tempted to dogmatism: to declare our intuition that liberty is a fundamental value that must not be sacrificed to equality. . . . But that is hollow, and too callous. If liberty is transcendentally important we should be able to say something, at least, about why" (121). Now, as Dworkin must know, defenders of liberty are able to say something about why it is, on occasion, more important than equality. What they say is that liberty is a precondition of any life worth living. And that is not hollow. As for its being callous, how could it be callous to try to protect the liberty of 87 percent of the citizens above the poverty level to control their legally owned property?

Dworkin's position, however, is open to the even more serious charge that the requirement he lays on his opponents, and which they certainly endeavor to meet, is one he himself admits that his own position does not meet. It is worth repeating what he was quoted as saying earlier:

I have tried to show the appeal of equality of resources, as interpreted here, only by making plainer its motivation and defending its coherence and practical force. I have not tried to defend it in what might be considered a more direct way, by deducing it from more general and abstract political principles. So the question arises whether the sort of defense could be provided. . . . I hope it is clear that I have not presented any such argument here. . . . My arguments are constructed against the background of assumptions about what equality requires in principle. . . . My arguments enforce rather than construct a basic design of justice, and that design must find support, if at all, elsewhere than in these arguments. (117–18)

Third, liberty is not the only political value that may conflict with equality. Some others are civility, criminal justice, decent education, healthy environment, high culture, order, peace, prosperity, security, toleration, and so forth. Egalitarians are committed to the view that if any of these values conflicts with equality, equality should override it. They may offer as an argument for this that equality is a precondition of the moral acceptability of all these values. But this is a bad argument. It is just false that equality is a precondition of the moral acceptability of, say, peace, prosperity, or security. A society can conform to these values and be morally better for it even if its citizens are not deprived of their legally owned property, as equality is said by Dworkin to require. Furthermore, defenders of the values that conflict with equality can claim with as great a plausibility as egalitarians that the value they favor is a precondition of the value they subordinate. The equal distribution of property without prosperity merely spreads poverty around more evenly; if the environment is unhealthy, the lives of people will be cut short and they cannot enjoy their equal share of property; if crime is rampant, people will soon be deprived of their property, regardless of whether its distribution is equal or unequal.

Egalitarians must face the fact of the political life in contemporary democracies that pluralists recognize. There are many political values and they conflict with each other. The welfare of a society requires that these conflicts be resolved, but for this no blueprint can be found. Politics is about defending the whole system of values, and this requires subordinating one of the conflicting values to the other. But which should be subordinated to which depends on complex historical, economic, sociological, religious, moral, technological, and other considerations, which are always in a state of flux. It is dangerously simpleminded to insist that one of the many political values should always override the others. Egalitarians are guilty of this charge, but they are not alone. The same charge convicts those who insist that liberty should be the overriding value. There is no value that should always override all other conflicting values. Pluralists recognize this, and that is why they reject egalitarianism, as well as all other ideologies that insist on the overridingness of any one or any small number of values.

The third problem concerns the question of why egalitarian policies are restricted to the citizens of a political community. Dworkin is emphatic that equal concern is the obligation of the *government* and that it holds in respect to all *citizens*. "No government is legitimate that does not show equal concern for the fate of all those citizens over whom it claims dominion" (1). But why *only* for citizens? The answer requires pointing at some characteristic or cluster of characteristics that all and only citizens have. In large multicultural democracies, however, there are no such characteristics to be found. Religion, ethnicity, language, education, race, history, attitudes to sex, death, marriage, child rearing, illness, work, and so forth divide rather than unite the citizens of a country like America. Nor are all citizens taxpayers, since the poor, children, and many others pay no taxes; they are not all the products of the same school system, since many are educated at home, or in private or religious schools; they are not all native born, since many are immigrants. They do have some of the same legal rights and obligations, but certainly not all, and the question is why equal concern should be among the rights shared by all and only citizens.

The temptation here is to say that it is obvious that people share such characteristics as the capacity for autonomy, rationality, moral agency, self-consciousness, language use, and so forth. But even if this were true, it would be of no help to egalitarians who restrict equal concern to citizens. For those characteristics are supposed to be shared by all human beings, not just by the citizens of a political community. If equal concern were justified by universally shared human capacities, then the government ought to treat everyone, not just citizens, with equal concern. And if equal concern required the redistribution of resources, then the government ought to make it worldwide.

That this would impoverish prosperous societies without relieving the poverty of the rest is only one of the absurdities that follows from this idea.

Furthermore, any government that committed itself to worldwide redistribution would betray its most basic obligation, which is to protect the interests of its citizens, not of other people. It is perhaps because egalitarians recognize this that they restrict equal concern to citizens. But then Dworkin should not try to justify equal concern by saying that there is "a natural right of men and women to equality of concern and respect, a right they possess not by virtue of birth or characteristic or merit or excellence but *simply as human beings*"; Kymlicka should not say that "the idea that *each person* matters equally is at the heart of all plausible political theories"; and Nagel should not say that "the impartial attitude is, I believe, strongly egalitarian . . . and takes to heart the value of *every person's* life and welfare"[26] (emphasis added).

Egalitarians thus face a hard choice. They can restrict equal concern to citizens or extend it to everyone. If they restrict it, they need a justification in order to avoid arbitrariness. The justification must point at some characteristic that all and only citizens have, but egalitarians have not found it. If they extend equal concern to everyone, then they must explain how a government can have the obligation to provide the same education, health care, police protection, roads, and so forth to the citizens of other countries as it has to provide for its own. It is, of course, not difficult to avoid having to make this hard choice. One can give up the indefensible claim that a government is obliged to treat people with equal concern.

The case against egalitarianism is that it deprives the large majority of the citizens who live above the poverty level of a sizable portion of their legally owned property. Egalitarians claim that equal concern for all citizens obliges the government to adopt this policy, but they not only fail to justify this claim, they explicitly acknowledge that it cannot be justified. On the basis of this unjustified and unjustifiable claim, they advocate depriving good, prudent, and law-abiding people of their legally owned property and giving it to people without asking whether they are bad, imprudent, or law-breaking. In advocating this injustice, they obfuscate the responsibility of individuals for the lives they lead, dogmatically elevate equality into a value that overrides all other values, and arbitrarily restrict equal concern to the citizens of a political community while their rhetoric demands that it be extended worldwide. It is an unjust, unjustified, inconsistent, and absurd policy of discrimination.

5.5 About Poverty

Notwithstanding the defects we have found in egalitarianism, it is true that if people through no fault of their own lack the basic necessities of a decent life, then, given the availability of resources, their society ought to alleviate their plight. Anti-egalitarians can endorse this policy, but they offer an account of its source, aim, and justification that egalitarians could not consistently accept.

The source of the policy is an obligation to help fellow citizens who live below the poverty level as a result of the contingencies of life beyond their control. The government, as well as individuals, should do what is reasonable to alleviate their misfortune. What makes this policy right, however, is not that inequality is morally objectionable but that people in one's society, through no fault of their own, are poor. And "poor" means not "has less than others" but "lacks the basic necessities of a decent life."

This point has been put forward with great clarity by Harry Frankfurt: "Economic equality is not as such of particular moral importance. With respect to the distribution of economic assets, what *is* important from the point of view of morality is not that everyone should have *the same* but that each should have enough. If everyone had enough, it would be of no moral consequence whether some had more than others."[27] It is not morally objectionable if billionaires have more than millionaires, or if people live below the poverty level as a result of immoral, imprudent, or criminal actions. If people are responsible for their poverty, there is no obligation to help them, and certainly no obligation to force on others a policy of helping them. Magnanimous people may be generous enough to help even those who are responsible for their poverty, but such actions are beyond the call of duty. There is no justification for laying it on people as a moral requirement.

An inappropriate expression of this requirement is, "How could it not be an evil that some people's prospects at birth are radically inferior to others?"[28] There are two things to be said about this. Given any population and any basis of ranking prospects, some will rank much lower than others. Lower-ranked ones will have radically inferior prospects in comparison with higher-ranked ones. Inveighing against this statistical necessity is like lamenting differences in intelligence. To call it an evil is a sentimental cheapening of the most serious condemnation morality affords. It misdirects the obligation people feel. If egalitarians would merely say that it is bad if undeserved misfortune befalls people and those who can should help them, then they could count on the support of decent people. But that support has nothing to do with equality.

Furthermore, the inappropriate expression just quoted invites the thought that our society is guilty of the evil of dooming people to a life of poverty. What this often repeated charge overlooks is the historically unprecedented success of our society in having only 13 percent of the population under the poverty level and 87 percent above it. The typical ratio in past societies is closer to the reverse. It is a cause for celebration, not condemnation, that for the first time in history a very large segment of the population has escaped poverty. If egalitarians had a historical perspective, they would be in favor of continuing this trend rather than advocating radical change that brings with it incalculable consequences.

A decent society should do what it reasonably can to raise above the poverty level those of its citizens who are not responsible for living below it. It should aim to alleviate the misfortune of fellow citizens if they have not brought it upon themselves. This policy differs from the egalitarian one in several basic respects. First, its intended beneficiaries are only those who live below the poverty level as a result of adversity they could not avoid or overcome. The egalitarian policy is intended to benefit the poor regardless of why they are poor. Second, the aim of the policy is not to equalize property but to alleviate poverty. The policy is intended to provide no more than whatever are the basic necessities of a decent life in a particular society. The egalitarian policy is designed to put in place a perpetual equalizing machinery that benefits the worst off regardless of whether and why they are poor. Third, the motivation for the policy is an obligation to help fellow citizens if they are impoverished by the contingencies of life beyond their control. The motivation for the egalitarian policy is the unfounded belief that those who have less are entitled to a portion of the legally owned property of those who have more.

The detailed formulation of the appropriate policy is a difficult practical question that is best left to experts. The aim of the present remarks is not to make policy but to point out the illusion and confusion on which egalitarianism rests, and to make clear how an anti-egalitarian policy differs from an egalitarian one. Egalitarians are rightly concerned with the undeserved poverty of their fellow citizens, but they wrongly suppose that its appropriate expression is equal concern. Its appropriate expression is concern for those citizens who are poor through no fault of their own.

The justification of this policy is prudential. It endangers the stability of a society if a substantial number of its citizens through no fault of their own lack the basic necessities of a decent life. Reasonable people recognize that a good society is a cooperative system in which the citizens participate because it provides the conditions they need to live as they wish. These conditions are lacking for people whose misfortune puts them below the poverty level. The more such people there are, the more the cooperative system is threatened. The justification of the policy of not allowing undeserved misfortune to deprive citizens of the basic necessities of a decent life is to protect the stability of the society by protecting its cooperative system. If prudence is a virtue, this justification is moral. But it is not a justification that has anything to do with the misguided egalitarian illusion that everyone ought to be treated with equal consideration. The truth is that reason and morality require that how people are treated should take into account their moral standing, what they deserve, and their responsibility for their past decisions and actions.

6/

The Myth of Equality

I seek to trace the novel features in which despotism may appear in the world. The first thing that strikes the observation is an immense multitude of men all equal and alike, incessantly endeavouring to procure the petty and paltry pleasures with which they glut their lives. . . . Above this race of men stands an immense and tutelary power, which takes upon itself to secure their gratifications, and to watch over their fate. That power is absolute, minute, regular, provident, and mild. . . . Such a government . . . provides for their security, foresees and supplies their necessities, facilitates their pleasures, manages their principal concerns, directs their industry, regulates the descent of property, and subdivides their inheritances—what remains, but to spare them all the care of thinking and all the trouble of living.

ALEXIS DE TOCQUEVILLE, *Democracy in America*

6.1 The Illusion

The conclusion of the preceding chapter is that there are decisive reasons for rejecting an economic egalitarianism that favors the redistribution of legally owned property. The egalitarian commitment to equality, however, need not be interpreted in this way. Egalitarians may argue for the general claim that on a fundamental level all human beings have equal worth and that morality requires treating them accordingly. The failure of the economic interpretation leaves the general claim intact. If human beings do have equal worth, then, on the fundamental level that egalitarians have in mind, even habitual evildoers ought to enjoy the same basic freedom, rights, and resources as everybody else.

The topic of this chapter is the illusion of equal human worth, which is deeply and often unquestioningly shared by countless people, even if they are not egalitarians. It may be said by religious believers that we are all children of God; by utilitarians that everybody is to count for one and no more than one; or by Kantians that all human beings are entitled to a basic respect simply because they are human. Many people hold on to this belief in the face of the undeniable fact, of which no one can be ignorant, that there are great moral differences between habitual evildoers, like the pusher, the prostitute, and the terrorist, on the one hand, and their decent, humane, and reflective counterparts, on the other. Yet the illusion is still accepted because it reflects the feeling that there is some good even in the worst of us and that is the source of our equal worth. Doubts about this feeling seem even to reinforce it, as Mill has observed in another context: "So long as an opinion is strongly rooted in the feelings, it gains rather than loses in stability by having a preponderating weight of argument against it. For if it were accepted as a result of argument, the refutation of the argument might shake the solidity of the conviction; but when it rests solely on feeling, the worse it fares in argumentative contest, the more persuaded are its adherents that their feeling must have some deeper ground, which the arguments do not reach."[1] But it has no deeper ground, and equal human worth is an illusion that falsifies the facts of moral life. The argument to this effect must begin with some necessary clarifications.

6.2 Clarifications

The most favorable interpretation of the claim that all human beings have equal worth is that it combines a descriptive and a prescriptive component. The first identifies a feature that all normal human beings are said to have, which is then taken to provide the basis of equal worth. (*Feature* is left deliberately vague to allow for quite different specifications of what it may be.) The second imposes the moral obligation to treat people as equals because of their equal worth. The description by itself lacks moral significance. It needs to be supplemented by a prescription that explains why the feature all normal human beings have should matter from a moral point of view. Why, for instance, might autonomy matter but having ten toes does not? The prescription alone is also insufficient because it leaves unanswered the natural question of what it is about people that makes it reasonable to regard them as having equal worth. The claim, then, that all human beings have equal worth is that they share a feature universally and equally, and this feature is morally significant because good lives depend on it. This interpretation, however, leaves open the obvious question of who has the obligation to treat people in this manner.

The obligation may be personal or political. If it were personal, it would oblige individuals to treat others as equals. The same needs would require the same response from them, regardless of whose needs they were. This would impose on people the surely unacceptable obligation to treat the needs of their family and friends as they treat the needs of strangers. It is far more reasonable, therefore, to interpret the obligation as political.[2] The government has the obligation to treat the citizens subject to it as equals. It should regard the goodness of each citizen's life as equally important. This may actually require unequal treatment, but that would be justified because some lives may face greater adversity than others.[3]

We still need further clarification however, to explain what the government ought to do to meet this obligation. One possibility is that it should guarantee for all citizens equal opportunity to make their lives good. This would inevitably result in great inequalities because people differ greatly in their genetic endowments and circumstances, and these differences affect the extent to which they can succeed. Egalitarians think that the government ought to do more. It should not only provide for all citizens the opportunity to live a good life but also make sure that even the least advantaged among them have the means to do so.

Rawls's first principle of justice may be thought to aim at equality of opportunity, and the second at equality of outcome. There is a tension between these two aims because equal opportunity tends to produce unequal outcome, and equal outcome requires making opportunities unequal by increasing the protection of some at the expense of others. Most egalitarians resolve this tension by balancing the claims of equal opportunity and equal outcome, but in their view, the balance ought to tilt in favor of equal outcome.

But this is still not the end of the necessary clarifications because we need to know how strong this obligation is supposed to be. After all, the government has many obligations, its resources are always scarce, and its obligations often conflict. It may be thought that if egalitarians regard equality as the most basic value, then the obligation is absolute. It does not, then, allow any exception, and if some obligation conflicts with it, the obligation to treat citizens as equals should override it. There is a general agreement that this requirement is too strong. Scarce resources, personal misfortune, natural disasters, criminal conduct, and so forth may make it impossible or wrong to treat all citizens as equals. These conflicts can be resolved only by treating them unequally. Whatever is done in such cases, the absolute obligation to treat people as equals would be violated.

In order to allow for this, the obligation is generally thought to be prima facie. There is a presumption in favor of the obligation to treat citizens as equals, but the presumption may be overruled if there are good reasons for it. The resulting view is that the obligation is said to hold normally, but if it is thought not to hold in a particular case, then the burden of explaining why it does not hold lies on those who claim that an exception should be made. Put succinctly: what needs justification is unequal, not equal, treatment. This, however, is not much help unless it is specified what would and would not be an acceptable justification for unequal treatment. The specification most egalitarians favor is that the only justification for the unequal treatment of any citizen is that thereby the equal treatment of citizens in general will be strengthened. It is, for instance, justified to allow physicians to have higher than average income if that is the best means for equalizing the available health care for all citizens.

In sum, the most reasonable interpretation of the claim that all normal human beings have equal worth is that it combines a descriptive and a prescriptive account of a morally significant, universal, and equal feature that the government has a prima facie political obligation to protect. We can now ask what reasons have been given by egalitarians in favor of this claim and whether these reasons are strong enough to defeat the reasons against it.

6.3 Vlastos on Equal Worth

Gregory Vlastos has formulated the classic egalitarian case for equal worth. He says that "individual worth" is a "value attaching to a person's individual existence, over and above his merit," and "it must hold in all human relations, including . . . those to total strangers, fellow-citizens or fellow-men." He sets out to "show that the concept of individual worth does meet this condition."[4] He points out that "if I see someone in danger of drowning I will not need to satisfy myself about his moral character before going to his aid. I owe assistance to any man in such circumstances, not merely to good men. . . . To be sincere, reliable, fair, kind, tolerant, unintrusive, modest in my relations with my fellows is not due to them because they have made brilliant or even passing moral grades, but simply because they happen to be fellow-members of the moral community" (47).

One wants to know whether this is still true if the following description fits my moral community: "Wherever you looked, in all our institutions, in all our homes, *skloka* was brewing. *Skloka* is a phenomenon born of our social order, an entirely new term and concept. . . . It stands for base, trivial hostility, unconscionable spite breeding petty intrigues, the vicious pitting of one clique against another. It thrives on calumny, informing, spying, slander, the igniting of base passions. Taut nerves and weakening morals allow one individual or group rabidly to hate another."[5] Would I not be, as Hume put it, "the cully of my integrity, if I alone shou'd impose on myself a severe restraint amidst the licentiousness of others"?[6]

Vlastos firmly denies that one's obligation changes in such circumstances. "The moral community is not a club from which members may be dropped for delinquency. Our morality does not provide for moral outcasts or half-castes. . . . We acknowledge personal rights which are not proportional to merit and could not be justified by merit. Their only justification could be the value which persons have simply because they are persons: their 'intrinsic value as individual human beings,' the 'infinite value' or the 'sacredness' of their individuality. . . . I shall speak of it as . . . 'human worth' for short" (48). He then explains that "the notion of human worth" is to be "understood to mean nothing less than the equal worth of the happiness and freedom of all persons" (56). Our morality, according to Vlastos, requires us to value equally the happiness and freedom of habitual evildoers, like the pusher, the prostitute, and the terrorist, and of kind, decent, and law-abiding people. Since on this view of "our morality" it is an obligation to treat good and evil people as equals, it requires convincing justification.

Vlastos says that according to "our code . . . in all cases when human beings are capable of enjoying the same goods, we feel that the intrinsic value of their enjoyment is the same. In this sense we hold that (1) *one man's well-being is as valuable as any other's.* And there is a parallel difference in our feeling for freedom. . . . For us (2) *one man's freedom is as valuable as any other's*" (51). From this it follows, says Vlastos, that "(3) one man's (prima facie) right to well-being is equal to that of any other, and (4) one man's (prima facie) right to freedom is equal to that of any other." Thus, "we believe in the equal worth of individual freedom and happiness," and this is the answer to the question, "What is your reason for your equalitarian code?" (52).

No one can seriously suppose, however, that Vlastos has given a *reason* for our supposed moral code. A *feeling* that Vlastos says *we* have that everyone's well-being and freedom have equal value is not a reason. A feeling may or may not be appropriate, and unless it is shown to be appropriate, it does not amount to a reason. But that this feeling is appropriate is the very claim for which Vlastos needs to provide a reason, so in citing it as a reason, he is simply assuming the truth of the conclusion he wants to reach. Nor has he shown that *we* have this feeling. Who are the "we"? Who is supposed to feel that the well-being and the freedom of terrorists and their hostages, drug dealers and children, torturers and their innocent victims are equally valuable? Where is the evidence on the basis of which Vlastos claims that *we* have this feeling? Instead of answering these questions, he says, in a footnote, "I am bypassing the factual question of the extent to which (1) and (2) [above] are generally believed" (51 n. 48).

If this were all, Vlastos's alleged reason for equal worth should be dismissed without further ado. But there is more. It is possible to extract two arguments from Vlastos's impassioned avowal of how he and some of his fellow egalitarians view human worth. The first rests on the distinction Vlastos draws between worth and merit, and the second focuses on the obligation to treat people equally being prima facie.

To begin with the distinction, Vlastos says that "the human worth of all persons is equal, however unequal may be their merit" (43). He explains that by merit he means "all the kinds of valuable qualities or performances in respect of which persons may be graded ... provided only it is 'acquired,' i.e., represents what its possessor has himself made of his natural endowments and environmental opportunities" (43). It follows, according to Vlastos, "that to speak of 'a person's merit' will be strictly senseless except insofar as this is an elliptical way of referring to ... those specifiable qualities or activities in which he rates well. So if there is a value attaching to the person himself as an integral and unique individual, *this* value will not fall under merit or be reducible to it. For it is of the essence of merit ... to be a grading concept; and there is no way of grading individuals as such" (43). And he says that the "value attaching to a person's individual existence, over and above his merit," is "individual worth" (45).

The importance of this distinction is that it permits Vlastos to acknowledge that there may be great inequalities among people in respect to their merit, and still hold on to their essential equality in respect to their worth. People can be graded on the basis of their comparative merits, but they cannot be graded on the basis of their worth because everyone has equal worth simply in virtue of being human. Good and evil people have, of course, unequal merit, but they still have equal worth. "We acknowledge personal rights which are not proportioned to merit and could not be justified by merit. Their only justification could be the value which persons have simply because they are persons: their ... human worth" (48).

Doubts, however, remain. Why should we think that merit is but worth is not a comparative grading concept? It makes good sense to speak of people having greater or smaller, higher or lower, more or less worth. When we speak in this way, we need not be speaking elliptically of their qualities. We may mean that some human beings qua human beings are better than others; that Roosevelt was a better human being than Hitler. Why could we not say that differences in their qualities reflect on the people whose qualities they are and have a bearing on their worth?

Vlastos's answer is to appeal to another distinction: between people's individuality and qualities. "If A is valued for some meritorious quality, m, his individuality does not enter into the evaluation. As an individual he is then dispensable; his place could be taken without loss of value by any other individual with as good an m-rating." He contrasts this with another case in which a father values A, his son, "as an individual . . . his affection will be for A, not for his M-qualities . . . his affection and good will are for A, and not only because, or insofar as, A has M-qualities. . . . Constancy of affection in the face of variations of merit is one of the surest tests of whether or not a parent loves a child" (44).

Vlastos, therefore, identifies the feature on which moral worth depends as the unique individuality that each person has. This feature is the subject of which various qualities are predicated. The qualities may change, but the subject remains the same. Worth attaches to each person's individuality, whereas merit attaches to each person's qualities. Worth is equal because there are and can be no differences among people in respect to *having* an individuality, whereas merit is unequal because people's qualities differ and change.

Vlastos's second argument is that the ascription of equal worth is prima facie, not absolute (37–40). There is a presumption that everyone is entitled to be treated as an equal because of equal worth. The presumption can be overruled in a particular case, provided the unequal treatment is required in order to achieve equal treatment. It is justified to treat good and evil people unequally if and only if by restricting the freedom of evildoers we make it more likely that people in general will be treated as equals. In this way, Vlastos could defend the belief in equal worth against the charge that it imposes the unacceptable obligation to treat good and evil people as equals.

6.4 Reasons against Equal Worth

The first reason against equal worth concerns the distinctions between worth and merit and between individuality and qualities. These distinctions are essential for Vlastos's justification of equal human worth. Only if equal worth is ascribed because of everyone's unique individuality, and unequal merit is attributed to different qualities, can Vlastos explain why good and evil people have equal worth. But the distinction between individuality and qualities cannot bear the weight Vlastos places on it.

Vlastos claims that people's individuality is independent of their qualities. People possess individuality necessarily but qualities only contingently. This leads to a dilemma that Vlastos can neither avoid nor resolve in a way that would allow the ascription of equal worth to all human beings. The dilemma is whether individuality is anything more than the logical subject of which qualities are predicated. If it is just the logical subject, then there is no reason to think that it is the individuality of a human being. Animals, plants, and material objects also have a logical subject in precisely the same sense, namely, as that of which their contingent qualities are predicated. If equal worth depends on individuality as a logical subject, then human beings, Ping-Pong balls, and cobwebs all have equal worth because everything that has a logical subject has equal worth. And then "our morality," as Vlastos understands it, ought to be equally concerned with the well-being of all entities. This, of course, is an absurdity that Vlastos neither intends nor can accept. Yet it follows from this attempt to resolve the dilemma.

The other possibility is that individuality is more than an empty logical subject. It must possess, then, some quality that distinguishes it from the individuality of other kinds of entities. There must be *something* that makes our individuality a *human* individuality. But Vlastos explicitly denies that our individuality is connected with any of our qualities. If the father in his example really loves his son, it is because of his son's individuality, not because of any of his qualities. "His affection and good will are for A, and *not only because* or *insofar as* A has the M-qualities" (44). But this makes no sense. If qualities had nothing to do with the father's affection and goodwill, then he could not reasonably direct them toward a recipient that has the qualities of being a person, alive, male, fathered by him, and so forth. There must be some quality that distinguishes the son from other human beings and entities. Unless Vlastos embraces the absurdity to which the first possibility leads, he must recognize that there is some quality that sets the individuality of a particular person apart from the individuality of other persons and entities. And—inconsistent as it is—he does suppose that there are such qualities. "A person's well-being and freedom are aspects of his individual existence as unique and unrepeatable as is that existence itself," and "their conjunction offers a translation of 'individual human worth'" (49).

If Vlastos opts for this second possibility, and thereby avoids the absurdity of the first, the consequences are equally fatal. First, the distinction between individuality and qualities collapses because he has recognized some qualities as necessary for human and personal individuality. In that case, however, the distinction between worth and merit also collapses because there is no individuality independent of qualities to which worth could be ascribed. Worth, then, becomes dependent on the possession of contingent and changeable qualities, and the necessity of equal worth disappears. Second, the qualities Vlastos identifies as definitive of worth—well-being and freedom—are obviously possessed in various degrees by different people, so they cannot have the same worth. Third, whether people possess well-being and freedom is a contingent fact. If their worth depends on well-being and freedom, then worth is also a contingent fact that some may have and others may lack. These consequences, of course, are just as unintended and unacceptable as the absurdity that follows from the previous possibility. The dilemma thus shows that Vlastos's attempt to justify the attribution of equal worth to all human beings is a failure.

Egalitarians who defend the belief in equal worth may follow a more promising line of argument, and Vlastos might have joined them. They may argue that there is a deep sense in which all human beings are equal, and that is why they ought to be treated equally. This is the moral center of their version of egalitarianism. Those who reject it must have a good reason for it. Such a reason, however, is not hard to find. And that is the second reason against equal worth.

It is a truism that there are great historical, cultural, and psychological differences among human beings. They differ in their talents, aspirations, intelligence, beliefs, attitudes; in their conceptions of a good life, virtues and vices, and values; in the multiplicity of roles they have in life, in the obligations they have, and in the excellence or deficiency of their conduct. Given these differences, and many others, it is natural to believe that it is reasonable to treat them as unequals. If egalitarians believe otherwise, it is incumbent on them to explain why human beings ought to be treated as equals even though they are different. The required explanation must point at a feature that would justify treating good and evil people as equals. A convincing explanation must meet several conditions. First, it must *identify* the shared quality, otherwise the explanation would be empty. Second, the quality must be shared by *all and only* human beings. For if not all human beings had it, then their equal treatment could not be based on it. And if some nonhuman beings also had it, then they ought also to be treated in the same way as egalitarians claim all human beings ought to be. Third, the quality must be shared *equally*, otherwise it could not be used to justify equal treatment. Fourth, the quality must be *morally important* because of its connection with a good life. It cannot be something like the possession of fingernails or the rate of hair growth because they do not affect the goodness of lives.

If there is such a quality, it would more likely be a potential than a developed one because people develop their potentialities at very different rates. So the most promising candidate is probably some capacity. But it will not be physiological, like digestion or aging, because that animals also have. Nor will it be an elementary psychological capacity, such as sentience or learning from experience, for many animals have that as well. The strongest candidate, then, is some more complex psychological capacity that is likely to have an important cognitive component. It may be the capacity for autonomy, or for reflective decisions, or for what Rawls calls "the capacity for moral personality," which he ascribes to people who "are capable of having . . . a conception of their good . . . and . . . a sense of justice . . . at least to a certain minimum degree."[7] This capacity would have to mark a threshold rather than a scale. For it must indicate a minimum level that all human beings have achieved, not the degree to which it has been achieved. So it must be something like the capacity to follow one's conception of a good life, or the capacity to evaluate one's actions on moral grounds, or the capacity to reflect and change one's conduct in the light of more distant and general goals. The egalitarian claim is, then, that this is the capacity that *all and only* human beings possess, that they possess it *equally*, that it is obviously *morally important*, and it is the capacity that warrants treating them as equals.

There are two reasons, however, why this claim is untenable. One is that the capacity in question indicates a scale, not a threshold; consequently, human beings do not possess it equally, and so equal treatment cannot be based on it. The capacity is scalar because its possession depends on the possession and development of other capacities, which are possessed and developed unequally. These other capacities include intelligence, sensitivity, attentiveness to others, memory, imagination, and so forth. The extent to which people can follow their conceptions of a good life, evaluate their conduct morally, or reflect on and change their conduct in the light of far-removed goals obviously depends on the extent to which they possess and have developed these other capacities. People vary greatly in these respects, and to treat them equally is to do violence to this fact.

Richard Arneson is an egalitarian who explicitly states and concedes the force of this objection.[8] It is instructive to see how he deals with its implications. He thinks that the problem is intractable "within the framework of standard alternatives to utilitarianism," but utilitarianism has the resources to defend "a sufficiently robust substantive equality." This, Arneson says, "is not a decisive defense of this doctrine . . . but to my mind utilitarianism's comparative success on this score is a non-trivial advantage."[9] These remarks reveal the egalitarian frame of mind: they hold the belief in equal worth as fundamental and then look for a theory that would justify it. If nonutilitarian theories fail to do it, then they turn to a utilitarian theory. And if that does not work, they look for another justification. The possibility that the belief is false is simply not considered by them. It seems, then, that they do not hold the belief because reasons have persuaded them of its truth. They start by regarding the belief as true and accept or reject theories depending on whether they confirm the belief. The usual name for this way of proceeding is prejudice.

The other reason why the egalitarian claim is untenable holds even if it were true that the capacity egalitarians seek could be found. For what is morally important is not the mere possession of a capacity but its exercise. It says very little morally important if it is true that people *could* follow their conception of a good life, evaluate their actions, or reflect on and change their conduct. What matters is whether they actually do what they could, whether they do it reasonably and to a sufficient extent, and whether what they do benefits or harms others. And of course, the extent to which people exercise whatever their equal capacity may be is going to be unequal. So once again, treating them as equals is a wanton disregard of the obvious moral reasons for treating them as unequals. It follows that egalitarians have not identified the shared quality that underlies human differences. It is most unlikely that a quality that meets the conditions enumerated earlier could be found. Egalitarians, therefore, must either provide some other basis that warrants treating good and evil people as equals or give up their position.

Let us suppose, however, that egalitarians somehow avoid this objection and succeed in identifying a universally human, equally possessed, and morally significant capacity. They would, then, have a basis for ascribing equal worth to all human beings. But the question would still remain why it is worth rather than merit that ought to be considered in determining the obligation of the government. Why should the capacity matter from the moral point of view rather than what people make of their capacity? Why should political obligation be based on a character trait rather than on actions? Even if it were true, which it is not, that people have equal worth as a result of some capacity, it is also true that they have unequal merit, that they develop their capacity unequally, and that their actions have unequal moral status. Why ascribe greater moral importance to the respect in which they are supposedly equal than to the respects in which they are unequal? People benefit and harm others not by their capacities but by their actions. Why, then, base the political obligation to treat them one way or another on their capacity rather than on their actions?

The third reason against equal worth is that egalitarians have no acceptable answer to this question. Vlastos does not even consider it, but Rawls does. His answer is that merit is a morally unacceptable basis for the government's treatment of people because it is arbitrary. People's merit depends on their genetic inheritance and upbringing. Neither is within their control, so it would be arbitrary to respond to them on the basis of considerations about which they can or could do nothing. As Rawls puts it: "It seems to be one of the fixed points of our considered moral judgments that no one deserves his place in the distribution of native endowments, any more than one deserves one's initial starting place in society. The assertion that a man deserves his superior character that enables him to cultivate his abilities is equally problematic; for his character depends in large part upon fortunate family and social circumstances for which he can claim no credit." The question, according to Rawls, is not what merit people have but how they should be treated regardless of their merit: "the natural distribution [of genes] is neither just nor unjust; nor is it unjust that persons are born into society at some particular position. These are simply natural facts. What is just and unjust is the way that institutions deal with these facts."[10] How, then, should institutions deal with them if not on the basis of merit?

Rawls's answer is that institutions should treat people on "the basis of equality, the feature of human beings in virtue of which they are treated in accordance with the principles of justice." This feature is "the capacity for moral personality [which] is a sufficient condition for being entitled to equal justice." Rawls stresses that this is a minimum: "the sufficient condition for equal justice, the capacity for moral personality, is not at all stringent. . . . There is no race or recognized group of human beings that lacks this attribute." He concludes: "To say that human beings are equal is to say that none has a claim to preferential treatment in the absence of compelling reasons. The burden of proof favors equality: it defines the procedural presumption that persons are to be treated alike. . . . The essential equality is . . . equality of consideration."[11]

The problem is that if merit is an arbitrary basis for determining how people should be treated, then the capacity for moral personality is also arbitrary, and for the same reason. If merit is arbitrary because it depends on genes and postnatal circumstances, then the capacity for moral personality is also arbitrary because it also depends on genes and postnatal circumstances. The capacity depends on the genes being human genes and nondefective, and the postnatal circumstances have to be such as to avoid incapacitating disease, natural disasters, abusive parents, extreme deprivation, and so forth.

Whether the genes and circumstances are favorable to people's possession of a capacity for moral personality is as little in people's control as, Rawls says, their native endowments and initial positions in society. If Rawls were right, merit and the capacity for moral personality would both be arbitrary. If the former makes unequal treatment unjust, then the latter makes equal treatment unjust. If Rawls's argument against treating people on the basis of their merit were correct, it would remove all bases on which people could be treated in a nonarbitrary and morally justified way.

It is perhaps because Vlastos realizes this that he insists—inconsistently—that worth is independent of all qualities, including the capacity for moral personality. As we have seen, however, that insistence does not help Vlastos's case because it makes worth depend on an empty logical subject that is devoid of all qualities. Such a subject, however, is possessed by all material and organic entities, so the equal worth of *human* beings cannot be based on it.

The fourth reason has to do with the supposed prima facie status of the egalitarian claim that the government ought to treat all citizens as equals. This obligation is said to be prima facie, not absolute, because there may be justifiable exceptions to it. As Vlastos puts it: "Reasons requiring a general pattern of action may permit, or even require, a departure from it in special circumstances. Thus . . . an equalitarian concept . . . may admit inequalities without inconsistency if, and only if, it provides grounds for equal human rights" (40). The exceptions, however, are rare, and the obligation of equal treatment is believed to hold most of the time. Moreover, it is always the exception, not equal treatment, that requires justification. In Rawls's words: "To say that human beings are equal is to say that none has a claim to preferential treatment in the absence of compelling reasons. The burden of proof favors equality."[12]

The problem with the prima facie claim is that it rests on the false assumption that there is a general presumption for equal treatment and that justified exceptions to it are rare. The truth is the opposite. There is a general case for unequal treatment, and equal treatment, given great human differences, is justifiable only in rare cases. The reason for rejecting the prima facie case for equal treatment is that it is rendered untenable by the countless justifiable exceptions to it. These exceptions show that unequal treatment is and ought to be the general practice.

Consider, to begin with, that equal treatment is in many cases impossible because of unavoidable statistical necessity. Equal treatment requires, for instance, equal access to good education, health care, and employment. But the quality of teachers and physicians varies greatly.

Good teachers and physicians will always be fewer than middling and bad ones taken together. The result is that some students and patients will get better education and health care than others. The same is true of employment. Some firms are better organized, are more successful, and place greater emphasis on retaining employees than others. Working at the first is better than working at the second, so some people will have better jobs than others. These and similar inequalities are unavoidable consequences of the unequal statistical distribution of talents and the contingencies of life. Such inequalities are the rule, not the exception, and no legislation of any government could eliminate them.

Next, take cases of moral differences. People who are honest, reliable, conscientious, kind, polite, or law-abiding are obviously entitled to better treatment than those who are dishonest, unreliable, careless, cruel, rude, or criminal. It is utterly implausible to suppose that the government has an obligation to ignore these moral differences among citizens. It would be unreasonable, for instance, for the government to make laws requiring employers not to take account of them, juries to discount them, or voters to disregard whether a candidate for political office has the virtues or the vices. The point is not that it would be unreasonable for individuals to ignore moral differences, but that it would be unreasonable for the government to legislate that they ought to be ignored.

Another group of cases in which unequal treatment is the reasonable rule, not the rare exception that needs special justification, has to do with differences between prudent and imprudent people. It makes a difference, for instance, to continued eligibility for welfare whether applicants are or are not actively seeking employment, whether they are in need because of misfortune or addiction, whether they seek unemployment benefits because they have been laid off or because they prefer not to work during the winter. It also makes a difference to whether people are entitled to receive mortgage, credit, or check-cashing privileges if they have gone bankrupt, have defaulted, or have a history of overdrawing their bank accounts or writing checks that bounce. It would be irresponsible if the government required ignoring such differences.

Yet a further type of perfectly justifiable unequal treatment occurs in the many cases when there is some reason for equal treatment but it conflicts with some other kind of consideration for which there are better reasons. Felons cannot vote; foreign-born American citizens cannot be president; residents in one state cannot be senators in another; pornographic books cannot be kept in school libraries; amputees cannot enlist as paratroopers; pedophiles cannot drive school buses; jockeys cannot bet on horse races; single parents cannot marry their children; and so on and on. Generally speaking, equal treatment may conflict with freedom, prosperity, peace, stability, security, and so forth. There often are good reasons to accept some unequal treatment in exchange for considerable gain in other respects.

The upshot of these examples is that statistical necessity, immorality, imprudence, and conflicts routinely require unequal treatment. Such cases are so numerous as to render untenable the claim that equal treatment is or ought to be the rule and unequal treatment the exception. Given the many deep and morally significant differences among people, it is far more reasonable to claim that the government has the obligation to treat citizens in a way that recognizes these differences among them and that what requires justification is ignoring the differences.

We may conclude that the failure of the distinction between worth and merit, of the identification of a quality on which equal worth could be based, of the explanation why a capacity rather than acting on it is morally important, and of the defense of the prima facie claim for equal treatment is sufficient reason for rejecting the egalitarian argument for equal worth.[13]

6.5 Moral Inequality

The reasons against equal worth are also reasons for unequal worth. The belief in unequal human worth—in moral inequality—is dangerous and has a very bad history. It was used to justify slavery, religious persecution, racism, colonialism, the inferiority of women, and other evils. It is right to regard it with suspicion. Yet there are good reasons for believing that it is true. True beliefs can be put to morally unacceptable uses, but that does not make the beliefs any the less true, nor their denial intellectually respectable. There is virtually no moral or political belief that has not been egregiously abused at some time or another. The belief in moral equality is no exception, as shown, for instance, by using it to justify the Terror spawned by the French Revolution. Surely, the reasonable procedure is to base beliefs on reasons for or against them. If the reasons favor them, and if the beliefs lend themselves to abuse, then one should guard against their abuse rather than deny their truth.

In addition to the reasons already given against equal worth or moral equality, here are two reasons for unequal worth or moral inequality. First, no one denies that human beings have unequal moral merit. They are judged on the basis of their actions, which differ greatly in being beneficial or harmful, right or wrong, virtuous or vicious, good or bad. Moral *performances* are thus acknowledged to be unequal. What sticks in the craw is the supposition that moral *capacities* are unequal. But how else could we know about people's moral capacities than by inference from their moral performances? Unequal performances, especially if they form habitual and predictable patterns, not only constitute evidence for moral capacities but are the *only* available evidence. Admittedly, the evidence is not conclusive. It is conceivable that behind lifelong patterns of unequal moral performances there are equal moral capacities. There is, however, no reason to believe that and there are good reasons to disbelieve it. Furthermore, any reason that could be offered in favor of equal moral capacities would have to rely on moral performances, so there is no way to sever the evidential link between performances and capacities. And since moral performances are unequal, so are moral capacities.

Second, no one denies that there are countless capacities that people possess unequally. Talents, skills, aptitudes, various temperaments, intelligence, energy, and so forth are recognized to be unequally distributed in any general population. The existence of unequal linguistic, mathematical, or musical capacities is simply taken for granted. Why, then, should moral capacities be different? The answer that the former are specific and the latter are general does not work because intelligence, for instance, is also general and yet is recognized to be unequally distributed. Nor does it help to say that the former are simple and the latter complex. For complex capacities are constituted of simple ones, and if simple ones are acknowledged to be unequal, then so must be the complex capacities that are constituted of the simple ones.

The conjunction of the reasons against moral equality and for moral inequality appears to be strong enough to create a presumption in favor of treating people on the basis of their moral performances rather than on the basis of the unfounded belief in their equal moral capacities. In that case, however, it needs to be explained why egalitarians are so reluctant to accept this glaringly obvious point. The explanation is that they fear its likely abuse. This fear needs to be laid to rest, and the following considerations are meant to do so.

To begin with, the inequality in question is based on moral performance, on what people do, on how their actions affect others. Its basis is not race, religion, sex, or ethnicity. People differ in these respects, but in normal circumstances, these differences are morally irrelevant. If they are thought to be morally relevant, then it must be explained why. But people's actions, in normal circumstances, are morally relevant because they affect others for better or worse. There is, therefore, nothing morally arbitrary in comparing people on the basis of their actions, as there is in comparing them on the basis of race, religion, sex, or ethnicity.

Next, moral inequality is compatible with equal treatment in some respects. It does not, for instance, rule out the equal right of citizens to vote in elections or their right to equal treatment under criminal law. The justification of equal treatment in some specific respect, however, relies on reasons that are independent of equality. The justification of the equal right to vote is that it is a necessary feature of democracy and democracy is the least imperfect form of government. The justification of the right to equal legal treatment is that criminal laws are meant to regulate people's actions. How they compare morally to others has no bearing on whether or not they have performed an action that is prohibited by a particular law. Generally, if it is claimed that people ought to be treated equally in some specific respect, it must be explained why that should be done and why their moral inequality has no bearing on the case at hand. We have seen, for instance, that the case for equal economic treatment fails since it is clearly morally relevant why some people have more and others less of economic resources.

Finally, moral inequality does not mean that there should be no restrictions on how even the worst evildoers ought to be treated. Moral inequality is compatible with holding that there ought to be a minimum level of decency. Not even moral monsters should be tortured, mutilated, starved, sexually abused, and so forth. The reason for this, however, is not the false belief in their moral equality. There are moral monsters who deserve such treatment, and yet they should not be treated as they deserve to be because of the importance of maintaining a minimum level of decency. Someone would have to inflict the deserved treatment, and that person would be corrupted. And the public knowledge that it has been done would tend to corrupt the prevailing moral sensibility by making actual a possibility that ought to be unthinkable. There may be a similar minimum level of shelter, nutrition, health care, education, and so forth below which not even criminal, imprudent, or immoral people ought to be allowed to fall. Once again, however, the justification for maintaining that level is not the illusion of moral equality but the requirements of social stability and decency.

In conclusion, equal human worth is an illusion. The truth is that there are good reasons to believe in moral inequality and there are safeguards that can prevent its abuse.

7 /

The Tyranny of Do-Gooders

The care of the universal happiness of all rational and sensible beings, is the business of God, and not of man. To man is allotted a much humbler department, but one much more suitable to the weakness of his powers, and to the narrowness of his comprehension—the care of his own happiness, of that of his family, his friends, his country.

ADAM SMITH, *The Theory of Moral Sentiments*

7.1 The Illusion

The egalitarian illusions we have so far considered occur in the context of a rights-based approach to politics. Its basic assumption is that there are some minimum requirements of all good lives, individuals have rights to them, and a good society will protect these rights. Beyond the minimum requirements, good lives will take a plurality of forms. According to this approach, rights must be secured before good lives can be achieved. The problem is that when the putative rights are specified, they lead to the denial of the responsibility of evildoers, to the corruption of justice by ignoring what people deserve, and to the indefensible egalitarian policy that requires treating good and bad, prudent and imprudent, law-abiding and criminal people with equal concern.

There is, however, another—welfare-based—approach that many egalitarians adopt. They begin with a thick, rather than a minimum, conception of a good life. They take human welfare to depend on living according to this conception, and they regard a society as good to the extent to which it makes this kind of life possible. According to this approach, the nature of a good life must be known before the rights that make it possible can be identified. Its defenders interpret the obligation to help others to live a good life much more widely than what has been found justifiable at the end of the preceding chapter. They attempt to defend their interpretation by appealing either to compassion or to the very nature of morality. The illusion at the core of the version of egalitarianism that we are about to discuss is that "any concern for the welfare of others, especially when it promotes the sense of equality, is . . . morally good."[1] In this chapter we shall consider the appeal to compassion; in the next, the appeal to morality itself.

7.2 Nussbaum on Compassion

Martha Nussbaum regards compassion as essential to morality.[2] She calls the account she defends Aristotelian social democracy, but in the interest of accuracy it is best to eschew this label. Aristotle favored slavery, thought that women were inferior to men and should not have the vote, and held that aristocracy, the rule of the best, is a good form of government, so his name should not be attached to an account that aspires to be democratic. But this aspiration is unsuccessful, whatever it is called, since Nussbaum makes clear that the account she favors is defended from "the onlooker's point of view, making the best judgment the onlooker can make about what is really happening to the person, even when that may differ from the judgment of the person herself."[3] It follows that democratic decisions are not trustworthy because people's judgments are unreliable. The onlooker—who apparently must be a woman—knows better than the people themselves what is good for them. It ill fits Nussbaum's position, therefore, to call it democratic. Accuracy, therefore, is best served by calling it maternalism.

If we accept Nussbaum as the onlooker who is making the best judgment she can, we may still want to know what the source of judgment is. She says that one main source is contemporary Scandinavian socialism.[4] Another source is "the commonness of myths and stories from many times and places, stories explaining to both friends and strangers what it is to be human rather than something else. The judgment is the outcome of a process of self-interpretation and self-clarification that makes use of the story-telling imagination far more than the scientific intellect."[5] Nussbaum apparently does not think that we should worry about the bewildering variety of incompatible stories told in different religions, cultures, and historical periods, and if these stories happen to conflict with our scientific intellect, then so much the worse for scientific intellect.

The aim of Nussbaum's maternalism is to provide a "comprehensive conception of good human functioning. . . . It is . . . an ethical-political account given at a very basic and general level, and one that can be expected to be broadly shared across cultures."[6] The various items that compose this comprehensive conception constitute the basic requirements of a good life. People's rights are defined by them. "A liberal political society is best advised to describe its basic entitlements as a set of *capabilities*, or opportunities for functioning. . . . Such a society should guarantee to all citizens a basic set of opportunities for functioning."[7] Nussbaum has given over the years a number of different lists of the capabilities she has in mind. Here we shall consider the most recent one (416–18). "The list," Nussbaum says, "shapes the judgment in a particular way: for what it tells citizens is not only that certain calamities are particularly grave, but also that they are unjust, wrong. . . . If institutions do not provide . . . citizens with recourse and support, the institutions . . . are defective. . . . Even when there is an element of natural necessity . . . we should not conclude prematurely that defective political arrangements are not involved. We really cannot say, without trying for an indefinitely long time, how much illness and misery we are capable of preventing" (418–19).

Nussbaum's list, "The Central Human Capabilities" (416–18), contains exactly ten items, no doubt because the myths and stories from which the list is derived hit upon the essential connection between good lives and the decimal system. The items are life; bodily health; bodily integrity; senses, imagination, thought; emotions; practical reason; affiliation; other species; play; and political and material control over one's environment. Nussbaum says that "all citizens should have a basic threshold level of each of these capabilities" (418), and she appends a brief explanation of each. It would be tedious and unnecessary to comment on every one of them. Sampling is sufficient to make patent their collective implausibility.

Nussbaum says about life, among other things, that there should be a guaranteed threshold of "being able to live to the end of a human life of normal length; not dying prematurely" (416). There should be "constitutional guarantees" of the conditions that enable people to live to a normal length. It follows that if smoking, sunbathing, driving a car, fatness, stressful or dangerous occupations make people vulnerable to premature death, then there should be a law against them since they are "unjust, wrong." Seat-belt laws and "restrictions on tobacco products," for example, are explicitly endorsed by Nussbaum, as requirements of "good human functioning . . . that can be expected to be broadly shared across cultures" (419). If in doubt, just think of all those stories told in all cultures that make not smoking and wearing seat belts part of good human functioning.

Bodily integrity includes "having opportunities for sexual satisfaction" (417). In a good society, therefore, there will have to be "constitutional guarantees" preventing the suffering of those who are sexually frustrated because they are physically unprepossessive, have bad breath, or seek unusual ways of sexual satisfaction. A good society, for instance, may establish tax-supported satisfaction centers in which well-trained social workers can alleviate the suffering of the thus afflicted. Failing to do that, or something like it, makes institutions and political arrangements "defective."

Under emotions, Nussbaum talks about the capacity "to grieve, to experience longing . . . and justified anger," and "supporting this capability means supporting forms of human association that can be shown to be crucial in their development" (417). Since one learns by doing, this means that the government should finance consciousness-raising groups, or some alternative, which will teach people to develop their facility in grieving, longing, and getting angry in preparation for the time when they actually encounter the causes that normally make these emotions appropriate. If the government does not do that, it is "unjust, wrong."

These implausible implications cannot be avoided by claiming that the constitutional guarantees do not require people to take advantage of them, or that it is left to the discretion of individuals whether they choose to develop their capabilities. For first, the constitutional guarantees are of services that have to be financed by taxation, which, in our society, would force people to support measures they find morally repugnant, intrusive meddling with private affairs, or unacceptable on religious, political, psychological, or aesthetic grounds. Second, having these guarantees is at present unconstitutional, so they would require a drastic revision of the constitution. Third, they would also require abandoning the principle that political arrangements ought to be justifiable to those who are subject to them, since many people, probably the majority of the country, would not consent to the arrangements Nussbaum recommends. Fourth, the constitutional guarantees do not merely provide possibilities but also outlaw activities, associations, and institutions that violate the basic threshold level of the capabilities that Nussbaum approves of on the unpersuasive bases of myths and stories and her Scandinavian experience. In short, Nussbaum's so-called constitutional guarantee is a euphemism for forcing on people her conception of a good life.

Nussbaum does not say much about practical reason here. She leaves it at "being able to form a conception of the good and to engage in critical reflection about the planning of one's life" (417). At another place, however, she makes clear that practical reason "is fundamental to our understanding of the list as a whole, and its political implications."[8] For practical reason enables citizens to formulate "good political principles," which are "principles for the adequate realization of . . . fully human capabilities in the citizens."[9] These capabilities—surprise!—turn out to be the ones that appear on Nussbaum's list. So the proper use of practical reason is to reach the conclusion she has reached. But what about people who dissent? What about the charge that "as government more and more fully supports well-being . . . it more and more removes from citizens the choice to live by their own lights"?[10] Nussbaum's response is that "choice is not only not incompatible with, but actually requires, the kind of governmental reflection about the good, and the kind of interference with laissez-faire, that we find in Aristotelian social democracy."[11]

If for "laissez-faire" we read what it really means, namely, freedom, then we arrive at what is most egregious about Nussbaum's list. Citizens are free to make choices—so long as they choose the conception of a good life that Nussbaum's list specifies. They are also encouraged to use their practical reason—so long as they use it to find the best means to implement that conception. If people choose a different conception or put their practical reason to a different use, they err: "people's judgments . . . can go wrong in many ways. Suffering and deprivation . . . brutalize or corrupt perception . . . they often produce adaptive responses that deny the importance of the suffering . . . people can become deeply attached to things that on reflection we may think either trivial or bad for them." To see whether this has happened, one should "take up the onlooker's [that is, Nussbaum's] point of view, making the best judgment the onlooker can make about what is really happening to the person" (309).

Nussbaum's fine words—"choice is an absolutely essential part, for the Aristotelian [i.e., Nussbaum], in promoting truly *human* functioning"[12]—ring hollow if it is understood that only those choices are to be countenanced that promote *her* idea of truly human functioning. Imagine the howl of protest from Nussbaum if fundamentalist Christians were to claim that choice is an essential part of their beliefs because they favor people deciding how best to live according to the teachings of the Bible. But the only difference between that claim and Nussbaum's is that they rely on different stories about what "truly human functioning" is. Nussbaum's maternalism permits people to use practical reason and choose how they live, provided they reason and choose as she thinks they should. If they choose or reason differently, it is because they have been brutalized or corrupted, and so, unlike Nussbaum, they do not know what is good for them. In short, Nussbaum knows best.

Nussbaum does not ask whether people could choose and reason differently because she is blind to the possibility that there may be alternatives to the capabilities approach. People may reasonably reject that approach because they do not think that the government should interfere with private lives. They may think that parents, churches, or private schools should develop capabilities, rather than some distant governmental agency that could not be expected to respond to individual and local differences. Or they may think that there are more important capabilities than some that appear on Nussbaum's list. They may think that the capabilities for discipline and self-control, or for competition and risk taking, or for faith and hope, or for service and self-denial are more important than the capability to live in harmony with animals, or to play, or to live a long life, or to enjoy sexual satisfaction. Nor does Nussbaum recognize that if her claim were true—namely, that a condition of good human functioning is that the government should guarantee the items on her list—then the absurd conclusion would follow that since no government has hitherto done that, no one has hitherto lived a life of good human flourishing. These objections, however, do not deter Nussbaum from her dogmatic commitment.

Nor is Nussbaum deterred from advocating this tyranny by the long tradition of liberal thought (to which she claims to belong) that stresses the central importance of freedom in a good society. She takes no notice whatever of Mill's view that the "only freedom which deserves the name is that of pursuing our own good in our own way, so long as we do not attempt to deprive others of theirs. . . . Each is a proper guardian of his own health, whether bodily *or* mental and spiritual. Mankind are greater gainers by suffering each other to live as seems good to themselves than by compelling each to live as seems good to the rest."[13] Or that "neither one person, nor any number of persons, is warranted in saying to another human creature of ripe years that he shall not do with his life for his own benefit what he chooses to do with it. He is the person most interested in his own well-being. . . . All errors which he is likely to commit against advice and warning are far outweighed by the evil of allowing others to constrain him to what they deem his good."[14] These views are echoed by countless liberal—and not just liberal—writers, but Nussbaum's maternalistic tyranny is contrary to them.

Nussbaum claims that she knows that people should live by the capabilities approach she favors, because her Scandinavian experience and myths and stories have taught her. But doubts about Scandinavian socialism have been expressed by Scandinavians in several elections, as well as by the electorates of many other democratic countries. The myths and stories of one culture are often anathema to another, and many myths and stories are false literally, symbolically, or both. In this light, one may ask with wonder about the source of Nussbaum's indifference to freedom, about the confidence with which she rides roughshod over how mature adults choose to live, and about her blindness to the unacceptable implications of her list. The answer is that their source is compassion. Nussbaum says that "compassion . . . lies at the heart of any good ethical code" (392), that "compassion gives public morality essential elements of ethical vision without which any public culture is dangerously rootless and hollow" (403), and that compassion is essential "to the political structure of a state that is both democratic and liberal" (401). Let us, therefore, consider what compassion is, when it is and when it is not appropriate, and how Nussbaum's understanding of it goes very wrong.

7.3 The Nature of Compassion

Compassion belongs to a family of which altruism, benevolence, charity, empathy, fellow feeling, humaneness, pity, and sympathy are some other members. There is no sharp division between them, and the words referring to them are in some contexts synonymous, in others not. *The Unabridged Random House Dictionary* (1987) defines *compassion* as "a feeling of deep sympathy and sorrow for another who is stricken by misfortune, accompanied by a strong desire to alleviate the suffering." This is a good starting point for beginning to understand what compassion is.

Compassion has a subject and a recipient. The subject is the one who has it, and the recipient is usually a person (although it might conceivably be a group or an animal) toward whom it is directed. People are recipients of compassion because some misfortune has befallen them. It affects them seriously, unlike a stubbed toe or a parking ticket. They have not brought the misfortune upon themselves by their vices but are *stricken* by it as its passive, undeserving victims. Their misfortune is analogous to what insurance companies call an act of God: an unexpected, unpredictable calamity that assails people through no fault of their own.

Compassion is stronger than merely feeling sorry for someone. It involves some degree of fellow feeling that leads the subject to identify to some extent with the recipients and wish for them the alleviation of their misery. It is this identification and well-wishing that makes possible the combination of deep sorrow and sympathy that characterizes compassion. One may feel sorry even for people who have brought their misfortune upon themselves, but if they did so as a result of selfishness or cruelty, for instance, then deep sorrow and sympathy are unwarranted.

Compassion motivates people to ease in some way the misfortune that elicits it. It calls for action, although it need not actually result in one because it may not be possible to ease the misfortune, as for the incurably insane; or there may be good reasons against trying to ease it, if it would be intrusive meddling; or there may be other, more important, although incompatible, actions that the subject of compassion is obligated to perform. But unless there are rightly countervailing considerations, compassion prompts corresponding action.

It may, then, be said that compassion has a *cognitive* component that concerns the subject's *beliefs* about the recipient and an *emotive* component that concerns the subject's *feelings*. Each must be justifiable if the compassion is to be appropriate. The justification of the cognitive component is that the subject has good reasons to believe that the recipient is indeed suffering from a misfortune, that it is serious, and that it is not the well-deserved outcome of the recipient's vices. In other words, the subject's beliefs must be *reasonable*, which means that the subject must hold the beliefs in a way that is responsive to evidence. The beliefs, then, are held because the available evidence favors them, and if additional evidence were to cast doubt on the beliefs, the beliefs would be adjusted accordingly.

The justification of the emotive component is that the subject's feelings are truly directed toward the recipient, that the feelings are indeed of deep sorrow and sympathy, and that their strength is commensurate with the misfortune. Self-deception, lack of self-knowledge, various defense mechanisms, and so forth may result in the subject's mistaking for sympathy and sorrow quite different feelings. And the subject's fear, shame, guilt, self-centeredness, and the like may make the feelings center on the subject rather than on the recipient, or they may make the feelings excessive or deficient. The emotive component, then, is justified if the feelings of deep sorrow and sympathy are *genuine*, rather than misdirected, misinterpreted, or disproportionate to the misfortune.

Reasonable beliefs and genuine feelings, having the recipient's misfortune in their focus, are necessary for the appropriateness of compassion. If the beliefs are unreasonable, the recipient is not suffering from serious, undeserved misfortune, and compassion is misplaced. If the feelings are not genuine, the subject's state is not compassion but some other feeling that has been falsified. If both components are present and justified, there is reason to ascribe compassion to the subject in a full sense. If in a particular situation a component is more or less lacking or has no or questionable justification, we can say that the subject in that situation either has no compassion or has compassion only partially. How such cases are described is a verbal question; as long as it is made clear what is meant, the actual words used do not matter.

We can now specify when compassion is and is not appropriate. It is appropriate if it meets each of the following three conditions. First, the subject's beliefs are reasonable and emotions genuine.

Second, the components of compassion are balanced. This means that neither overwhelms the other and the two jointly motivate corresponding action. If the cognitive component is overwhelming, the subject's feelings are suppressed and little room is left for the deep sorrow and sympathy necessary for compassion. If the emotive component is overwhelming, it escapes cognitive control, and the subject's beliefs respond to feelings, not to evidence. The subject, then, is ruled by feelings, which prompt beliefs, rather than allowing beliefs to keep feelings within reasonable limits. The two components are balanced if the subject's feelings are based on reasonable beliefs and if the beliefs are informed by genuine feelings. This balance is the best guarantee that the subject's actions will actually achieve the purpose of compassion, namely, easing the recipient's misfortune.

Third, if the first two conditions are met, there is a prima facie reason for the subject to have and to act on compassion. But this prima facie reason may be overridden by the subject's having other and more important obligations that have little to do with compassion. Such obligations may be created by justice, conscientiousness, professional or familial commitments, or the interests of others whom the subject has agreed to serve. Compassion may conflict with the discharge of these obligations, and there may be good reasons to regard the obligations as more important than compassion. So the third condition of the appropriateness of compassion is that there is no conflicting obligation that ought to override the compassion.

If these conditions are met, compassion is appropriate, but it is not easy to meet them, as Aristotle knew: "To do this to the right person, to the right extent, at the right time, and in the right way, *that* is not for everyone, nor is it easy; that is why goodness is both rare and laudable and noble." And he also knew that "it is possible to fail in many ways . . . while to succeed is possible only in one . . . to miss the mark easy, to hit it difficult."[15] Compassion is inappropriate if it fails in one of the many ways of meeting the three conditions of appropriateness.

7.4 Doubts about Compassion
We have been discussing compassion and its appropriateness in order to evaluate Nussbaum's claims that compassion is essential to any good ethical code, to public morality, and to the political structure of a

democratic and egalitarian state.[16] It is now possible to show that these claims are unacceptable because the compassion to which Nussbaum appeals is not just inappropriate but inappropriate many times over. Furthermore, since Nussbaum's attitude to freedom and to mature adults' conceptions of a good life which differ from her own was meant to be justified by her appeal to compassion, the inappropriateness of her compassion leaves her attitude without justification.

Let us begin with Nussbaum's claim that "compassion takes up the onlooker's point of view, making the best judgment the onlooker can make about what is really happening to the person, even when that may differ from the judgment of the person herself" (309). If compassion is appropriate, it cannot possibly take up *merely* the onlooker's point of view. For the reliability of the onlooker's judgment depends on whether the onlooker's beliefs are reasonable and feelings genuine. But whether or not they are depends on the evidence, which is independent of what the onlooker believes or feels. To think otherwise is to lapse into a form of subjectivism that accepts any belief or feeling so long as the onlooker holds it. To avoid this, it must be admitted that the onlooker's judgment may be mistaken. To determine whether or not it is mistaken requires going beyond the onlooker's point of view.

In that case, however, Nussbaum must explain why the onlooker's judgment is bound to be more reliable than that of the recipient of compassion. Why should we suppose that if the judgment of the recipient differs from the onlooker's, then this is because "suffering and deprivation . . . brutalize or corrupt [the recipient's] perception" (309)? Why should we not suppose instead that it is the onlooker's judgment that has gone astray, especially since the onlooker is bound to be far less familiar with the recipient's circumstances and preferences than the recipient? To these questions Nussbaum gives no answer. She simply asserts the superiority of the onlooker's point of view, as illustrated by a concrete case she presents.

"R, a woman in a rural village in India, is severely undernourished and unable to get more than a first-grade education. She does not think her lot a bad one, since she has no idea what it is to feel healthy, and no idea of the benefits and pleasures of education. So thoroughly has she internalized her culture's views of what is right for women that she believes that she is living a good and flourishing life" (309). Now a reasonable person would begin with taking seriously the woman's point of view. If the woman believes that although she is poorly nourished and educated, her life is good and flourishing, then she may have reason for it. Perhaps some aspects of her life compensate for the undoubted hardships of her existence. Maybe she takes great pleasure in her children or has a glorious sex life; or participates with pride in the traditions and customs of her village that have gone on since time immemorial, enabling the villagers to cope with their bad circumstances; or prizes the independence and self-reliance of her family; or she is optimistic because of recent improvements in their conditions; or she may be consoled by religious faith; and so forth. But Nussbaum ignores these and countless other possibilities. She ascribes the woman's judgment to suffering and deprivation, dismisses out of hand the woman's point of view, and does not even begin to consider the possibility that the woman may have reasons for what she thinks. This is condescension indeed, which Nussbaum ought not to present, as she does, to illustrate what it is to treat people with equal respect and concern.

What Nussbaum thinks compassion requires in such cases can be seen when she recommends, in discussing a similar case in Bangladesh, undertaking "a searching inquiry, carried out in women's cooperatives, in partnership between the local and the foreign women, into the role of education in their functioning, and in its relationship to other valuable functionings."[17] So these ill-nourished and ill-educated local women engage in a searching inquiry under the tutelage of foreign women who know everything better than they, except the circumstances of the lives that they are hell-bent on improving. Suppose their searching inquiry reveals that the local women lack education. Then what? Does that provide the education or the resources for it? Does it make the local women better nourished? Of course not. What it does is to make it harder for the local women to cope with their lives by adding dissatisfaction to the already present hardships. Then, mission accomplished, the foreign women go home to their well-nourished and well-educated lives and feel good about their compassionate nature. This kind of thinking gives a bad name to compassion because it ignores whether the do-gooders' beliefs are reasonable and whether their feelings are genuine. As a result, what Nussbaum takes to be compassion is inappropriate to the misfortune it is meant to relieve.

Consider next Nussbaum's view about who should be the subjects of compassion. The natural view is that it should be individuals, but this is not what Nussbaum thinks. Her view is that "the psychological mechanisms by which human beings arrive at compassion . . . typically rest on the senses and imagination in a way that makes them in principle narrow and uneven," and "any approach to social welfare that relies on individual philanthropy . . . typically produces uneven and at times arbitrary results" (386). Consequently, "we should not depend on the vicissitudes of personal emotion, but should build its insights into the structure of rules and institutions" (392). This requires that "the public culture of a pluralistic liberal democracy would involve an extension of something like equal respect and concern to all citizens" (420–21), which depends on a "good constitution" that should "specify a basic social minimum that should be available to all citizens" (416). There will be "institutional guarantees" and "institutions of corrective justice" (418) to make sure that equal respect and concern prevail. The subjects of compassion, therefore, should be the political rules and institutions enshrined in a constitution, which is good if it guarantees equal respect and concern and excludes the narrow, uneven arbitrariness of individual compassion.

The problem for this view is to explain how rules, institutions, and constitutions could be compassionate. To begin with, strictly speaking, these entities are incapable of having beliefs and feelings necessary for compassion. To say that they should be compassionate must be an elliptical way of saying that the individuals who design and maintain them should be compassionate. But if this is what is meant, then why would not the narrow, uneven arbitrariness that characterizes individual compassion be built into the rules, institutions, and constitutions that these unsatisfactory individuals design and maintain?

It is most implausible to reply that when individuals act on behalf of rules, institutions, and constitutions, then they leave behind their personal point of view, which is narrow, uneven, and arbitrary, and adopt an impartial point of view, which calls for treating people with equal respect and concern. Anyone who knows anything about how politicians acting in their official capacity actually make decisions knows that they rarely, if ever, proceed from an impartial point of view. They are guided by such considerations as the bearing of their decisions on their prospects for reelection; the requirements of political bargaining in which they support policies they disagree with in exchange for support of policies close to their hearts; the chronic shortage of and conflicting demands on funds; the interests of the small part of citizenry by whom they have been elected; the pressures on them by the political party to which they belong; the limits their consciences do not allow them to trespass; the ebb and flow of public opinion; the favorable or unfavorable opinion of the media; and so forth. It has been well said that all politics is local.

If Nussbaum concedes that this is how politicians in fact proceed but claims that she is talking about how they ought to proceed, then she has given up her claim that compassion requires abandoning the narrow, uneven, arbitrary point of view of individuals and adopting the impartial point of view of rules, institutions, and constitutions.

For the one is as partial as the other. If the injunction that politicians should leave their partiality behind can be effective, then it can be just as effective for individuals acting as such as it can be for individuals acting on behalf of rules, institutions, and constitutions. Nussbaum shares the illusion of egalitarians that political arrangements can correct individuals' lack of compassion. But they cannot, because political arrangements are made by individuals, and if individuals lack compassion, then the political arrangements they make will also lack it. It is only individuals who can make political arrangements compassionate; political arrangements cannot make individuals compassionate, because they are abstract entities that could not make individuals hold beliefs and have feelings. If Nussbaum is right to distrust the compassion of individuals, then she must give up her view that compassion "lies at the heart of any good ethical code" (392), "gives public morality essential elements of ethical vision" (403), and is essential "to the political structure of a state that is both democratic and liberal" (401). This is not to claim, of course, that since compassion is flawed, there cannot be good ethical codes, public moralities, and political structures—it is to claim rather that good ones will not be based on compassion.

The next problem with Nussbaum's claim that compassion is the basis of egalitarianism is that it is inconsistent. Nussbaum begins her account of compassion by discussing "the cognitive structure of compassion" (304–27). She says that "insofar as we believe that a person has some grief through his or her fault, we will blame and reproach, rather than having compassion. Insofar as we do feel compassion, it is either because we believe the person to be without blame for her plight or because, though there is an element of fault, we believe that her suffering is out of proportion to the fault. Compassion then addresses itself to the nonblameworthy increment" (311). In the following many pages the point that compassion is appropriate only if its recipients are not responsible for their misfortune is not only ignored but contradicted.

Nussbaum says over and over again that appropriate compassion is egalitarian. "Compassion . . . standardly includes the thought of common humanity. . . . And the respect we have for the equal humanity of others should . . . lead us to be intensely concerned with their material happiness. . . . The fact that a certain individual is a bearer of human capacities gives that person a claim on our material concerns, so that these capacities may receive appropriate support. We do not properly respect these capacities if we neglect the needs they have for resources" (371). The idea that compassion is inappropriate if its recipients are responsible for their misfortune has dropped out of consideration. We ought to be compassionate, Nussbam says, to everyone equally who shares our common humanity; we should respect them all just because they are bearers of human capacities.

But this is not all. We should "acknowledge the extent to which we are at the world's mercy—the extent, for example, to which people who are malnourished, or ill, or treated with contempt by their society have a harder time developing their capacities for learning and choice—even ethical choice—without denying that our basic capacities and our agency deserve respect and sustenance, just by being there in whatever form" (372). So it makes no difference if people are at fault. Even if they are immoral or criminal, they still deserve our compassion. "The standard occasions for compassion . . . involve losses of truly basic goods, such as life, loved ones, freedom, nourishment, mobility, bodily integrity, citizenship, shelter" (374). If a terrorist blows himself up by mishandling the bomb he intends for innocent people, we should feel compassion for him. We should also feel compassion for the jailed torturer, because he lost his freedom and mobility; for the drug lord maimed by a competitor, because his bodily integrity has been compromised; for the cruel woman left by her partner, because she has lost her loved one; and so on. "It seems right," says Nussbaum, commenting on a literary character, "for society to acknowledge its own share in creating the personality of a criminal . . . by a compassionate response to his alarming and forbidding personality" (412).

If Nussbaum is right in her earlier view that compassion is appropriate only if fault is absent, then she must be wrong in her later view that common humanity and being a bearer of human capacities are sufficient for compassion. If Nussbaum is right in her later view that compassion requires "equal respect and concern to all citizens" (421), that "a liberal political society . . . should guarantee to all citizens a basic set of opportunities for functioning" (416), then she must be wrong in her earlier view because she now thinks the presence or absence of fault makes no difference to the appropriateness of compassion; only its recipient's misfortune matters. If compassion is directed toward *all* citizens regardless of their faults, then Nussbaum cannot think of it as appropriate; if it is directed only toward nonblameworthy citizens, then Nussbaum cannot think that it warrants equal respect and concern for *all* citizens. One or the other claim must be given up, and whichever it is will essentially damage Nussbaum's attempt to base egalitarianism on compassion.

The last objection we shall discuss is a further reason for rejecting Nussbaum's claim that compassion is essential to any good ethical code, public morality, and egalitarian democratic state. This reason is that even if we have an obligation to be compassionate, we also have obligations that follow from justice, conscientiousness, our work or profession, and so forth. These other obligations often conflict with the obligation to be compassionate. It is by no means a foregone conclusion that in such conflicts the obligations of compassion should always override whatever other obligations conflict with them. If the obligations of compassion are to be considered as important as Nussbaum claims, then she owes an explanation of why they should always override conflicting obligations. Nussbaum, however, provides no such explanation and shows no awareness that one is needed.

Just because Nussbaum fails to provide the required explanation does not mean, of course, that one could not be found. But if one reflects on some of these conflicts, it is very hard to suppose that reasons could be found for the overridingness of the obligation to be compassionate. If the deliberations of judges and juries are dominated by compassion rather than by the facts of guilt or innocence, they violate their far more basic obligation to be guided by the law, not by their feelings. If teachers assign grades on the basis of compassion rather than performance, they are failing in their duties. If soldiers treat attacking enemies with compassion rather than force, they betray their oath. If diplomats are guided in their negotiations with foreigners by compassion rather than the interests of the country they represent, they are irresponsible and incompetent. If the founders or reformers of a nation design a constitution in which compassion dominates over checks and balances, or the independence of the judiciary, or the opportunity to replace the government that lost the confidence of the electorate, they invite disaster.

Compassion, of course, may play a role in all these matters, but it is unreasonable to suppose that compassion should always override all other obligations if they come in conflict. Furthermore, participants can make morally right decisions in all these contexts without compassion entering into their deliberations. So there is no good reason to accept Nussbaum's claim that "compassion . . . lies at the heart of any good ethical code" (392), or that "compassion gives public morality essential elements of ethical virtue" (403), or that compassion is essential "to the political structure of a state that is both democratic and liberal" (401).

The point of this objection is not that Nussbaum is mistaken in assigning to compassion an essential place in morality because something else has that place. Its point is rather to reaffirm the pluralism to which Nussbaum claims to be committed, but which she uses only when it suits her rhetorical purposes and ignores when it does not. According to pluralism, there are no states of mind, values, or conceptions of a good life that should always override whatever comes in conflict with them. Conflicts, of course, need to be settled, but how they are settled varies from case to case depending on the particular circumstances of the individuals or societies that face the conflicts. Pluralism is thus incompatible with the kind of ideological mentality that permeates Nussbaum's egalitarianism. She moralizes from the allegedly superior point of view of the onlooker who knows that whatever conflict occurs, it should be settled according to her conception of a good life and her compassion. And from that point of view she treats pluralism as opportunistically as we have seen her treat freedom. The freedom she values is only the freedom to choose the conception of a good life she favors, namely, the capabilities approach. The pluralism she values is only the plurality of options provided by the same capabilities approach. If people choose a different conception of a good life, or if they prefer options other than those countenanced by the capabilities approach, then, like the woman in India or the women in Bangladesh, they are to be educated because their judgments have gone wrong as a result of suffering and deprivation that have brutalized and corrupted their perception (309). Nussbaum's maternalism leaves no room for the thought that these women, and other people who reject her egalitarianism, may have reasons for their views, and that it is disrespect to treat what they say as a symptom of brutalization or corruption. This is especially so in view of the implausible implications of the capabilities approach and various other objections to it that have been made in the course of the preceding argument.

Nussbaum's tumid prose and tyrannical do-goodism are inadequate supports for a position bereft of reasons. Nor does the sex-change operation render what used to be paternalism less of a threat to the freedom of individuals. Compassion, like all passion, ought to be controlled and not inflicted on others in the misguided belief that it is for their own good.

7.5 The Limited Importance of Compassion

The argument of this chapter is now complete. There follows from it a critical and a constructive conclusion. The critical conclusion is that Nussbaum's attempt to base egalitarianism on compassion rests on an indefensible illusion that renders her appeal to compassion inappropriate many times over.

First, it violates the freedom of its recipients and ignores the reasons they may have for living as they do. It imposes on them Nussbaum's conception of a good life that is vitiated by its implausible implications. It attributes the recipients' reluctance to accept this flawed conception to brutalization and suffering that distorts their judgment.

It is thus an unreasonable, intrusive, and disrespectful interference with its recipients' lives.

Second, it requires governments to be the subjects of compassion because it distrusts the partiality of individuals. But it fails to see that it must always be individuals who act compassionately because governments can act only through the individuals who represent them. If it is true that individuals are always partial in their compassion, then they are partial also when they represent governments. In that case, however, the requirement that compassion should be impartial and egalitarian cannot be met. If governments should be impartial and egalitarian, as Nussbaum claims, then they cannot be based on compassion.

Third, it is inconsistent because it claims both that compassion is appropriate only if the recipients' misfortune is not their fault and that compassion must be impartially and equally directed toward all people who are bearers of human capacities and suffer from misfortune, regardless of whether they are at fault. This inconsistency can be avoided only by giving up either the appropriateness or the egalitarianism of compassion. The first would make compassion unreasonable; the second would violate the basic requirement of Nussbaum's position.

Fourth, it puts compassion forward as essential to any good ethical code, public morality, and egalitarian democratic state. But it ignores obligations of justice, profession, work, and conscientiousness, which often conflict with the obligation to be compassionate. It provides no reason why compassion should always override all conflicting obligations. And it is committed to an ideological dogmatism that arbitrarily assumes the superiority of the conceptions of a good life and compassion which it favors and which are shown to be unacceptable on independent grounds.

The constructive conclusion that follows from the argument is that compassion is a fine sentiment when it is appropriate. It is appropriate if it is based on the reasonable belief that its recipients suffer from serious misfortune through no fault of their own and on genuine feelings of sorrow and sympathy that are directed toward their recipients and are proportionate to their misfortune. Compassion is appropriate, next, if the subject's beliefs and feelings are balanced. They then mutually reinforce each other, and their joint forces motivate the subject, whose beliefs and feelings are not distorted by the domination of one or the other of these components. And compassion is appropriate, last, if it does not conflict with other obligations that are more important than it in a particular context.

It is in this sense that it may be appropriate for the citizens of a society to be compassionate toward their fellow citizens if, through no fault of their own, they have the misfortune of lacking the basic necessities of life. But compassion is not an appropriate reaction to fellow citizens if they are responsible for their misfortune through immorality or criminality; if they do not suffer from misfortune but merely own less property than others; or if its recipients are people outside their society about whose possible misfortune it is very hard to form reasonable beliefs or genuine feelings. Of course, just because compassion is not appropriate in such cases does not mean that there may not be some other obligation that requires people to help. In the next chapter we shall consider the claim that it is morality itself that imposes such an obligation on people.

8/

The Menace of Moralism

The man who works from himself outwards, whose conduct is governed by ordinary motives, and who acts with a view to his own advantage and the advantage of those who are connected with himself in definite assignable ways, produces in the ordinary course of things more happiness to others (if that is the great object of life) than a moral Don Quixote who is always liable to sacrifice himself and his neighbors. . . . [A] man who has a disinterested love for the human race—that is to say, who has got a fixed idea about some way of providing for the management of the concerns of mankind—is an unaccountable person . . . capable of making his love for men in general the ground of all sorts of violence against man in particular.

JAMES FITZJAMES STEPHEN, Liberty, Equality, Fraternity

8.1 The Illusion

In this chapter we shall consider another welfare-based version of egalitarianism and show that it rests on an illusion that is as indefensible as the one discussed in the preceding chapter. The illusion is that there is an obligation to help equally all those who lack the basic necessities of a good life. The basis of this supposed obligation, however, is not compassion but the very nature of morality. The claim is that the mere fact of commitment to morality places people under this obligation, and to fail to honor it is immoral. This is an illusion that involves a gross exaggeration of the requirements of morality and leads to rampant moralism. Moralism is to morality what scientism is to science. Both aberrations inflate reasonable claims either by exaggerating their importance or by extending them to inappropriate contexts. As monetary inflation weakens the currency, so moralistic and scientistic inflation weaken morality and science. Those who value morality and science will oppose moralism and scientism. If moralism is rampant, then according to *The Unabridged Random House Dictionary*

(1987), it is "1. violent in action or spirit, raging, furious . . . 2. growing luxuriantly, as weeds. 3. in full sway; prevailing or unchecked."

Moralism *is* rampant. It is very hard to think of an area of life that is free of the exhortation of one or another group of moralizers. We are told what food is right or wrong to eat; how we should treat our pets; what clothing to wear; how we should spend our after-tax income; how precisely we should phrase invitations for sex; what kind of bags we should carry our groceries in; when and where we are permitted to pray or smoke; what jokes we are allowed to tell; who should pick the fruit we buy at the supermarket; how we should invest our money; what chemicals we should use in our gardens; by what method of transportation we should go to work; how we should sort our garbage; what morality requires us to think about cross-dressing, sex-change operations, teenage sex, and pot smoking; we are forbidden to inquire after the age, marital status, drug use, or alcoholism of job applicants; we are liable to be accused of sexual abuse if we spank our children or hug our neighbor's; our nineteen- and twenty-year-olds are permitted to fight our wars, but they are not permitted to buy a beer; we are not supposed to say that people are crippled, stupid, mentally defective, fat, or ignorant; and we must not use words like *mankind* and *statesman*, or *He* when referring to God.

One influential attempt to make a reasoned case for moralism is Peter Singer's. He endeavors to provide a utilitarian justification for a version of rampant moralism. Singer has views on many controversial subjects, but we shall concentrate here only on what he says about the obligation to relieve famine.

8.2 Singer on Morality

Singer says that when people are starving, it is immoral to have such things as "stylish clothes, expensive dinners, a sophisticated stereo system, overseas holidays, a (second?) car, a larger house, private schools for our children, and so on."[1] If the "so on" is taken as broadly as Singer undoubtedly intends, it becomes obvious that a very large majority of people in affluent societies is immoral. If, for instance, we put the poverty level in America at 13 percent,[2] then it is a reasonable estimate that about 87 percent of Americans are guilty of what Singer regards as immorality. Similar estimates hold in other affluent societies. Most people above the poverty level, and many below it, spend money on things that are not necessities. Those to whom this kind of moral exhortation gives an uneasy conscience may be cowed into thinking that there is something to Singer's claim. But not many of them would think that the immorality they are charged with is terribly serious. If it is a sin to have more than what is necessary, it is a venal, not a deadly, sin. In a different moral vocabulary, it is a minor omission that involves a failure of generosity, not a major commission of a wrong that causes serious unjustified harm to others.

Singer, however, strongly disagrees. He says that "by not giving more than we do, people in rich countries are allowing those in poor countries to suffer from absolute poverty [i.e., having less than basic necessities], with consequent malnutrition, ill health, and death. This is not a conclusion that applies only to governments. It applies to each absolutely affluent individual [i.e., one who has more than basic necessities], for each of us has the opportunity to do something about the situation; for instance, to give our time or money to voluntary organizations like Oxfam."[3] In saying this, Singer states no more than a factual possibility: we *are* allowing absolute poverty, and we *could* spend our time and money to try to alleviate it. The question is whether there is a moral obligation to do so, and if there is, how strong is this supposed obligation. Singer's moralism enters with a vengeance in his answer. Since "allowing someone to die is not intrinsically different from killing someone, it would seem that we are all murderers."[4]

This is not a slip or a momentary exaggeration. Singer really means it. When we stay at home after work and read a book, listen to music, watch television, or, God forbid, go out to a restaurant instead of doing volunteer work or writing a check to Oxfam, we are allowing someone to die, and we are murderers. He asks: "Is this verdict too harsh?" He knows that "many will reject it as self-evidently absurd."[5] He allows that there are obvious differences between killing and allowing to die, but "these differences need not shake our previous conclusion that there is no intrinsic difference between killing and allowing to die. They are extrinsic differences, that is, differences normally but not necessarily associated with the distinction between killing and allowing to die."[6] It should not be overlooked that when Singer attempts to argue for his claim that we are all murderers, he drops the talk about murder and speaks instead of killing. But the concession he slips in makes the claim only a little less outrageous: we are merely all killers, not murderers, of people who live in absolute poverty.

Singer also makes clear that the obligation to alleviate absolute poverty is very strong. It is not the obligation of charity, which is usually thought to be right to do but not wrong not to do. The obligation is not just right to do but also wrong not to do. It is a clear positive duty, and the failure to discharge it is equivalent to killing those we could have saved. He says: "We ought to give money away, rather than spend it on clothes which we do not need to keep us warm. To do so is not charitable or generous. Nor is it the kind of act which philosophers and theologians have called 'supererogatory'—an act which it would be good to do but not wrong not to do. On the contrary, we ought to give money away, and it is wrong not to do so."[7] Singer realizes that the general acceptance of what he says would lead to "the revision of our conceptual moral scheme" and would have "radical implications,"[8] but given the suffering from absolute poverty, nothing less is called for. This makes obvious that what Singer is saying is that if people do not think about their moral obligations the way he does, then they should change the way they think. It will perhaps be seen that it is not inappropriate to describe what Singer is doing as rampant moralism.

Describe it as we may, the question remains whether Singer is right. Reason may be on the side even of rampant moralism. Let us, therefore, see what reason Singer gives in support of the claim that affluent people are killers if they do not alleviate absolute poverty. He begins by saying: "Suppose that . . . I notice that a small child has fallen in [a pond] and is in danger of drowning. Would anyone deny that I ought to wade in and pull the child out? This will mean getting my clothes muddy . . . but compared to the avoidable death of a child this is insignificant." And he goes on, "We have an obligation to help those in absolute poverty that is no less strong than our obligation to rescue a drowning child from a pond."[9]

Those willing to use their critical faculties will notice that most people in absolute poverty are not small children and to think of them as such is a crass paternalistic insult. They will also notice that it makes a great difference who the person is who is in danger of drowning. If it is a contract killer in pursuit of a victim, we are unlikely to acknowledge a strong obligation to pull him out. Furthermore, if there is a lifeguard on duty whose job it is to rescue those in danger of drowning, we should let him do it. And of course, the equivalent is precisely the job of the governments of the countries in which people in absolute poverty live. Singer's putative analogy is a rhetorical stratagem that misleads the uncritical and provokes the critical.

The example, however, is dispensable to Singer's argument. What he really wants is to propose and defend a principle that underlies the example. We shall call it the *Prevention Principle:* "If it is in our power to prevent something very bad from happening, without sacrificing anything of comparable moral significance, we ought to do it." And he claims, "This principle seems uncontroversial."[10] But this claim is patently false, as the following considerations show.

First, it obviously makes a great difference who is threatened by the very bad thing. If the very bad thing is defeat in war and it threatens unjust aggressors, or if it is imprisonment for life of justly convicted murderers, then the obligation to prevent it is hardly uncontroversial. Second, it is no less obvious that it is folly to prevent a very bad thing from happening without asking about the consequences of doing so. These consequences concern not those who could prevent it but those who are prevented from suffering it. The consequences could be even worse than the very bad thing that is prevented. Death is presumably very bad, but if the consequence of preventing it is to live in great pain attached to a life-support system, then an increasingly large number of people (including Singer) would not recognize the obligation to prevent it. Third, it is equally obvious that it affects the supposed obligation why the very bad thing is threatening some people. What if they brought it upon themselves by imprudent risks (such as taken by recreational drug users) or by lack of foresight that reasonable people can be expected to have (such as ignoring the notice to evacuate from the path of a flood or a rapidly spreading fire)? Is the obligation to prevent the very bad thing obvious then? Fourth, it is similarly questionable whether the obligation holds if the people threatened by the very bad thing are proud, independent, and refuse help. Fifth, should it not be asked also how good are the chances of preventing the very bad thing from happening? Is it not more reasonable to prevent merely bad things from happening if the chances of success are good, rather than expend efforts and resources by risking the strong likelihood of failure to prevent very bad things? These considerations render the putatively uncontroversial Prevention Principle controversial.

The implication is that before it is reasonable to acknowledge the obligation whose violation, according to Singer, makes us killers, we should ask: Are we obliged to prevent very bad things regardless of whether they are deserved? regardless of consequences? regardless of whether people have brought them upon themselves? regardless of people's refusal of help? regardless of the likelihood of success? These questions should be asked not in order to justify doing nothing, but in order to determine whether our obligations would not be better met by concentrating on helping people in our own context where the answers could more easily be found rather than in distant contexts in which our unfamiliarity makes it unlikely that we can find reasonable answers. Singer, in offering his simpleminded argument, fails to consider these complexities. Of course, he could consider them. But then he would have to show that the answers to these difficult questions would favor his case. That, however, he has not even begun to do.

8.3 The Obligation to Prevent Suffering
Let us go on, however, and ask what makes Singer so confident that the Prevention Principle is uncontroversial. The answer is that he sup-

poses that the principle is a straightforward implication of morality. He thinks that if morality is rightly understood, then commitment to it commits one to the Prevention Principle. We need to ask, therefore, what his understanding of morality is. (Singer tends to speak of ethics rather than morality, but the two are treated here as synonymous.)

According to Singer, morality is egalitarian. "Equality is a basic ethical principle . . . the principle of equal consideration of interests. The essence of the principle . . . is that we give equal weight in our moral deliberations to the like interests of all those affected by our actions . . . an interest is an interest, whoever's interest it may be."[11] Singer makes clear that the equal consideration of interests may require unequal treatment in circumstances where some people require more than others in order to satisfy their interests equally. It is, for instance, in the interests of both healthy and sick people to be able to function normally, but the sick require medical help whereas the healthy do not. "This," says Singer, "is in line with the principle of declining marginal utility, a principle well known to economists, which states that for a given individual, a set amount of something is more useful when people have little of it than when they have a lot." Unequal treatment, however, can be justified only if it "is an attempt to produce a more egalitarian result."[12]

There are many serious problems with this "basic ethical principle" which Singer does not consider. First, it commits one to the absurdity of considering equally the interests of terrorists and their hostages, of criminals and their victims, of benefactors and scourges of humanity, and so forth. Second, it does not say how people's interests are to be determined. The interests cannot be what people believe them to be because, as a result of ignorance, indoctrination, self-deception, and the like, people are often mistaken about their interests. Are the interests, then, what the relevant experts say that they are? This would make it a moral requirement to treat people in ways they regard as contrary to their interests, which is surely an unacceptable form of paternalism. If Singer nevertheless accepts it, he should provide reasons for it and should make clear that the "basic ethical principle" commits one to paternalism. Singer, however, does neither. Third, the principle rests on the severely criticized principle of diminishing marginal utility, and the criticisms have not been met.[13] The latter, economic, principle assumes that the utility functions of people are commensurable, but they are not. As a result, it is often impossible to say what interests are equal or unequal. Let us put these problems aside, however, and ask the more basic question: Why should people's interests be equally considered?

Singer's answer is that it is the very nature of morality that requires it. "Ethics," he says, "takes a universal point of view." "Ethics requires us to go beyond 'I' and 'you' to the universal law, the universalizable judgment, the standpoint of the impartial spectator or ideal observer, or whatever we choose to call it."[14] And he goes on, "The universal aspect of ethics, I suggest, does provide a persuasive, although not conclusive, reason for taking a broadly utilitarian position." This means that "at some level in my moral reasoning I must choose the course of action that has the best consequences, on balance, for all affected," where " 'best consequences' is understood as meaning what, on balance, furthers the interests of those affected."[15] Because morality is committed to the universal point of view, it must be impartial. Because morality is impartial, it must consider the interests of everyone equally. Because morality requires the equal consideration of interests, it must prevent something bad from happening to anyone, anywhere, if it does not involve the sacrifice of something of comparable moral significance.

Every step in this argument is questionable as a result of serious difficulties that Singer does not consider. That morality need not be committed to the universal point of view is shown by the long tradition of Aristotelian eudaimonism, which has been an influential moral theory for more than two thousand years, and by value pluralism, which is perhaps the most significant contemporary contribution to morality. Eudaimonists and pluralists argue that there are many reasonable conceptions of a good life, many reasonable ways of ranking many reasonable values, and they deny that there is a universal point of view from which the one true blueprint for reasonable lives, rankings, and values could be derived. That the universal point of view does not commit one to impartiality is made evident by the fact that obligations that people everywhere have to their family, friends, and country often take justifiable precedence over impartial obligations that may be owed to everyone. That impartiality does not require the equal consideration of the interests of all those who are affected by one's action is obvious if it is remembered that treating the interests of good and bad people with equal consideration cannot be a requirement of morality; that it is often hard to know what people's interests are; that treating interests with equal consideration presupposes that interests are commensurable, which they are not; and that treating people with equal consideration would often involve a morally highly objectionable form of paternalism. Lastly, that the equal consideration of interests does not impose the obligation to prevent something bad from happening to anyone, anywhere, is clear if it is borne in mind that it makes a great difference whether people deserve the bad thing that threatens them, whether they have brought it upon themselves, whether the consequences of preventing it are acceptable, and whether expending resources in this way is warranted by practical considerations, such as the likelihood of success. Singer's assertion about the obligations that the commitment to morality creates systematically ignores these serious difficulties.

Such force as Singer's rampant moralism has derives from this failure. He counts on the fact that most affluent people claim to be committed to morality and will be disturbed by the claim that the implication of their commitment is that they must either donate what they do not need for basic necessities, or recognize that by failing to do so they are letting people in absolute poverty die, which makes them killers. If they cannot fault the argument, they must accept its consequence: they must either radically change the way they live or accept the guilt and shame of being killers. What they ought to do, of course, is to fault the argument. The difficulties just enumerated show that its faults are many.

Suppose, however, that Singer can dispose of all these difficulties and he is correct in claiming that commitment to morality requires commitment to the Prevention Principle. Suppose, further, that when reasonable people understand this and see that morality requires them to change their lives and society radically, to give up the comforts that make their lives pleasant, they consider giving up their commitment to morality. What has Singer to say to such people?

He says that people in that position must make an "ultimate choice" in which their "fundamental values come to the fore." They are "choosing between different possible ways of living: the way of living in which self-interest is paramount, or that in which ethics is paramount, or perhaps some trade-off between the two."[16] And he goes on: "If we are honest with ourselves, we will admit that, at least sometimes, where self-interest and ethics clash, we choose self-interest, and this is not just a case of being weak-willed or irrational. We are genuinely unsure what it is rational to do, because when the clash is so fundamental, reason seems to have no way of resolving it."[17] What about those who choose self-interest over morality and its supposed universal point of view? Does this "mean that the person who acts only from a narrow perspective—for the sake of self, family, friends, or nation, in ways that cannot be defended even indirectly from an impartial perspective—is necessarily acting irrationally?" The answer is, "If to be irrational is to make a mistake, there is no mistake here."[18] Singer acknowledges, "Since reasoning alone proved incapable of fully resolving the clash between self-interest and ethics, it is unlikely that rational argument will persuade every rational person to act ethically."[19]

This calls for three comments. First, having arrived at the view that he can provide no reason against preferring self-interest to morality, Singer should heed the words of Mill, from whom he has learned so much: "An opinion on a point of conduct, not supported by reasons, can only count as one person's preference; and if the reasons, when given, are a mere appeal to a similar preference felt by other people, it is still only many people liking instead of one."[20]

Second, to suppose that the choice people face is between self-interest and morality is a misrepresentation. The choice is really between accepting the obligation that Singer's moralism lays on them to help people in absolute poverty regardless of why they are poor, regardless of consequences, regardless of the likelihood of success and accepting the obligation to help others in their own context even if they are not in absolute poverty. The choice, therefore, is typically not between morality and immorality but between different moral obligations. Not making the choice Singer prescribes need not, therefore, make people immoral.

Third, Singer's answer to reasonable people who are considering whether they should radically change their lives is that he cannot offer a rational argument to persuade them to do so. What he offers instead is rampant moralism that tries to achieve by bullying what it cannot achieve by reasoning. If we look beyond Singer's rhetoric, recognize the complexities he ignores, bear in mind the difficulties he does not face, we find that he cannot provide a rationally persuasive grounding for his position. And in the name of this simpleminded and rationally unpersuasive position that is riddled with problems, he urges people to change radically their lives and the society in which they live, and calls them killers if they do not.

8.4 Responsibility for Poverty

Consider now the following defense of Singer's position. Perhaps he overstated the case in talking about killing and the obligation to change one's life and society radically, but surely decent people will recognize that they ought to do *something* to alleviate the suffering of those who live in absolute poverty. In other words, a suitably revised version of the Prevention Principle *does* state a genuine obligation, the suffering of people in absolute poverty *is* reason enough to try to help them, and affluent people *are* in the position to do so. There are, however, good reasons to reject even this much weakened position.

Singer presents the Prevention Principle in isolation from any other moral principle. But of course, there are other moral principles, they also create obligations, and commitment to morality involves commitment to these other principles and obligations. Here is, then, another moral principle that reasonable and morally committed people will accept: people should be held responsible for the easily foreseeable consequences of their voluntary actions. Let us call this the *Responsibility Principle*.

It is a simple principle, so there is no need for a great deal of explanation of it. If I decide to do something when nothing forces me, if I understand both the decision and the surrounding circumstances, and if a normally intelligent person could be expected to see that the action is likely to bring about certain specific results, then it is justified to praise or blame, reward or punish, approve or condemn me for the action. The Responsibility Principle is obviously a basic moral principle, for without it we could not hold people morally or legally accountable. Without the principle the systems of morality and law, as we at present understand them, would have to be fundamentally revised.

One reason for rejecting even the weakened form of the Prevention Principle that we have some obligation to alleviate the suffering of people in absolute poverty is that this supposed obligation is obviously affected by the Responsibility Principle. It surely makes a difference to the obligation whether the people living in absolute poverty are responsible for their own suffering. If their suffering is an easily foreseeable consequence of their immoral or imprudent actions, then it is hard to see why other people would have an obligation to alleviate *their* plight rather than the plight of others who have not brought their suffering upon themselves. Say that some people live in absolute poverty because they have been impoverished by waging an unjust foreign or civil war (as in Rwanda), or because they have murdered or exiled many of those among them who had the necessary know-how to raise living standards (as in Iraq), or because they are strongly devoted to a religion that teaches resignation and whose practice is incompatible with improving their lot (as many are in India). It would be absurd to deny that such considerations require a further revision of even the weakened version of the Prevention Principle. It should be revised to say that affluent people have some obligation to alleviate the suffering of those who live in absolute poverty if the sufferers are not responsible for their own suffering. And it should be remembered that if it turns out that affluent people do not have the obligation to alleviate the suffering of some group of people, it does not mean that they have no obligation to alleviate the suffering of some other group. The choice is not between honoring the obligation and doing nothing but between honoring *that* obligation and some other obligation.

Now all this is likely to strike rampant moralizers as evasive pedantry because they believe that people living in absolute poverty are not responsible for their own suffering. But whether this belief is true is a factual question, and we have no lesser authority than Singer for suspecting that the belief is false. He says, "The major cause of absolute poverty is overpopulation,"[21] and he repeats the point, "I accept that the earth cannot support indefinitely a population rising at the present rate . . . the best means of preventing famine, in the long run, is population control."[22] If Singer is right, then the question of whether or not people living in absolute poverty are responsible for their own suffering is answered by considering whether or not they are responsible for overpopulation.

Overpopulation is the cumulative result of the combination of individual actions and certain conditions. No individual is responsible for overpopulation. But individuals are responsible for the size of their families. It is an easily foreseeable consequence of their actions that if they increase the size of their families, they will have to divide their resources among more people. If they live in poverty, absolute or other, this will worsen their condition. No reasonable person can fail to see this. If people nevertheless increase the size of their families and end up in or perpetuate their absolute poverty, then they are responsible for their own and their children's easily foreseeable suffering. Increasing the size of their families is clearly a voluntary action because they could refrain from sexual intercourse, they could enjoy sex without its leading to conception, they could practice such traditional methods of contraception as are available in their context, and they could abort unwanted fetuses. If overpopulation is the major cause of absolute poverty, then it is the imprudent voluntary actions of people living in absolute poverty that is a major contributing factor to their own and their children's suffering.

Singer takes no notice of this whatsoever. He does say, however, that "the best means of preventing famine, in the long run, is population control. It would then follow . . . that one ought to be doing all one can to promote population control. . . . Since there are organizations working specifically for population control, one would support them rather than more orthodox methods of preventing famine."[23] These organizations distribute contraceptive devices and teach people how to use them. The implication of Singer's view is that affluent people have the obligation to give up what they do not need for basic necessities in order to enable people in absolute poverty to enjoy the pleasures of sex without having to worry about feeding their offspring. And if affluent people fail to do so because they regard it more important to help others in their own context who do not live in absolute poverty and are not responsible for their suffering, or because they want to give their children the best education their money can buy, then they are immoral. Singer urges this absurd view on his readers with the deadly earnestness that is the hallmark of rampant moralism. We may conclude, then, that given the Responsibility Principle and the suffering of others who do not live in absolute poverty but who are not responsible for their own suffering, the obligation is to help only those who have not brought their misfortune on themselves.

The discharge of this obligation requires morally committed people to ask and answer the question of why people suffer. The mere fact of suffering is not enough to impose an obligation on anyone because the suffering may be the responsibility of the sufferer. Whether it is can be determined by the application of the Responsibility Principle. Its application requires making reasonable comparative judgments about the likelihood that the discharge of the obligation in one context rather than another will be effective in alleviating suffering. Singer agrees: "We have no obligation to make sacrifices that, to the best of our knowledge, have no prospect of reducing poverty in the long run."[24] We should, therefore, revise the Prevention Principle once more: affluent people have some obligation to alleviate suffering if the sufferers are not responsible for their suffering and if it is likely that the aid will reduce their suffering in the long run.

One consequence of the latest version of the Prevention Principle is that whether the obligation holds depends on being able to make reasonable judgments about the sufferers' responsibility and about the likelihood that the aid will be effective in the long run. Making such judgments requires considerable knowledge of the context in which the sufferers live. The vast majority of affluent people cannot be expected to have such knowledge. They would have to be able to answer such questions as whether the aid is likely to reach its intended recipients, rather than being wasted as a result of inefficient distribution, or being stolen by corrupt officials, or being distributed to favored groups, or being in a form that the recipients would find unacceptable. They would have to be able to judge whether the aid is going to result in superficial short-term relief that merely prolongs suffering or whether it brings about long-term structural changes that would relieve suffering in the long run. If they could not make reasonable judgments of this sort, they would have to accept the judgments of various local politicians and aid workers, and they would have to decide whether these judgments are trustworthy. Since both the politicians and the aid workers have a vested interest in attracting aid, there would be a prima facie reason not to take their judgments at face value.

Even if these questions were satisfactorily answered, there would be further questions about the causes of the suffering. Is it the result of a natural disaster, corruption, inefficiency, an unjust political system, religious practices, outdated customs, or the voluntary actions of the sufferers? The likelihood is that several factors have contributed to causing the suffering. Judging the effectiveness of the aid is possible only if these causes and their relative contributions are known. Without such knowledge, the aid may just be wasted, and as Singer rightly says: "Any consequentialist ethics must take probability of outcome into account. A course of action that will certainly produce some benefit is to be preferred to an alternative course that may lead to a slightly larger benefit, but is equally likely to result in no benefit at all."[25] Since it is extremely unlikely that people have the knowledge on which reasonable attempts to take probability into account would have to be based, it is hard to see how the conditions stated by the latest revision of the Prevention Principle could be met.

It will strengthen this point if we consider two questions that are likely to occur to those who think about Singer's claim and the reasons against them. One is about the fate of the children born to imprudent parents who live in absolute poverty: is there no obligation to aid these children? The other is about the division of responsibility between the leaders of people who live in absolute poverty and the people themselves: is there no obligation to aid people if their wretched conditions are largely the consequences of the stupidity or immorality of their leaders?

It must be granted, of course, that the children are not responsible for the conditions into which they are born and that the leaders, for example, of China, India, Iraq, and various African countries must bear a major share of the responsibility for the awful conditions that prevail in the domains they rule. Decent people cannot but be affected by the miserable lives of many millions of people. Acknowledging widespread misery is one thing, however, and accepting the obligation to do something about it—an obligation that would be wrong not to meet—is quite another.

The hard fact is that the aid that may be given will be only window-dressing that produces, at best, short-term relief and perpetuates the conditions that produce absolute poverty. For the children who are helped will grow into adults who will have children. The temporary improvement of their condition will make the population living in absolute poverty grow faster than it would without aid. And that will make poverty worse in the long run, not better. Nor will the acceptance of the obligation be seen as reasonable if it is borne in mind that it will strengthen the rule of the stupid or immoral leaders who are more or less responsible for absolute poverty. It is not easy to behold the pictures of emaciated children that television reports are so eager to inflict on their viewers. The fact remains, nevertheless, that the aid will produce even more emaciated children unless their leaders are replaced by honest and practical reformers and unless the people who would be the parents of yet unborn miserable children exercise sufficient self-control to avoid having offspring with doomed lives. Given this fact, we must conclude with Singer that "we have no obligation to make sacrifices that, to the best of our knowledge, have no prospect of reducing poverty in the long run."[26]

8.5 Helping Others in Need

In the light of the foregoing considerations, reasonable and decent people living in affluent circumstances would be well advised to reject Singer's rampant moralism. Such people are not murderers, killers, or immoral if they do not donate what they earn beyond the basic necessities to alleviate the suffering of people in absolute poverty. Singer has given no acceptable reason for the illusion that affluent people are morally obligated to change radically their lives and society, that morality requires the equal consideration of the suffering of all people regardless of whether they are responsible for their suffering, and that the mere existence of absolute poverty creates an obligation to alleviate it. What Singer has given is a shoddy argument that plays on the emotions of decent people who regret, as they should, the existence of so much suffering in the world.

It will be asked, is regret enough? Should not people *do* something? In answer, consider, for instance, an American family of four: two parents and two children. They have an annual income of $100,000, which makes them affluent. Taking various exemptions into account, they are likely to pay about $30,000 in federal and state taxes and in their contributions to Social Security and Medicare. In addition, they have to pay property and school taxes, as well as sales tax on various articles they buy. It is not unreasonable to estimate that all in all they pay about $35,000 in various forms of taxes. Approximately 60 percent of the federal and state budget is spent on social programs.[27] (The figure is higher in other affluent countries.) We may say, then, that roughly 60 percent of their total annual taxes of $35,000, or $21,000, is spent on social programs. So the answer to the question of whether they should not *do* something is that they *are* doing something: they are spending about one-fifth of their income, one dollar out of every five, on helping others. This is more than double the tithe Singer regards as the morally acceptable minimum. Of course, they may give more. But as to the supposed obligation to give more—an obligation that would be immoral not to meet—the case for it has not been made.

We may conclude, then, that it is an illusion that everyone has an obligation to help equally all those who lack the basic necessities. The truth is that there is an obligation to help others provided they are not responsible for their situation, the help is likely to be effective, and there is no more pressing obligation.

The Ideology of Freedom

There is no consideration of any kind that overrides all other considerations in all conceivable circumstances.

STUART HAMPSHIRE, *Innocence and Experience*

9.1   The Illusion

Egalitarianism has different versions, depending on whether equality of freedom or rights or resources is regarded as most important. The discussion up to now has focused on versions that stress the importance of equal rights and/or resources. The version we shall consider in this chapter aims to defend the fundamental importance of equal freedom. In our own times, it has been defended by Judith Shklar, Robert Nozick, and Joseph Raz, among others.[1] A clear initial statement of this view is, "Liberalism has only one overriding aim: to secure the political conditions that are necessary for the exercise of personal freedom. Every adult should be able to make as many effective decisions without fear or favor about as many aspects of her or his life as is compatible with the like freedom of every adult. That belief is the original and only defensible meaning of liberalism."[2] This version of egalitarianism thus regards the equal freedom of all adults as the basic value. The very idea of there being a value that is basic, however, rests on the illusion that a value can be found that should always override any other value that may conflict with it. This illusion is the source of all ideological politics, not just of this version of egalitarianism, but the illusion is unsustainable. We shall focus on Joseph Raz's attempt to defend it.

9.2   Raz on Freedom

Raz begins with the claim that "the specific contribution of the liberal tradition to political morality has always been its insistence on the respect for individual liberty. . . . The argument of this book will demonstrate how far-reaching are the implications of political liberty, how they affect our conception of justice, equality, prosperity and other political ideals."[3] The ideal of individual freedom is the "liberal foundation for a political morality" (3). And "the whole purpose of this book [i.e., Raz's] is to defend a concept of political freedom" (16). "Liberalism is a doctrine about political morality which revolves around the importance of personal liberty" (17). Raz uses *freedom* and *liberty* interchangeably, and he sometimes refers to it as *individual* and sometimes as *political*. We shall call it *individual freedom*.

Raz distinguishes between core and derivative rights (168–70), and claims that the "right to personal liberty is the right from which the other[s] derive" (169). He explains why individual freedom is so important with reference to "the humanistic principle which claims that the explanation and justification of the goodness or badness of anything ultimately derives from its contribution, actual or possible, to human life and its quality" (194). This principle provides "the goal of all political action," which is "to enable individuals to pursue valid conceptions of the good and to discourage evil or empty ones" (133). Raz then quotes with approval the following passage from John Mackie: "If we assume that, from the point of view of the morality we are constructing, what matters in human life is . . . diverse activities determined by successive choices, we shall . . . take as central the right of persons progressively to choose how they shall live" (203).[4] This, says Raz, "suggests that the fundamental right is . . . a right to liberty" (203). And he continues: "One common strand in liberal thought regards the promotion and protection of personal autonomy as the core of the liberal concern for liberty. This is also the view argued for in this book" (203).

Raz then goes on to explain what he means by autonomy. "An autonomous person is part author of his own life. His life is, in part, of his own making. . . . A person is autonomous only if he has a variety of acceptable options available to him to choose from, and his life became as it is through his choice of some of these options" (204). Since autonomy presupposes the existence of a plurality of valued options, "valuing autonomy leads to the endorsement of moral pluralism" (399). Thus Raz's view is, "Freedom is valuable because it is . . . a concomitant of the ideal of autonomous persons creating their own lives through progressive choices from a multiplicity of valuable options. The perception of freedom as constituted by the ideals of personal autonomy and value-pluralism is familiar. . . . It would not qualify as an interpretation of liberalism if it were not" (265).

But "the defence of pluralism and autonomy calls for an explanation of . . . individual well-being." This is a moral task, for morality is "concerned with the advancement of the well-being of individuals" (267). The concept of individual well-being "captures one crucial evaluation of a person's life: how good or successful is it from his point of view? . . . The value of various situations for a particular person depends to a large extent on his actual goals, as they are or will be throughout his life" (289–90).

Raz, then, sets out a version of egalitarian liberalism whose primary commitment is to create the political conditions of individual well-being. Freedom—constituted of individual autonomy and value pluralism—is the basic value, according to this view, because it is the essential requirement of well-being. The ideal that this version of egalitarianism aims at is a society in which individual freedom is limited only by the protection of the freedom of other individuals. The ideal promises a society in which there is a great deal of freedom for everyone, and it gives rise to the expectation that provided its policies are followed, the ideal will be better served by it than by any other approach to politics.

Given this promise and expectation, it is a considerable surprise to find Raz saying that "autonomy is valuable only if it is directed at the good" and that there is "no reason to provide, nor reason to protect, worthless let alone bad options" (411); or that "it is the function of governments to promote morality" (415); or that it is justified "to use coercion in order to force [people] to take actions which are required to improve peoples' options and opportunities" (416); or that "a government . . . is entitled to redistribute resources, to provide public goods, and to engage in the provision of other services on a compulsory basis" (417); or that "the perfectionist principles espoused in this book suggest that people are justified in taking action to assimilate [a] minority group, at the cost of letting its culture die or at least be considerably changed by absorption" (424); or that "the autonomy-based doctrine of freedom advocated here deviates from some liberal writings on the subject . . . in its ready embrace of various paternalistic measures" (422); or that "the perfectionism advocated here goes beyond means-related paternalism . . . in sanctioning measures which encourage the adoption of valuable ends and discourage the pursuit of bad ones" (423).

If there were agreement about what is good and bad, these views could perhaps be reconciled with the promise made and the expectation created by Raz's version of egalitarian liberalism. But since there is no such agreement, someone's views about good and bad are going to be imposed on others. A society may have to do this. To do it, however, in the name of freedom, autonomy, and pluralism makes one suspect Raz's understanding of these notions. In any case, it is hard to see how the yawning gap could be closed between the initial statement of Raz's view and the views expressed in the passages just quoted. These passages could have been written by the socialists, religious fundamentalists, or communists whose views Raz is eager to repudiate. But they could not have been written by the author of *On Liberty*, whose views Raz is "reformulating," or by Isaiah Berlin, whose warnings against the dangers of the positive freedom that Raz advocates go unheeded. Something has gone very wrong between the cup of egalitarian liberalism that Raz is offering and the lip that delivers the quoted views. We have to see now how and why Raz got from a liberal beginning to an illiberal conclusion.

9.3 Freedom and Evil

The short explanation of what drives Raz from claiming that equal freedom is a basic value to approving policies that drastically curtail freedom is his acknowledgment that evil is widespread and human well-being requires curtailing the freedom of evildoers. Raz, therefore, recognizes the problem that was shown (in chapter 2) to present a fundamental difficulty for egalitarian liberalism. It is in order to cope with it that he approves of policies that restrict the freedom of evildoers. What Raz does not recognize is that if evil is indeed widespread, then the restriction of freedom has to be so extensive as to render unfulfillable the promise of egalitarian liberalism to create a society in which individuals are equally guaranteed a great deal of freedom to pursue what they take to be their well-being. Raz is right to value freedom, right to see that evil requires restricting freedom, but he fails to see the unavoidable inconsistency between doing both and the consequent failure of his version of egalitarianism. This short explanation must now be expanded in order to provide reasons for it.

To begin with, Raz does not say what he means by evil, but there is no reason to think that he would be opposed to the view of evil (formulated in chapter 2) as serious unjustified harm caused by human beings to other human beings. He does say, however, that "it is the goal of all political action to enable individuals to pursue valid conceptions of the good and to discourage evil or empty ones" (133). Let us concentrate for the moment on political actions that discourage evil. Raz says that "the main source of deviation between morality and a person's concern for his own well-being arises where the social forms available to him in his society are morally wicked. . . . Such cases do arise. They arise all too often" (319–20). Elsewhere he says that "dishonesty, indolence, insensitivity to the feelings of others, cruelty, pettiness and the other vices and moral weaknesses are logically inseparable from the conditions of a human life which can have any moral merit," and he recognizes "their prevalence" (381). Moreover, "autonomy itself is blind to the quality of options chosen. A person is autonomous even if he chooses the bad" (411). It is clear from these passages that Raz believes that evil is widespread, that it is caused by free actions (he says autonomous actions, but autonomous actions are free), and that a good society will curtail the freedom of evildoers. From these beliefs it follows that in a good society freedom will have to be extensively curtailed. For the more freedom there is, the more widespread will evil be; and to make evil less widespread requires curtailing freedom. Furthermore, if Raz is right in claiming that freedom is essential to well-being, then the decrease of freedom will also decrease well-being. These implications are contrary to the promise of Raz's egalitarian liberalism and thus present a serious objection to it.

Raz may reply to this objection by stressing two points. The first is that the objection would be serious only if he had supposed that freedom is an absolute value that overrode all other values that may conflict with it. However, he supposed no such thing. According to him, freedom is a basic value, but it is prima facie, not absolute. The freedom of an individual may be reasonably overridden if the freedom of other individuals requires it. What Raz says about autonomy applies also to freedom: "A moral theory which values autonomy highly can justify restricting the autonomy of one person for the sake of the greater autonomy of others or even of that person himself in the future" (419).

This reply, however, is unsatisfactory. For the claim that a value is prima facie means that although it normally overrides other values that conflict with it, there may be exceptional circumstances in which this is not so. But if evil is widespread and curtailing it depends on curtailing freedom, then the circumstances in which freedom is reasonably overridden will not be the exception but the rule. If Raz is right in claiming that "dishonesty, indolence, insensitivity to the feelings of others, cruelty, pettiness and the other vices" are prevalent (381); if there is "no reason to provide, nor reason to protect, worthless let alone bad options" (411), then freedom will be often and reasonably overridden. To claim in the face of this that freedom is the basic value is no more plausible than to claim that any other frequently overridden value is basic. The case Raz makes for freedom being basic can be made for peace, prosperity, security, justice, civility, and so forth being basic. The conclusion that follows is that the claim that freedom is the basic value ought to be given up. If that were done, however, then the foundation on which egalitarian liberalism rests would collapse.

Raz, however, may opt for another response. He may claim that curtailing freedom in order to decrease evil is justified by the consequent increase in well-being. This is probably true, but its consequence for egalitarian liberalism is no less damaging than the consequence of the preceding response. For if an increase in well-being requires a decrease in freedom, then freedom can hardly be the essential condition of well-being that Raz claims it is.

Given the failure of these two responses, the objection stands. Raz's version of egalitarianism does no better at overcoming the inconsistency between the constructive and corrective aims of egalitarianism than the other versions we have considered. Egalitarian policies cannot increase the chances of human well-being. To his credit, Raz sees this, and that is why he is driven from liberal beginnings to such illiberal conclusions as urging the government to enforce morality, advocating paternalism, and coercively preventing people from pursuing their own ideals of well-being.

9.4 Autonomy and Pluralism

Inconsistency is only one problem with Raz's version of egalitarianism. There are two others that we shall discuss. Both stem from his commitment to pluralism and his view of freedom. The first problem (discussed here) is that it is a mistake to regard autonomy as essential to well-being. The second problem (the topic of 9.5) is that it is also a mistake to regard freedom—regardless of whether or not autonomy is constitutive of it—as the basic value. Both problems arise because Raz's understanding of the place of autonomy and freedom in well-being is incompatible with his commitment to pluralism.

Let us begin with moral or value pluralism, as Raz understands it.

Moral pluralism is the view that there are various forms and styles of life which exemplify different virtues and which are incompatible. Forms or styles of life are incompatible if, given reasonable assumptions about human nature, they cannot be exemplified in the same life. . . . Moral pluralism claims not merely that incompatible forms of life are morally acceptable but that they display distinct virtues, each capable of being pursued for its own sake. If . . . lives are not merely incompatible but also display distinctive virtues then complete moral perfection is unattainable. Whichever form of life one is pursuing there are virtues which elude one because they are available only to people pursuing alternative and incompatible forms of life. (395–96)

So pluralism, for short, holds that there are forms of life and values, such as virtues, which are incommensurable, incompatible, and conflicting (chaps. 13–14).

The question that leads to the first problem with Raz's position is whether the autonomous life is one among a plurality of morally acceptable forms of life, or whether all morally acceptable forms of life must be autonomous. One would expect pluralists to opt for the first possibility, but Raz opts for the second. That is where he goes wrong.

Raz says,

the autonomous person's life is marked not only by what it is but also by what it might have been and by the way it became what it is. A person is autonomous only if he has a variety of acceptable options available to him to choose from, and his life became as it is through his choice of some of these options. . . . It should be clear . . . that autonomy is here construed as a kind of achievement. (204)

Raz thinks of this as an ideal, and he says that "the ideal of personal autonomy . . . holds the free choice of goals and relations as an essential ingredient of individual well-being" (369). He asks about autonomy: "Is it just one option among several that one can choose or leave alone, or is it an essential ingredient of the good life so that anyone's well-being suffers if his autonomy is incomplete?" (390). The answer he gives is, "The moral outlook the implications of which we have explored is one which holds personal autonomy to be an essential element of the good life. We saw that such a morality presupposes . . . that people should have available to them many forms and styles of life incorporating incompatible virtues. . . . Such an autonomy-valuing pluralistic morality generates a doctrine of freedom" (425).

Raz, therefore, is committed to the view that autonomy is a necessary condition of human well-being, an essential ingredient of all good lives. Pluralism about forms of life holds only on a level above autonomy. First the conditions of autonomy must be met by all good lives, and only thereafter could good lives take a plurality of forms, embodying a plurality of virtues. It is because Raz subscribes to this view that he holds a form of "pluralism which allows that certain conceptions of the good [namely, non-autonomous ones] are worthless and demeaning, and that political action may and should be taken to eradicate or at least to curtail them" (133). And it is because of this view that Raz's answer to the "troubling problem concern[ing] the treatment of communities whose culture does not support autonomy" is that according to "the perfectionist principles espoused in this book . . . people are justified in taking action to assimilate the minority group, at the cost of letting its culture die or at least be considerably changed by absorption" (423–24).

It takes a good deal of perversity to call this view pluralistic, but let that pass. The question is whether it is defensible, not what it is called. There are strong reasons for regarding it as indefensible. First, the view is inconsistent with the ideal of well-being that Raz has earlier developed. According to that view, "individual well-being . . . captures one crucial evaluation of a person's life: how good or successful it is from his point of view?" and "the value of various situations for a particular person depends to a large extent on his actual goals, as they are or will be throughout his life" (289–90). But it is either irrelevant to the evaluation of the goodness of a life that other people find it "worthless" or "demeaning" or it is a mistake to evaluate the goodness of a life from the point of view of the person whose life it is. In the first case, non-autonomous lives may be good, and then autonomy cannot be an essential ingredient of all good lives. In the second case, the absurdity follows that how people think and feel about their own lives is irrelevant to the goodness of their lives. Not only is that an absurdity; it also implies that there is some external standard acceptable to all reasonable people that determines the goodness of a life. If there were such a standard, pluralism, committed to denying that there is such a standard, would be mistaken. If there were no such standard, then the external evaluation of lives, according to Raz, would be arbitrary. Raz, therefore, must abandon either the view that autonomy is an essential ingredient of all good lives or the view that good lives may take a plurality of forms. Since he views "freedom as constituted by the ideals of personal autonomy and value-pluralism" (265), and these two constituents are incompatible, his view of freedom is incoherent.

The second reason for rejecting Raz's claim that autonomy is a necessary condition of well-being is that his account of autonomy is as incoherent as his notion of freedom. Raz says that "autonomy is here construed as a kind of achievement" (204), not as a capacity, because the value of the capacity derives from the value of the autonomous life that it makes possible (372). The achievement of an autonomous life is intrinsically valuable whereas the capacity for autonomy is only instrumentally valuable. But what is the achievement that the autonomous life exemplifies? Another incoherence in Raz's account emerges in the incompatible answers he gives to this question.

Raz says, on the one hand, that "personal autonomy is the ideal of free and conscious self-creation" (390), and he speaks of "the ideal of autonomy as a life freely chosen" (371). But he also says, on the other hand, that "the autonomous life depends not on the availability of one option of freedom of choice. It depends on the general character of one's environment and culture," and that "for those who live in an autonomy-supporting environment there is no choice but to be autonomous" (391). If Raz is right in claiming that "the autonomous person is marked not by what he is but by how he came to be what he is"

(391), then he must make up his mind whether the mark of an autonomous life is that it is freely chosen or that it is lived in an autonomy-supporting environment that makes autonomous life unavoidable.

If it must be freely chosen, then very few lives indeed are autonomous because very few people live according to "the ideal of free and conscious self-creation." The vast majority of people just follow the patterns that prevail in their context: they earn a living, get married, buy a house, drive a car, have children, save for retirement, and so on, for no better reason than that is the accepted norm in their context. They certainly make choices, but the choices are between means, not ends. They choose the ways in which they conform to the prevailing patterns, which they take for granted.

If, on the other hand, the autonomous life is unavoidable in a particular context, then it can no more be an achievement than speaking one's mother tongue or buying groceries. It is then just the form of life that is presented to people by their circumstances, much as Christianity was presented to Europeans in the Middle Ages. Raz must choose between the autonomous life's being a rare achievement and its being frequent but not an achievement. If it is rare, then his egalitarian liberalism is committed to imposing a form of life favored by a few on a large unreceptive majority, which cannot very well be reconciled with freedom's being a basic value. If it is frequent because it is unavoidable in certain contexts, then Raz's view and the policies it prompts amount to no more than an endorsement of a way of life that would be followed regardless of whether people choose it freely and regardless of what Raz's kind of egalitarians say or do.

The third reason for rejecting Raz's claim that autonomy is an essential ingredient of good lives is that it is obviously false. According to Raz, "the autonomous person has or is gradually developing a conception of himself, and his actions are sensitive to his past. . . . He must be aware of having the pursuits he has, and he must be aware of his progress in them. Normally one needs to know of one's progress with one's projects in order to know how to proceed with them (unless one tries to pursue them rationally then they are not one's projects any more" (385). And he goes on: "One creates values, generates, through one's developing commitments and pursuits, reasons which transcend the reasons one had for undertaking one's commitments and pursuits. In that way a person's life is (in part) of his own making. It is a normative creation, a creation of new values and reasons" (387).

If we grant that this is an accurate description of the autonomous person, then it follows that being one requires much time and leisure for reflection; the reflection must be directed inward, rather than outward toward the world; it must be based on accurate self-knowledge and the absence of self-deception; it must involve the critical examination of the conventional values in one's context; it must subordinate one's emotions, will, and imagination to reason; it must involve a high degree of intelligence and articulateness; it must be based on strong self-confidence; and it must require a life that is sufficiently prosperous, secure, independent, and unburdened by contrary obligations to make these pursuits possible. Lives like that can be found, especially among successful academics who write books about good lives. But the lives of workers, farmers, athletes, soldiers, devout religious believers, commercial artists, pop stars, computer programmers, forest rangers, and stock car racers are rarely like that.

Now it might be said that the autonomous life is none the worse for being rare, but this is not something that Raz could reasonably say. For he holds that "autonomy is a constituent element of the good life. A person's life is autonomous if it is to a considerable extent his creation" (408), and that "the value of personal autonomy is a fact of life. Since we live in a society whose social forms are to a considerable extent based on individual choice, and since our options are limited by what is available in our society, we can prosper in it only if we can be successfully autonomous" (394). So Raz is committed to holding that a life in our society cannot be good unless it is autonomous. It follows that the lives of workers, farmers, athletes, and so forth—lives that do not meet the requirements listed above—cannot be good. Raz, therefore, not merely recommends the autonomous life as an ideal; he also calls all lives bad that fail to conform to the ideal; he regards them as "worthless and demeaning" for being non-autonomous; and he thinks that "political action may and should be taken to eradicate or at least to curtail them" (133). And, let it be remembered, he holds all this while claiming commitment to equal freedom as the basic value and to pluralism as part of it.

It makes matters even worse for Raz that the lives he calls bad actually meet the conditions of good lives that he specifies earlier in the book. He claims that "individual well-being . . . captures one crucial evaluation of a person's life: how good or successful is it from his point of view?" (289), that "the value of various situations for a particular person depends to a large extent on his actual goals" (290), and that "some of these goals a person may have . . . chosen. Others he may have drifted into, grown up with, never realized that anyone can fail to have them, etc. It makes no difference from our point of view which is which. What matters is that they are his goals, and I use the term broadly to cover his projects, plans, relationships, ambitions, commitments, and the like" (290–91). Since these conditions can clearly be met by non-autonomous lives—they are not without goals—Raz's claim that autonomy is an essential ingredient of good lives is false in any case, but it is false also by Raz's own showing.

The conclusion that follows from these criticisms is that Raz is mistaken in claiming that autonomy is a necessary condition of all good lives. He is right in believing that an autonomous life may be good, but he is wrong to hold that a life cannot be good unless it is autonomous. A consistent pluralist would recognize that good lives may take many different forms, of which autonomous lives are only one. But it is instructive to trace the reasoning that has led Raz to a position that is inconsistent with his avowed pluralism. Its first premise is that equal freedom is the basic political value, because good lives cannot be lived without it. Its second premise is that the freedom good lives require must involve autonomy. The conclusion is that lives cannot be good without autonomy. The argument in this section was intended to show that the second premise is false, so the conclusion does not follow. In the next section we shall consider the first premise.

9.5 Pluralism and the Basic Value

We have seen (in 9.2) that Raz interprets egalitarian liberalism as the view that equal freedom is the basic political value. The goodness of a society, according to this view, depends on how closely it approximates the ideal of equal freedom. Egalitarian liberalism promises to come closer to it than any other approach; it creates the expectation that its policies will lead to a society in which there will be a great deal of freedom for everyone equally; and it will thus provide the political conditions in which all citizens can live good lives. We have also seen that widespread evil, whose existence Raz acknowledges, makes the promise unfulfillable and the expectation unmeetable. The argument will now show that a good society will not regard equal freedom as its basic value, not just because evil requires radically curtailing it but also because the very idea of a value being the basic one is deeply flawed.

Raz says that

three main features characterize the autonomy-based doctrine of freedom. *First,* its primary concern is the promotion and protection of positive freedom . . . consisting of the availability of an adequate range of options, and of the mental abilities necessary for an autonomous life. *Second,* the state has the duty not merely to prevent denial of freedom, but also promote it by creating the conditions of autonomy. *Third,* one may not pursue any goal by means which infringe people's autonomy unless such action is justified by the need to protect or promote the autonomy of these people or of others. (425)

Let us waive the problems connected with autonomy and agree that these actually are the features of freedom. There are two reasons for denying that freedom, thus understood, is the basic value of a good society.

The first is that these features make obvious that freedom is possible only if a variety of other values are realized in a society. There must be at least moderate prosperity, peace with other countries, internal stability, a reliable system of justice, a decent level of education, dependable health care, a healthy environment, some measure of civility among citizens, a fair degree of law-abidingness, and so forth. If these values are not protected and promoted in a society, citizens lack "an adequate range of options" or "the mental abilities" and the opportunities to realize them, and then they cannot have freedom. Since freedom depends on these values, it cannot be that it is more basic than the values on which it depends.

The second reason is that freedom does not merely presuppose that these other values are in place; it also conflicts with them, and there are often good reasons to resolve the conflicts in favor of the other values. Maintaining prosperity, security, and justice, for instance, may well be worth the sacrifice of some freedom. If the cost of having a good system of education, health care, or environmental protection requires foregoing some measure of freedom, both individuals and societies may reasonably decide that it is worth it. Since these other values may on occasion override freedom when they conflict with it, freedom cannot be more basic than they are.

Raz may respond by claiming that these two reasons show only that freedom is not an absolute value, but not that it is not basic. Raz insists that even a basic value may be reasonably curtailed in appropriate circumstances. But he thinks that these circumstances can be appropriate only if the curtailment of the freedom of an individual promotes freedom in general. If this were so, it would still be reasonable to regard freedom as a basic value.

It is, however, plainly not so. A good reason for curtailing freedom may be the protection of life, even if that means a net decrease in freedom. Or a good reason for curtailing freedom may be the reduction of poverty, even if the cost is a net loss of freedom. It cannot be reasonably denied that a considerable gain in some values, like life expectancy, security, or justice, may be worth the sacrifice of some freedom. The belief that freedom can be reasonably curtailed only if it increases freedom overall is, therefore, mistaken. Consequently, there is no reason to believe that freedom is more basic than those other values that may override it in some conflicts.

The reason for denying that freedom is the basic value, however, is not merely that other values may override it but also that regarding it as basic is incompatible with pluralism. Raz says that "value-pluralism . . . is here employed in a wide sense in which it encompasses the complete art of the good life. . . . It is in fact used in a sense which encompasses all values" (397). In that case, however, it will also encompass freedom. And if incompatible values cannot be "strictly ordered according to their moral worth" because there are no over-arching "impersonal criteria of moral worth" (396–97), then this must be true of freedom as well. So according to pluralism, there may be perfectly reasonable conceptions of a good life in which freedom is not regarded as the basic value.

Raz may reply that freedom is a necessary condition of all good lives, and that is why it is basic. But if that makes freedom basic, then security, justice, moderate prosperity, social stability, adequate education and health care are also basic. If basic values conflict, as they routinely do, then freedom cannot be reasonably claimed to override other values that are as necessary for good lives as freedom is on the grounds that freedom is basic. For the conflicting values are also basic.

The conclusion that follows is not that freedom is not a basic value but that it is not *the* basic value. If pluralism is correct, there is a plurality of basic values, they conflict with one another, and there is no impersonal criterion that would resolve these conflicts always in favor of any one value. Raz, therefore, must choose between his commitment to pluralism and his commitment to freedom as the basic value. If he gives up pluralism, he gives up what he claims is an essential constituent of freedom. If he gives up freedom as the basic value, he gives up his version of egalitarian liberalism.

9.6 Ideological Politics

All the problems we have found in Raz's version of egalitarianism would be avoided if the idea of equal freedom as the basic value were abandoned. Abandoning it would not mean that the value and importance of freedom for good lives could not be recognized. Of course freedom matters a great deal; of course a good society would be free. But acknowledging this should be accompanied by the acknowledgment that there are other values that also matter a great deal and that a good society needs them too. Peace, prosperity, order, justice, law-abidingness, education, health care, and so forth are also important values. This may seem like a platitude hardly worth saying, but it is one with which Raz's position is incompatible. It is worth considering the assumption that underlies Raz's denial of this platitude.

If the existence of a plurality of basic values is acknowledged, and if it is recognized that these values are apt to conflict, then it becomes a pressing question whether these conflicts can have a reasonable resolution. Raz's underlying assumption is that finding such a resolution depends on identifying one of the plurality of basic values as the most basic. Once this is done, the conflicts can be reasonably resolved by determining which of the conflicting values is more important for the promotion of the most basic one.

Raz is not alone in holding this assumption. All the egalitarians we have discussed in chapters 3–8 subscribe to it. The differences among them concern the value they identify as the most basic. Rawls thinks that "justice is the first virtue of social institutions."[5] Dworkin holds that "equal concern is the sovereign virtue of political community."[6] Singer claims that "ethical judgments must be made from a universal point of view."[7] Nussbaum says that "compassion . . . lies at the heart of any good ethical code."[8] There are also others, whom we have not discussed, who think that the basic value is autonomy, or rights, or toleration; and so forth. This assumption commits those who hold it to a certain approach to politics.

We shall refer to this approach as ideological. It has been acutely identified and criticized by numerous political thinkers.[9] They have been relegated, however, to the margin of contemporary political thought. The focal question debated is not whether politics should be ideological but rather which version of egalitarian ideology should prevail. The debate is between freedom-, rights-, and resource-based egalitarians; between deontological and consequentialist egalitarians; and between egalitarians who are relativists, naturalists, or conventionalists about values. All of them assume, however, that there is some one value that is the most basic, and that conflicts among values can be reasonably resolved only by ascertaining the respective importance of the conflicting values to the realization of the most basic value.

Dworkin makes this assumption explicit:

Political theories differ from one another . . . not simply in the particular goals, rights, and duties each sets out, but also in the way each connects the goals, rights, and duties it employs. In a well-formed theory some consistent set of these, internally ranked and weighted, will be taken as fundamental or ultimate within the theory. It seems reasonable to suppose that any particular theory will give ultimate pride of place to just one of these concepts; it will take some overriding goal, or some set of fundamental rights, or some set of transcendent duties, as fundamental, and show other goals, rights, and duties as subordinate and derivative.[10]

The identifiability of some value as most basic is an essential assumption of ideological politics. Another is that the cause of the ills a particular society faces is that the society has failed to promote the basic value and that the aim of policies should be to specify the steps that need to be taken to promote it. A third essential assumption of ideological politics is an explanation of why the most basic value should be in that privileged position in terms of some supposed truth about the nature of the world or human beings. The explanation aims to show that, given that truth, it is human well-being that makes the favored value most basic. These assumptions may be called, in order of presentation, normative, practical, and factual. They are interdependent, separable only for the purposes of analysis. Ideological politics, then, is the approach that takes the reasonable resolution of conflicts among values to depend on the outlook in the background that is constituted of these normative, practical, and factual assumptions.

The ideological approach to politics has deplorable consequences. It postulates an ideal, represented by whatever is taken to be the most basic value, and it regards the pursuit of the ideal as a requirement of rationality and morality. It recognizes that there may be legitimate political disagreements, but they are about the best means of pursuing the ideal, not about the ideal itself. There may also be disagreements with the ideal, but since the ideal is wrongly supposed to be required by rationality and morality, disagreements with it are dogmatically attributed to the failure of rationality or morality. The rejection of the ideal, therefore, is irrational, immoral, or both. Ideological politics thus becomes a conflict between "us" and "them." "We" have rationality and morality on our side, but "they"—our opponents—are benighted or corrupt. "We" may try to educate "them" by patiently explaining why it is right to regard our ideal as the ideal, but "they" may be too far gone, and then education must be replaced by coercion.

If people reject Rawls's conception of justice as the first virtue of social institutions, they must fail to be as fully rational as those in the original position, or their selfishness prevents them from acting as if they were behind the veil of ignorance. Those who reject Dworkin's equal concern as the sovereign virtue are "immoral" and what they do is "shameful." Going against the universal point of view of which Singer speaks makes people murderers, killers, or, at the very least, immoral. The failure to accept compassion as the most basic value that Nussbaum says it is results from such impediments as "pathological narcissism," delusions of "male omnipotence," and "the intolerance of humanity in oneself." And it is the same ideological politics that leads Raz to regard the lives of those who reject his notion of freedom as "worthless and demeaning" and as warranting "political action . . . to eradicate or at least to curtail them."

These attitudes are bad enough, but the attempt to disguise their true repressive nature makes them even worse. For Rawls represents himself as a defender of pluralism; Dworkin claims to be neutral about all interests regardless of whose interests they are; Singer claims to be committed to impartiality; Nussbaum champions multiculturalism; and Raz justifies the repression he calls for by an appeal, of all things, to freedom. What these commitments really mean, however, is that pluralism, neutrality, impartiality, multiculturalism, and freedom apply only to those who accept as most basic the value that these egalitarians regard as such. Those who think that some other value is most basic and those who deny that there is a most basic value are to be reeducated or coerced to prevent them from acting irrationally or immorally.

These deplorable consequences do not show that ideological politics is mistaken. It may be the correct approach to politics, even if it is coercive and vilifies its opponents. It is not hard to show, however, not only that ideological politics is an enemy of those who wish to dispose of their own lives and property as they see fit, but also that it rests on the untenable normative assumption that there is a most basic value. If this assumption is false, the approach to politics based on it becomes unacceptable.

The main reason for denying that there can be a most basic value is that values are interdependent, and a particular value can be realized only if the other values on which it depends are also realized. We have seen (in 9.5) that freedom, as Raz understands it, depends on peace, prosperity, order, security, justice, and so forth. The same is true of the other values that defenders of other versions of egalitarianism regard as most basic. Justice, equality, impartiality, and compassion can be pursued only by people who live above the subsistence level, have adequate intelligence and education, feel secure, have decent housing and health care, are not teetering on the brink of war, and so forth. Egalitarians who regard some value as the most basic simply take for granted that these conditions are met. They are normally entitled to do so in contemporary Western societies. But they are not entitled to ignore the fact that the value they favor depends on other values and claim that their favored value is the first, or sovereign, or the one that ethical judgments must reflect, or at the heart of all good ethical codes. And they are entitled even less to present themselves as champions of pluralism while coercing dissenters to conform to the value they favor. The mistake, therefore, in regarding a value as the most basic is not that some other value is most basic. The mistake is that the interdependence of values rules out the possibility that there could be a most basic value. Ideological politics rests on this mistake, and that is why it is untenable.

There is, however, a consideration that makes this normative assumption attractive. If there is a plurality of values, they will conflict, and their conflicts should have a reasonable resolution. But if the normative assumption is mistaken, then there is no most basic value on which reasonable resolutions could be based. Are we then left with only arbitrary resolutions of conflicts among values? Is that not too high a price to pay for giving up ideological politics?

The answer is that there is an alternative to ideological politics: pluralistic politics. This is not the place to provide a full account of it or to answer the many questions it raises.[11] Here, however, is a brief sketch of it. In an enduring and fairly stable society, such as ours, it is possible to identify numerous values that are generally recognized as important and attract the allegiance of many people. An impressionistic list of these values includes freedom, justice, rights, pluralism, order, stability, civility, peace, law-abidingness, prosperity, education, health care, healthy environment, and so forth. This list is not meant to be complete, and it is not meant to imply that there is general agreement about the interpretation of the values appearing on it. Many of these, and other, values are incommensurable, incompatible, and conflicting. The welfare of the society requires that their conflicts be resolved in a reasonable manner. The pluralistic approach to conflict resolution is to appeal to an objective standard: namely, the whole system of values that are prized and regarded as important by the people whose lives they inform. The question to be asked about the conflicting values is, which is more important to the protection of the whole system of values? And the answer will provide the reason for resolving the conflict in favor of one of the conflicting values.

Finding this answer is neither simple nor easy. It normally requires good judgment, which is based on historical reflection, political experience, and the ability to see the current state of the political life of one's society steadily and as a whole. It depends on avoiding the temptations of inflated hope and fear, of sentimentalism, of popularity, and of foolhardy risks. It is difficult to make such judgments, but the judgments made are objectively right or wrong. For one or the other value *is* more important to the protection of the whole system of values. Statesmen are those who have a good record in getting the judgments right. Mere politicians often err. But even if a judgment is right, it is right only under the conditions in which it was made. The conditions—economic, cultural, international, technological, moral, and so forth—continually change, and judgments will have to be made again and again to take account of and cope with changes, new conflicts, and the need to continue to attract the allegiance of the people whose well-being depends on getting the judgments right. These conditions, changes, conflicts, and judgments constitute the political life of a society. That life can go well or badly. But to suppose that it will go well if the ever-shifting scene were judged from the point of view of some most basic value that is given precedence over everything else is to guarantee failure. Pluralistic politics consists in a ceaseless struggle to cope with these complexities. Ideological politics is a doomed attempt to cope by theorizing the complexities away.

We may conclude, then, that the illusion that equal freedom is the basic political value is doubly at fault. Freedom is no more basic than many other values necessary for human well-being. But there is no reason to regard anything as the basic value, if that means that it should always override whatever may conflict with it. The truth is that there are many basic values, that is, many values without which human well-being is impossible.

10/

The Burden of Double-Mindedness

Purify your hearts ye double-minded.

The Epistle of James

10.1 The Illusion

Perfectionism is the view that the task of moral and political theory is to provide a reasoned account of the good life and the good society. Once the account is in place, it is possible to derive from it the rules, principles, and institutions that make the achievement of the good life and the good society possible. In other words, first must come knowledge of the good, and then the right course of action will follow from it. Perfectionism, then, may be understood as the view that the good is prior to the right.

We have seen (in chapters 7, 8, and 9) that Nussbaum, Singer, and Raz hold different versions of perfectionism because they accept different accounts of the good. Each version has been found untenable for several reasons, but one of these reasons counts against all three in the same way: the commitment to what they take to be the good. Armed with their supposed knowledge of the good, they pronounce on how others should live and what their moral and political obligations are. They believe that it is justified to impose their views on others because those who do not share them are either ignorant of the good or willfully pit themselves against it. These repressive attitudes are among the dangerous consequences of perfectionism. Many egalitarians—and not just they—find these consequences unacceptable. This makes them receptive to a nonperfectionist view.

Nonperfectionism is characterized by a principled refusal to take a position on what the good is. Egalitarians who follow this course recognize that the nature of the good is controversial, and they leave it to the discretion of individuals to decide for themselves what to think about the good. According to nonperfectionist egalitarians, a good society is one that protects the conditions in which people can decide and pursue what they regard as the good. The protection is provided by both freedom and welfare rights, which guarantee the opportunities and distributive shares that all conceptions of the good require, regardless of how they differ in other respects. The right is defined by what protects these conditions. Nonperfectionist egalitarianism thus may be characterized as the view that the right is prior to the good. This is supposed to avoid the unacceptable consequences of perfectionist egalitarianism because, being uncommitted about the good, it will not impose a conception of it on unwilling people.

Nonperfectionist egalitarianism, however, rests on yet another illusion. This is that it is psychologically possible to remain politically uncommitted to any conception of the good while maintaining a personal commitment to a particular conception of it.

10.2 Nonperfectionist Egalitarianism

Nonperfectionist egalitarians agree that their first task must be to give an account of the right, but they disagree about the form it should take. One suggestion is to approach it through the idea of neutrality: the egalitarian state ought not to favor any reasonable conception of the good. Its task is merely to prohibit the pursuit of unreasonable conceptions and to protect the conditions that the pursuit of all reasonable conceptions requires.[1] Another suggestion is that the egalitarian state ought to be based on the consent that all reasonable people living in it would give if they understood the reasons for the prevailing political arrangements.[2] A further suggestion is that the egalitarian state ought to be able to justify its political arrangements to the people who are subject to them, provided the people are fully informed and rational.[3] These suggestions overlap, and there are others as well, but such details are irrelevant to the present purposes.

The salient point is that the egalitarian state is intended to protect the freedom of its citizens to live according to their conceptions of the good, maintain just institutions that distribute the needed resources equally, favor conditions in which the widest possible plurality of lives can be lived, guarantee everyone's right to live in this manner, and thus treat all citizens with equal respect. The nonperfectionist egalitarian view of this underlying equal respect is expressed by Dworkin as, "From the standpoint of politics, the interests of the members of the community matter, and matter equally"; by Nagel as, "To give equal weight, in essential respects, to each person's point of view"; and by Vlastos as, "The human worth of all persons is equal, however unequal may be their merits."[4]

If the citizens of an egalitarian state understand that the justification of prevailing political arrangements is that they protect the conditions they need for living according to their different conceptions of the good, then they will support these arrangements. When people are motivated in this way, they have *political* reasons to treat all citizens and all reasonable conceptions of the good with equal respect, where "equal respect" embodies conformity to the conditions just adumbrated. People, of course, are not motivated solely by political reasons. They are motivated also by their specific conceptions of the good. They want to live according to these conceptions, and political reasons motivate them, at least in part, because they make it more likely that people can live as they wish. Political reasons motivate people, therefore, partly because they are also motivated by *personal* reasons, which they derive from their conceptions of the good.

In an egalitarian state, the main political reasons are the same for everyone whereas personal reasons vary with individual conceptions of the good. If two people have the same political reasons, it is because they support the same political arrangements. If two people have the same personal reasons, it is because they have the same conception of the good. The justification of both political and personal reasons derives from the conceptions of the good that motivate people, but political reasons hold equally for all reasonable conceptions whereas personal reasons hold only for the specific conceptions that are a person's own.

Perhaps it is not pedantic to stress that the distinction between the personal and the political should not be confused with the distinction between the private and the public, or the subjective and the objective, or the self-regarding and the other-regarding. The personal has to do with individuals living according to their conceptions of the good. Such conceptions, however, can be, and often are, as public, objective, and other-regarding as any political arrangement that political reasons may lead people to value. The difference between the personal and the political is that the personal is concerned with specific people living in specific ways, whereas the political is concerned with the conditions that enable all citizens to live in the various ways that seem good to them, so long as their ways are reasonable.

By way of illustration, consider religious or sexual attitudes. The egalitarian state is committed to arrangements that recognize a plurality of reasonable religious and sexual attitudes, protect the right to live according to them by providing the needed resources, and treat all reasonable attitudes with equal respect. The political reason people have to support such arrangements is that they foster whatever religious or sexual preferences citizens happen to have. The personal reason is that the arrangements help the people themselves to live as Catholics, atheists, or Buddhists, or as heterosexuals, homosexuals, or celibates.

If people had no personal reason to live in a particular way, then the political reason for protecting the conditions required for living in that way would be less likely to motivate them. If they recognized only personal but no political reasons, then they would undermine the conditions that their personal reasons ought to lead them to want to protect. For reasonable people, therefore, personal and political reasons ought to coexist harmoniously, even if different considerations give them the force of reasons.

The aim of this chapter is to show that nonperfectionist egalitarianism is no more acceptable than other versions of egalitarianism, although this is so for a reason peculiar to itself. Nonperfectionist egalitarians are unavoidably and lastingly doomed to double-mindedness because they must acknowledge the strength of two mutually exclusive reasons they have: the personal and the political. They are thus forced to be either inconsistent or conflicted, frustrated, and thus dissatisfied with a crucial aspect of their lives. The psychological cost of being an egalitarian who is faithful to these incompatible reasons is therefore great enough to present a serious obstacle to living a good life. If nonperfectionist egalitarians become aware of the cost of their double-mindedness, they will want to avoid bearing it, if they can. And they can, but only by giving up this version of egalitarianism.[5]

10.3 Double-Mindedness

Double-mindedness is best understood in contrast with single-mindedness. To be single-minded is to have a strong enough reason that overrides any other reason that may conflict with it. To be double-minded is to have two strong reasons that exist in a state of tension because acting on one excludes acting on the other. People in this state feel the strength of both reasons, but neither obviously overrides the other. Consequently, they waver, they are ambivalent, they are of two minds about what they should do.

Double-mindedness may be a temporary state or a lasting disposition. As a temporary state, it is a common experience that most people have when they try to decide, as they must, between immediate and more distant satisfactions, between the demands of morality and self-interest, between institutional and personal loyalties, between duty and pleasure, and so forth. Such a state is intrinsically undesirable because it involves frustration, but if it is temporary and occurs infrequently, it does no great harm, for reasonable people can tolerate much frustration and still live a good life. If, however, double-mindedness is a lasting disposition, if it is an essential feature of people's psychological profile, then it is a threat to their prospects of living a good life, because it habitually and predictably dooms them to frustration. It is reasonable, therefore, to want to avoid it.

To see why this is so, consider the psychological condition of people who are committed to living according to some reasonable conception of the good. This conception will shape their beliefs and feelings about significant features of life as it is lived in their particular context. They will have beliefs and feelings, which may or may not be conscious or articulated, about race, religion, sex, violence, beauty, authority, family, work, death, and so forth. Clusters of these beliefs and feelings may be called "formative attitudes." They are formative because a normal human life cannot be lived without having beliefs and feelings about such matters and because such beliefs and feelings are crucial elements of individual conceptions of the good.

Formative attitudes are internally complex. They are not simply what people happen to believe and how they happen to feel about some feature of their lives, like having children or dying. They include also the importance people attribute to the particular feature. And that is a matter not just of regarding some feature as important or unimportant in their lives but also of judging a feature's importance in comparison with other significant features of life toward which normal people in normal circumstances will also have some attitude or another. Understanding people depends on understanding the hierarchical structure of their formative attitudes, to know what they believe and what feelings they have about the significant features of life. Because the features are significant, beliefs and feelings about them are powerful. The formative attitudes embodying these powerful beliefs and feelings constitute perhaps the strongest personal reasons people have for doing whatever they do.

Such personal reasons motivate people to evaluate ways of living and acting as on balance good, bad, or indifferent. What conforms to their formative attitudes they tend to regard as good, what violates them as bad, and what neither conforms to nor violates them as indifferent. What is important in the present context is that nonperfectionist egalitarians will often encounter ways of living and acting that their formative attitudes prompt them to regard as bad. There will be people whom they regard as racist or sexist; people who maltreat children, women, and homosexuals; who scorn the achievements of nonwhites; who side with corporations rather than the workers; who are moved by greed rather than by solidarity; who believe in making use of American power rather than accepting guilt for the terrible things America is supposed to have done. These are common and well-known egalitarian attitudes, and they provide strong personal reasons for those who hold them to regard their targets as bad. And they are regarded as bad even if they stay within the bounds of the law. They are condemned on moral grounds.

Contrast now the motivating force of strong personal reasons with that of political reasons. Nagel puts the point thus: "The basic insight that appears from the impersonal [i.e., what is here called political] standpoint is that everyone's life matters, and no one is more important than anyone else. . . . At the baseline of value in the lives of individuals . . . everyone counts the same. For a given quantity of whatever it is that's good or bad—suffering or happiness or fulfillment or frustration—its intrinsic value doesn't depend on whose it is."[6]

Those who share what Nagel regards as a basic insight unavoidably find their political and personal reasons in conflict. Their political reasons prompt them to regard their own conceptions of the good, their own formative attitudes, their own judgments about what is on balance good, bad, and indifferent as having exactly the same importance as the conceptions of the good, formative attitudes, and judgments about what is on balance good, bad, and indifferent of others, even if the conceptions, attitudes, and judgments of others are incompatible with their own. Political reasons thus often oblige people who agree with Nagel to act contrary to their personal reasons.

For nonperfectionist egalitarians, this conflict between personal and political reasons is not a rare occurrence, a consequence of pushing the logical implications of a political theory too hard, but a regular and predictable feature of daily experience. These egalitarians live in a society and must respond to the countless people they encounter. If their responses are motivated by political reasons, they will treat others with equal respect, regardless of whether they live and act in ways the egalitarians have personal reasons to find good, bad, or indifferent. If, on the other hand, their responses are motivated by personal reasons, then they will not treat with equal respect those whose lives and conduct they find good, bad, or indifferent. If nonperfectionist egalitarians remain consistent, they will be normally motivated by their personal and political reasons in mutually exclusive ways. This will make them double-minded. However they respond to others, they will act contrary to one or another set of their own deeply held reasons.

To show just how serious is the psychological burden of double-mindedness, consider an illustration of the kind of conflict that nonperfectionist egalitarians may encounter. A woman learns that her son's schoolteacher believes that there are inherited racial characteristics, that intelligence is one of them, that blacks are on the average significantly less intelligent than whites, that this makes whites as a group superior to blacks as a group, and that this superiority ought to be reflected in policies affecting education, employment, private association, and other areas of life. The teacher is vocal in his views, and although he breaks no laws, he is, in the woman's opinion, a racist. She finds his racial attitudes deplorable, she does not want him to be teaching either her son or other students, and she regards the racial views he expresses as deeply offensive. For all this, she has perfectly good personal reasons, which derive from her conception of the good and from her formative attitudes.

If she is consistent, she also has political reasons to regard the racist teacher with the same respect as her son's other teachers, or indeed as she is obliged by her political reasons to regard any other citizen in her society. Her political reasons will tell her to think with Dworkin that the views of the teacher "matter, and matter equally"; with Nagel "to give equal weight . . . to each person's point of view," including the teacher's; and with Vlastos to treat the teacher with equal respect, since "the human worth of all persons is equal."[7]

This kind of conflict cannot be minimized by fastening on the unlikelihood of encountering a racist teacher. The woman's case is meant merely to illustrate one way in which the conflict may arise. It arises also in countless other ways and with great frequency for nonperfectionist egalitarians, as they encounter what they regard as bad attitudes in others about abortion, capital punishment, suicide, euthanasia, reverse discrimination, corporal punishment of children, foreign aid, drugs, prayer in schools, pornography, and so forth. These egalitarians live with others, and they cannot help learning about the details of others' lives. They must respond to the details, and their personal and political reasons prompt incompatible responses. On the basis of their personal reasons, nonperfectionists must often find attitudes contrary to their own morally suspect. On the basis of their political reasons, however, they must respect these attitudes equally to their own, they must be guided by the thought, as Nagel says, that the "attempt to give equal weight, in essential respects, to each person's point of view . . . might even be described as the mark of an enlightened ethic."[8]

Nonperfectionist egalitarians, therefore, are bound to be frequently double-minded about whether they ought to treat others in accordance with their personal or political reasons. They must routinely choose between responding to others in a way that reflects their own moral attitudes about what is good, bad, and indifferent and responding to them with equal respect, regardless of the moral qualities their lives and actions are thought to have. The point is not that nonperfectionist egalitarians cannot choose. They can, and they often do. The point is rather that they must choose, and whatever they end up choosing, they will act contrary to their deeply held personal or political reasons. This makes them double-minded.

10.4 The Conflict

Nonperfectionist egalitarians may try to avoid the conflict between their personal and political reasons by distinguishing between the political and the personal levels of action. When they encounter concrete situations as participants, they are guided, as other people are, by their personal reasons. When they stand back and think about such situations, not as participants but as reasonable people trying to figure out what political arrangements their society ought to have, they are guided by their political reasons. Personal reasons may be said to motivate them directly on one level; political reasons motivate them indirectly on another. They can then point out how innocuous are the actions that their political reasons lead them to take. The equal respect for all points of view translates into equal rights to vote, to use public facilities such as roads, libraries, and parks, to express private views, to run for political office, and the like. Equal respect is just respect for the rights of citizenship in an egalitarian society which should be accorded to all citizens regardless of whether their points of view are thought to be good, bad, or indifferent. Equal respect, it may be said, is perfectly compatible with having personal reasons to find morally deplorable the manner in which some citizens exercise their rights.

This way of trying to avoid the conflict between the personal and the political, and thus avoid double-mindedness, will be seen as a failure once it is realized that equal respect implies much more than the innocuous rights mentioned above. In the case of the racist views, for example, it includes having an equal claim to the funding of research into racial superiority and inferiority, to having racist views fairly represented in the school curriculum, to recognizing it as one important element in some conceptions of the good, to licensing television and radio stations that advocate such views, to permitting businesses to follow personnel policies that reflect them, to having private schools, clubs, organizations, apartment buildings, and housing developments that exclude blacks, and so forth. If equal respect is taken seriously, it must be recognized to include equal respect and public support not just for racism but also for the advocacy of anti-Semitism, slavery, cannibalism, sadism, the repatriation of blacks, the public flogging, mutilation, and execution of criminals, and similar views, just so long as their advocates do not break the law.

If the implications of equal respect are recognized, then this attempt to avoid the conflict between personal and political reasons will also be recognized to fail. Even if the personal and political levels of actions are to be distinguished, they will still place incompatible requirements on nonperfectionist egalitarians. On the political level, they are committed to treating their fellow citizens with equal respect, to regarding their realization of their conceptions of the good as just as intrinsically valuable as anyone else's, including the egalitarians' own, even if they are racists, sexists, homophobes, anti-Semites, and the like. On the personal level, they find such lives and conduct morally unacceptable. So the distinction between the personal and the political levels of action does not help avoid the conflict nonperfectionist egalitarians face.

If it is accepted that the conflict is unavoidable, there may be three ways in which nonperfectionist egalitarians may try to resolve it and thus avoid double-mindedness. One is to deny that the conflict occurs frequently; another is to resolve it in favor of personal reasons; and the last is to resolve it in favor of political reasons. What has been said so far ought to be sufficient to show that the conflict is frequent and that its denial would be mistaken. In this respect, at least, the present argument is in agreement with Nagel and those who agree with him.

Nor is there need to say much about resolving the conflict in favor of the personal. If nonperfectionist egalitarians adopt a policy of allowing their personal reasons to override their political reasons whenever there is a conflict between them, they cease to be egalitarians. Egalitarianism, after all, is a political position, and it requires its adherents to treat everyone with equal respect. If personal reasons overrode political reasons, then only those people would be regarded with equal respect whose ways of living and acting conformed to the personal reasons of egalitarians. This would make the racial, religious, sexual, and other attitudes of egalitarians the standards of political correctness. Although such an arrangement would be congenial to egalitarians, they should try harder than they in fact do to resist the temptation to favor it. For it violates their own standards of legitimacy, namely, neutrality, or the consent of people to the political arrangements to which they are subject, or being able to justify the arrangements to dissenters. If egalitarians were to resist this temptation, they would have to become evenhanded in their attitudes toward right- and left-wing hate speech, the condemnation and the advocacy of homosexuality, the Christian celebration of and the radical feminist opposition to the conventional family, fundamentalism and atheism, cigarette smoking and pot smoking, and so forth. It will perhaps be agreed that egalitarians have some way to go to achieve evenhandedness in these respects.

There remains the third option: to resolve the conflict between the personal and the political in favor of the political. This is by far the most widely accepted approach. Its chief inspiration is Rawls's work. He sums up his position as providing a standpoint that is

objective and expresses our autonomy . . . it enables us to be impartial. . . . To see our place in society from the perspective of this position is to see it *sub specie aeternitatis*. . . . The perspective of eternity is not a perspective from a certain place beyond the world, nor the point of view of a transcendent being; rather it is a certain form of thought and feeling that rational persons can adopt within the world. And having done so, they can . . . bring together into one scheme all individual perspectives and arrive together at regulative principles that can be affirmed by everyone as he lives by them, each from his own standpoint. Purity of heart, if one could attain it, would be to see clearly and to act with grace and self-command from this point of view.[9]

Rawls does not put forward this perspective as an alternative to what has been called here the personal. Even if nonperfectionist egalitarians succeed in adopting this objective and impartial outlook, they will still have specific racial, religious, sexual, and other attitudes in respect to which they will differ from others. Rawls's point must be that when their personal reasons, prompted by these attitudes, conflict with their political reasons, prompted by the perspective Rawls favors, then their political reasons will or ought to override their personal reasons. Their hearts will not be pure in the sense that they will only one thing; they will be pure in the sense that they will subordinate their personal attitudes to what Rawls regards as a higher purpose.

This is not a trivial point. Even if the political reasons of nonperfectionist egalitarians are provided by this impartial perspective, and even if they override their personal reasons, their personal reasons will not be silenced. They will continue to have formative racial, religious, sexual, and other attitudes. It is just that their political reasons will not permit them to act according to the conflicting personal reasons these attitudes provide. The conflict, in other words, will not disappear; it will be resolved by favoring one of the conflicting reasons. But the defeat of the personal by the political exacts the heavy psychological cost from nonperfectionist egalitarians of acting contrary to their own formative attitudes toward what is good, bad, and indifferent.

Egalitarians who try to resolve the conflict in this way will find themselves time after time unable to act on some of their deepest judgments of what is good or bad. Their political reasons will prevent them from acting according to their racial, religious, sexual, and other attitudes. For the actions that would reflect their attitudes would strengthen what they regard as good and weaken what they regard as bad. To do either, however, would be contrary to their political reason, which requires of them to treat all attitudes with equal respect, to support them with corresponding shares of scarce resources, and to maintain political arrangements that favor none of them over the others.

If egalitarians allow their political reasons to override their personal reasons, they will lack integrity. They cannot commit themselves to any of their formative attitudes without reservation, lest they show too much or too little respect for ways of living and acting they regard as good and bad, so they will never be wholehearted. Their formative attitudes, the core of their moral identity, the source of much of what they value in their lives, will be defeated, and defeated again, in the civil war of their soul. By allowing the political to override the personal, they will permanently maim themselves.

10.5 Nagel on Impartiality

Some egalitarians are aware of this problem. Nagel, who in numerous publications has struggled with it perhaps more than anyone, says: "It is clear that in most people, the coexistence of the personal standpoint with the values deriving from the . . . impersonal [i.e., political] standpoint produces a division of the self. From his own point of view within the world each person, with his particular concerns and attachments, is extremely important to himself. . . . But from the impersonal standpoint which he can also occupy, so is everyone else: *Everyone's* life matters as much as his does, and his matters no more than anyone else's. These two attitudes are not easy to combine."[10] Nonperfectionist egalitarians labor mightily to overcome this problem and to combine the personal and political reasons that their position obliges them to have. But their efforts fail because they underestimate both the seriousness of the psychological burden that doublemindedness imposes on them and the acuteness of the conflict between their personal and political reasons.

Nagel nevertheless thinks that there is a good reason to bear these high costs. The case he makes for it is perhaps the most influential one available: the political ought to override the personal because morality requires it. This is because the political is moral, the personal is nonmoral, and decent and reasonable people will realize that moral considerations ought to take precedence over nonmoral considerations. What makes the political moral and the personal nonmoral is impartiality. The political, as Nagel views it, is impartial, and that is why it is moral, whereas the personal, varying with individuals, is partial, and so it is nonmoral.

Nagel is careful in formulating his case to leave room for nonmoral personal attitudes and reasons within conceptions of a good life. Impartial institutional arrangements ought to take into account personal attitudes and reasons, which he acknowledges to be basic features of human motivation. Nevertheless, the political and the personal will come into conflict, and when that happens, impartial political reasons ought to override partial personal reasons. As he puts it: "My own view is that . . . moral considerations are overriding. . . . While doing the right thing is part of living well it is not the whole of it, nor even the dominant part: because the impersonal standpoint that acknowledges the claims of morality is only one aspect of a normal individual among others." There will be times, however, "when doing the right thing may cost more in other aspects of the good life than it contributes to the good life in its own right."[11] The content of morality that determines the right action derives from a "universal standpoint that does not distinguish between oneself and anyone else [and] reveals general principles of conduct that apply to oneself because they apply to everyone. There is a natural tendency to identify this higher standpoint with the true self, weighed down perhaps by individualistic baggage. There is a further tendency to accord absolute priority in the governance of life to its judgments."[12] "As a matter of moral conviction," Nagel writes, "I am inclined strongly to hope, and less strongly to believe, that the correct morality will always have a preponderance of reasons on its side, even though it needn't coincide with the good life."[13]

According to this view, the conflict between the political and the personal, between the impartial and the partial, is a particular form of the familiar conflict between morality and personal preference. Nonperfectionist egalitarianism, implying that impartial political reasons ought to override partial personal reasons, just is the moral point of view. To reject it by allowing personal reasons to override political reasons is a violation of one central requirement of morality. The reason for paying the heavy cost of having political reasons override personal reasons consequently is that morality requires it. This makes it hard to be moral, but that is how it is.[14]

It would be natural to expect that, having described his hopes, beliefs, and moral convictions, Nagel will go on to provide reasons for them. That, however, he does not do. His account is full of deft distinctions, perspicuous clarifications, elegant turns of phrase, descriptions of what it would be like if what he hopes and believes to be true were true, but the most he provides by way of an argument for why "the correct morality" and "this higher standpoint" ought to override personal reasons is that the "demand on the ordinary individual—to overcome his own needs, commitments, and attachments in favor of impersonal claims that he can also recognize— ... does not necessarily mean that it would be irrational for someone who can do so to accept such demands, or rather impose them on himself."[15] There is, however, a very large gap between saying that ordinary individuals may not be irrational in allowing impartial political reasons to override their personal reasons and saying that their impartial political reasons ought to override their personal reasons. It is one thing to say to the woman that it would not be irrational for her to squelch her indignation with her son's racist teacher and quite another that the higher standpoint of the correct morality requires her to squelch it.

The amazing feature of Nagel's position is that, instead of arguments designed to close the gap, he offers again and again frank admissions that he does not have them. These admissions, listed in chronological order, are as follows:

In "Equality" Nagel writes: "There are two types of arguments for the intrinsic value of equality. ... I am going to explore the individualistic one, because that is the type of argument that I think is most likely to succeed. It would provide a moral basis for the kind of liberal egalitarianism that seems to me plausible. I do not have such an argument."[16]

In "Moral Conflict and Political Legitimacy" Nagel advances an epistemological argument for "a higher-order framework of moral reasoning . . . which takes us outside ourselves to a standpoint that is independent of who we are."[17] But he says about this argument in *Equality and Partiality* that "while I still believe the conclusion, I no longer think that [the] 'epistemological' argument works."[18]

In *The View from Nowhere* he writes: "This book is about a single problem: how to combine the perspective of a particular person inside the world with an objective view of that same world." In moral theory, this becomes the question of "how to combine objective and subjective values in the control of a single life." However, "I believe that the methods needed to understand ourselves do not yet exist," and "I do not feel equal to the problems treated in this book. They seem to me to require an order of intelligence wholly different from mine." In discussing in the same book the specific conflict between the political and the personal, Nagel writes: "The basic moral insight that objectively no one matters more than anyone else, and that this acknowledgment should be of fundamental importance to each of us . . . creates a conflict in the self too powerful to admit an easy resolution. I doubt that an appealing reconciliation of morality, rationality, and the good life can be achieved."[19]

In *Equality and Partiality* he writes: "My claim is that the problem of designing institutions that do justice to the equal importance of all persons, without making unacceptable demands on individuals, has not been solved—and that is partly because . . . the problem of the right relation between the personal and impersonal standpoints within each individual has not been solved."[20]

What follows is that Nagel has provided no reason to think that morality requires resolving the conflict between the political and the personal in favor of the political. The need to provide reasons for these highly controversial claims is made particularly acute by there being very strong reasons for not resolving the conflict between the political and the personal in the way nonperfectionist egalitarians favor. These reasons are the great psychological costs of doing so: the loss of integrity, wholeheartedness, and coherence; the inability to live and act consistently with some of their formative attitudes; and being doomed to a permanent state of double-mindedness. Nonperfectionist egalitarians demand that people, in the name of morality, pay these costs, but since they are unable to provide reasons why their demand ought to be met, they offer only specious moralizing.

10.6 The Rejection of Impartiality

We have so far granted for the sake of argument the assumptions of nonperfectionist egalitarians: the moral point of view is impartial; political arrangements ought to be similarly impartial; the right should have priority over the good; and the purpose of political arrangements is to enable people to live according to their conceptions of the good. The criticism has been that, given these assumptions, the political and the personal will conflict and their conflict will be acute and frequent enough to make it impossible for people to live according to their conceptions of the good. The political arrangements of nonperfectionist egalitarianism, therefore, fail to serve their purpose, even if the assumptions on which they are based are accepted.

The upshot is a dilemma that nonperfectionist egalitarians face about how to resolve the conflict between the political and the personal. If they resolve it in favor of the personal, they violate their political commitment to equal respect for all law-abiding conceptions of the good. If they resolve it in favor of the political, they violate their personal commitment to their own conception of the good. The double-mindedness of nonperfectionist egalitarians is a symptom of this dilemma. The dilemma can be avoided, but only by abandoning one of the assumptions whose inconsistency causes it. The assumption that should be abandoned is that the moral and the impartial points of view are identical. There are strong reasons for regarding the assumption as mistaken, reasons that hold independently of this dilemma. These reasons will emerge if we note an ambiguity.

The impartial point of view may be interpreted as a universal or an anthropocentric point of view. Universal impartiality is the point of view of God or the Universe. It is to view the whole of reality, as it were, from the outside, *sub specie aeternitatis*. This view is totally objective, neutral, dispassionate, uncommitted, impersonal, neither favoring nor disfavoring anything that it beholds. It just sees things as they are. No human being can adopt the attitude of universal impartiality, but we can aspire to it. The aspiration has notable successes to its credit through the enormous achievements of the physical and biological sciences. The emerging scientific view of the world comes as close as humanly possible to universal impartiality.

Unless one believes in a benevolent God who arranged the Universe for the benefit of humanity, the point of view of universal impartiality will be seen as morally uncommitted. (Since such a belief is rejected by most nonperfectionist egalitarians, and if they accepted it, they would have to give up the view that the right is prior to the good, for the arrangements of the benevolent God would surely be the good, we shall disregard this possibility.) The point of view *is* taken by human beings, but that implies no moral commitment, for the extent to which the view is true is the extent to which it would be the same for all intelligent beings who are capable of arriving at it. Universal impartiality is our best approach to the truth about the nature of reality, but it cannot be identified with the moral point of view, for the moral point of view is evaluative and concerned with human well-being whereas the point of view of universal impartiality is not.

The point of view of anthropocentric impartiality—the view *sub specie humanitatis*—is evaluative and concerned with human well-being. It is not the view from nowhere, as Nagel put it in the title of one of his books, but the view from here, from the sublunary world where we are trying to make good lives for ourselves. That is why it is anthropocentric. And the reason why it is impartial is that from its point of view the well-being of each human being matters equally. If the moral point of view were identified with the impartial point of view, it would have to be the anthropocentric interpretation of impartiality. The arguments against their identification, however, are decisive.

To begin with, it is next to impossible to imagine an action that anyone could take that would equally affect the well-being of each human being. For even if the action were the destruction of the whole of humanity, it would not affect equally those who were dying anyway and those who were in the prime of life. If impartiality is interpreted more realistically to involve the equal treatment only of those who are affected by an action, then impartiality is unattainable, for different people will be affected by an action quite differently. Killing someone, for instance, will affect quite differently those who loved and those who hated the victim. But perhaps impartiality is supposed to mean only that people should take into account the well-being of everyone affected by an action, regardless of how the action might affect them. This, however, is an impossible requirement to meet because it is impossible to know who will be affected by an action. Who could tell, for instance, who would be affected by the publication of a book, the bombing of a building, or the amnesty of a prisoner? If impartiality meant this, no one could be impartial. Furthermore, surely the requirement of impartiality cannot just be equal concern for everyone's well-being, for that would rule out perfectly justified actions that enhance the well-being of some and diminish the well-being of others, such as imprisoning criminals, failing poor students, or waging war against unjust aggressors. The very idea of anthropocentric impartiality is incoherent.

Suppose, however, that it is not incoherent, that it has some plausible interpretation. It would still not be true that the moral point of view could be identified with the impartial point of view. For the vast majority of actions that morality requires people to perform occur in contexts where partiality is essential. Love, friendship, family life, citizenship, professional responsibilities are what they are because participants in them treat one another quite differently from the way in which they treat nonparticipants. Such partiality, resulting in caring much more about the well-being of some people than about the well-being of others, is a requirement of morality. Morality, therefore, cannot be identified with impartiality.

It does not help avoid this point to say that what morality requires is an equal but minimum impartial concern for everyone's well-being. For even if that were true, it would make impartiality only a part of morality, not identical with it. In which case, however, countless actions would be morally right or wrong quite independently of impartiality. No one can reasonably deny that morality sometimes requires people to act impartially. Judges, umpires, graders, referees, and so forth ought to be impartial toward those whom it is their responsibility to evaluate. But parents and children, lovers, friends, comrades, and fellow citizens ought not to be impartial toward one another, they ought not to treat one another in the same way as they ought to treat strangers. The result is that when the political and the personal conflict, it is an open question whether impartial or partial considerations ought to guide the resolution of the conflict.

Finally, even if it were true that in such conflicts the political should always override the personal, the reason for this could not be the impartiality of the political and the partiality of the personal. For the political is always partial. The political obligations of a government are not toward the well-being of everyone equally but, at most, only toward the well-being of all citizens equally. And the political obligations of citizens are not toward the equal well-being of all human beings but only, at most, toward the equal well-being of fellow citizens. Governments or citizens would be irresponsible if they failed to recognize their special obligations toward citizens or fellow citizens. Since partiality is a characteristic of both the political and the personal, impartiality cannot be appealed to in resolving their conflicts.

For these reasons, the moral point of view cannot be reasonably identified with the impartial point of view. Moreover, even if they could be reasonably identified, it would still not follow that if the political and the personal conflict, then the political should prevail. Since nonperfectionist egalitarianism is based on the identification of the two points of view and on the overridingness of the political, it is mistaken.

We have been considering nonperfectionist egalitarianism because of its promise to avoid the repressive tendencies of perfectionist egalitarianism. The criticisms we have just presented show that the promise cannot be kept because the view as a whole is untenable. But it is worth pointing out that its promise could not be kept even if the view were otherwise defensible. For a view that advocates that political considerations should always override conflicting personal considerations, that in cases of conflict the well-being of a society should always take precedence over what individuals regard as their well-being, is no less repressive than the view of perfectionist egalitarians. Nonperfectionists advocate coercing individuals in the name of the common good to go against their own conceptions of the good. Perfectionists advocate coercing individuals in the same way, except they do it in the name of a conception of the good they regard as superior. There is a difference, but it does not make a difference to the repression of individuals. Both versions of egalitarianism end up being intolerant, even though their rhetoric implies the contrary. This, of course, raises the question of what should and should not be tolerated, of how much coercion a good society can inflict on its citizens. That is the topic of the next chapter.

The illusion we have been considering, therefore, is misguided. The principled refusal to make a political commitment to any conception of the good can coexist with a personal commitment to some particular conception of the good only at a psychological cost that no reasonable person would wish to pay. The truth is that personal conceptions of the good unavoidably influence political commitments. This provides an additional reason for making sure that one's personal conception of the good is well founded.

The Rhetoric of Toleration

Liberalism has been supposed to advocate liberty; but what the advanced parties that call themselves liberal advocate is control, control over property, trade, wages, hours of work, meat and drink, and in a truly advanced country . . . control over education and religion; and it is only on the subject of marriage . . . that liberalism is growing more and more liberal.

GEORGE SANTAYANA, *"The Intellectual Temper of the Age"*

11.1 The Illusion

The illusion is that egalitarian liberalism is the ideology of toleration. An egalitarian liberal society is supposed to be tolerant, and the liberal attitude is supposed to be virtually synonymous with the tolerant attitude. The rhetoric of egalitarian liberals cultivates this illusion. Dworkin says that "liberal tolerance . . . is not only consistent with the most attractive conception of community but indispensable to it."[1] According to Charles Larmore, "At the heart of the liberal position stand two ideas . . . *pluralism* . . . and *toleration*, or the idea that because reasonable persons disagree about the value of various conceptions of the good life, we must learn to live with those who do not share our ideals."[2] Rawls claims, "The success of liberal constitutionalism came as a discovery of a new social possibility; the possibility of a reasonably harmonious and stable pluralist society. Before the successful and peaceful practice of toleration in societies with liberal institutions there was no way of knowing of that possibility."[3] This is the illusion and the rhetoric. But what is the truth?

The truth is that egalitarian liberals advocate toleration of discrimination in favor of minorities and women (but not against them); of obscenity that offends religious believers and patriots (but not blacks and Jews); of unions' spending large sums in support of political causes (but not corporations' doing the same); of pot smoking (but not cigarette smoking); of abortion (but not capital punishment); of the public lies of Clinton (but not of Nixon); of hate speech against fundamentalists (but not homosexuals); of sex education in elementary schools (but not prayer); of jobs open only to union members (but not private clubs open only to males); of lies about American imperialism (but not the Holocaust); of sacrilegious language (but not of language that uses *he* to refer to all human beings); of scientific research into just about anything (except racial differences in intelligence); and so on and on.

Egalitarianism is an ideology, and like all ideologies, it is committed to some values and policies. When other values and policies conflict with the ones they favor, egalitarians oppose them, and do what they can to prevail. This is the normal business of politics. But to pass off their own ideology as the exemplar of toleration is misleading rhetoric. Egalitarian liberals are tolerant of a wide range of sexual practices. Others are just as tolerant of a wide range of economic, educational, or religious practices. When egalitarian liberals prevail, sexual limits are few, but the limits on the market, private schooling, or worship are many. No doubt, if others prevailed, the limits would shift. Complex contemporary societies must impose limits on their members. But egalitarian liberals are unique in favoring limits on what they dislike while claiming to champion toleration.

11.2 The Enforcement of Morality

A full-blown example of the egalitarian rhetoric about toleration is the notorious controversy about the enforcement of morality. It began with a lecture Sir Patrick Devlin, a highly placed British judge, gave to the British Academy in 1959.[4] The topic was the recommendation of a British Royal Commission to decriminalize homosexuality and prostitution. Devlin's concern was not with the recommendation but with the weakening of moral bonds. He argued that "societies disintegrate from within more frequently than they are broken up by external pressures. There is disintegration when no common morality is observed and history shows that the loosening of moral bonds is often the first stage of disintegration, so that society is justified in taking the same steps to preserve its moral code as it does to preserve its government and other essential institutions."[5]

The egalitarian response was an avalanche of indignation because Devlin was—falsely—taken to oppose the commission's recommendation. Dworkin wrote: "Lord Devlin concludes that if our society hates homosexuality enough it is justified in outlawing it, and forcing human beings to choose between the miseries of frustration and persecution."[6] Herbert Hart said that "the case presented by Lord Devlin justifying the legal enforcement of morality . . . liberals . . . consider an unjustifiable extension of the scope of the criminal law,"[7] and he thought that Devlin's case is "likely to be merely a projection of the judge's own morality or that of the social class to which he belongs."[8] Graham Hughes claimed that "here is an overt rejection of rationality."[9] And Richard Wollheim held that Devlin's position is "totally irrationalist" because it excludes "what it has been the triumph of civilization to establish: the taming of conscience by reason."[10] From this it appears that egalitarian liberals oppose the legal enforcement of morality and favor toleration.[11]

The appearance, however, is misleading. As the following passages show, egalitarian liberals are unequivocally in favor of the legal enforcement of morality. Dworkin gives a list of egalitarian liberal policies in his often reprinted article on liberalism: "Liberals demand that inequalities of wealth be reduced through welfare and other forms of redistribution financed by progressive taxes. They believe that government should intervene in the economy. . . . They support racial equality and approve government intervention to secure it."[12] And he claims that "the distribution of wealth is the product of a legal order . . . no government is legitimate that does not show equal concern for the fate of all those citizens over whom it claims dominion," and that "equal concern requires that government aim at a form of material equality that I have called equality of resources."[13]

Nagel says, "I am concerned with the problem of altering those features of individual motivation and human interaction which make it necessary to accept large inequalities in order to benefit the worse off. The kind of egalitarianism I am talking about would require a system much more equal than now exists in most democratic countries." He is concerned because "it is appalling that the most effective social system we have been able to devise permits so many people to be born into conditions of harsh deprivation which crush their prospects for leading a decent life." And he claims that "any political theory that aspires to moral decency must devise and justify a form of institutional life which answers to the real strength of impersonal values."[14]

Rawls proclaims that "justice is the first virtue of social institutions . . . laws and institutions . . . must be reformed or abolished if they are unjust." He says that "viewing the theory of justice as a whole, the ideal part presents a conception of a just society that we are to achieve if we can. Existing institutions are to be judged in the light of this conception and held to be unjust to the extent to which they depart from it without sufficient reason."[15] And elsewhere Rawls asserts that "the long-term goal of (relatively) well-ordered societies should

be to bring burdened [by unfavorable conditions] societies, like outlaw states, into the Society of well-ordered Peoples. Well-ordered
people have a *duty* to assist burdened societies."[16]

These passages make obvious that Dworkin, Nagel, and Rawls regard egalitarian liberalism as a moral position that requires the transformation of existing unequal political institutions in order to conform to what they think of as morally right. They propose to
accomplish this by legislation. They are, of course, not alone among
egalitarians in thinking that they have good reasons for wanting the
laws to conform to what they think of as the requirements of morality.
What else are laws against racial and sexual discrimination, religious
education in public schools, laws mandating affirmative action, union
membership, redistribution of wealth through progressive taxation
and high inheritance taxes but the legal enforcement of what egalitarians regard as morality? To abuse Devlin because he does the same is
misleading rhetoric. Their real objection is that they disagree with the
particular moral requirement that they falsely believe Devlin wants to
enforce. In any case, the enforcement of morality, as we shall see, does
not conflict with toleration. The conflict is about what should be enforced and what should be tolerated. We must get clear, therefore,
about toleration and about which aspects of morality should be enforced and tolerated.

11.3 Toleration
"Toleration is intentionally allowing, or refraining from preventing,
actions which one dislikes or believes to be morally wrong. Questions
of toleration arise in circumstances which are characterized by diver-
sity, coupled with dislike or disapproval. These circumstances serve
to distinguish toleration from liberty, and from indifference, where
there need be no reference to dislike. Moreover, toleration requires
that the tolerator have power to intervene, but refrain from using that
power."[17] Or, put more succinctly, if less circumspectly, "To tolerate is
first to condemn and then to put up with."[18]

Toleration is generally thought to be a good thing, but it is not obvious why. How could it be good to allow what is morally wrong? It
seems that toleration betokens weakness of will or of moral conviction. The usual response to such doubts is that toleration is necessary
because of moral disagreements. As Rawls puts it: "The problem of
political liberalism is: How is it possible that there may exist over
time a stable and just society of free and equal citizens profoundly divided by reasonable though incompatible religious, philosophical,
and moral doctrines?"[19] Toleration, then, may be the solution of this
problem.

Let us grant for the moment that toleration does solve the problem. Even so, it is a political, not a moral, solution. From the moral point of view, toleration may be accepted as a necessary evil, but it still is an evil because it requires people to go against their moral convictions and allow what is morally wrong even though they could prevent it. A tolerant society in which the citizens are profoundly divided by incompatible religious, philosophical, and moral doctrines will unavoidably seem to the citizens to be a society that cultivates the immorality of all those of their fellow citizens with whom they so profoundly disagree. It is hard to see why citizens would have allegiance to such a society. Their natural inclination would be alienation and the desire to secede and form a society with their like-minded fellow citizens in which morality will prevail. This cannot very well be the key to stability.

But even if this problem is ignored, others remain. One is that the acceptance of toleration as a general policy leaves open the question of what should and what should not be tolerated. Toleration obviously has limits. What are they? Where are they to be drawn? Who draws them? The egalitarian answer is that there are some conditions all good lives require; the violation of these conditions should not be tolerated, but differences about good lives that conform to the conditions should be. Everything, however, depends on how the conditions are specified. Rawls, speaking for most egalitarians, specifies them as conditions that guarantee stability, justice, freedom, and equality. What he has in mind, however, is justice that involves economic redistribution regardless of desert; freedom that is severely curtailed in order to eliminate differences due to greater or lesser natural abilities; and equality that requires ignoring the differences between habitual patterns of good and evil, prudent and imprudent, law-abiding and criminal actions. The result is that what should be tolerated turns out to be what egalitarians think should be tolerated and what should not be tolerated just happens to be what is contrary to their preferences. This kind of toleration even the worst dictatorships can claim as a virtue.

The other problem is that it must be made clear what action is called for by toleration. If toleration is passive, it involves no more than allowing people to do what one regards as morally wrong even though one could stop them. If toleration is active, it involves the provision of resources for and the maintenance of a climate of opinion that encourages the morally wrong activities. Egalitarians are committed to the active toleration of all those activities that conform to the conditions all good lives require. They insist again and again that all citizens must enjoy equal concern and that means the equalization of economic resources. "No government is legitimate that does not show equal concern for the fate of all those citizens over whom it claims dominion . . . equal concern requires . . . equality of resources";[20] "everyone's life matters, and no one is more important than anyone else";[21] and "each person has an equal claim to a fully adequate scheme of equal basic rights and liberties."[22] According to egalitarians, therefore, toleration must take the form of supporting activities seen as morally wrong with the same share of resources as activities seen as morally right. This requires that, provided only that they do not violate the conditions of all good lives, members of the Ku Klux Klan and the ACLU, pedophiles and pediatricians, pornographers and politicians, victims of the Holocaust and those who deny its occurrence are entitled to equal concern and equal share of economic resources. Few would accept such absurdities, and egalitarians are not among them. Consistency requires, however, that they should either accept them or abandon the rhetoric of active toleration.

These problems of toleration cry out for a reasonable answer to the questions of what should and should not be tolerated and whether toleration, when appropriate, should be passive or active. A precondition of arriving at such an answer is to recognize that morality has different aspects and that the answer varies with the aspects.

11.4 Aspects of Morality

Morality has a universal, social, and personal aspect, and they jointly protect the values necessary for living good lives. Within each aspect there are limits that define what should and should not be tolerated. The enforcement of these limits is a legitimate aim of morality. They may be enforced in various ways, but our concern is with the political approach, which includes legal enforcement.

Values in general are benefits, whose possession makes a life better than it would be without them, and harms, whose infliction makes a life worse than it would otherwise be. It is possible to be mistaken about a value, so there is a difference between being a value and being valued. The essential point is that values are connected with benefits and harms. Mistakes about values may occur because what is regarded as beneficial or harmful may not in fact be so. The key to values, therefore, is to understand the benefits and harms on which they depend. There are some benefits and harms that must count as such for everyone in normal circumstances, and others that vary with societies and individuals. Primary values derive from the former, and they are the concern of the universal aspect of morality. Secondary values are derived from the latter, and they belong to the social and personal aspects of morality.

The universal benefits and harms from which primary values are derived are to be understood in terms of basic human needs set by socially invariant and historically constant human characteristics. The obvious place to start looking for them is the body: nutrition, oxygen, protection from the elements are necessary for survival; the need for rest and motion, pleasure and the avoidance of pain, consumption and elimination, sleep and wakefulness are physiological requirements of all human lives. These truisms may be enlarged because there are also psychological needs shared by all human beings to satisfy their physiological needs in particular ways. These ways differ with individuals, societies, and ages, but there is no difference in the psychological need to go beyond primitive life ruled by necessity and enjoy the luxury of satisfying needs in whatever ways are regarded as good. Everyone prefers civilized life. It is possible to go still further in describing universal human needs because contact with others is also an inevitable part of good lives. Vulnerability, scarce resources, and limited strength, intelligence, energy, and skill force cooperation and social life on human beings. They require the establishment of some authority, the maintenance of institutions and conventional practices, the development and enforcement of rules, which make it possible to satisfy basic needs. These aspects of society impose restrictions on what can be done and provide forms for doing what is allowed. Social life thus establishes moral possibilities and limits. No society can do without them, and human beings cannot live good lives without some participation in society.

These basic needs make it possible to identify many benefits and harms that are the same for everyone, always, everywhere, in normal circumstances. Primary values are the satisfactions of basic needs. They are universal because it is beneficial for all human beings to satisfy their basic physiological, psychological, and social needs. It is a truism that any human life is better if it possesses these benefits and worse if it does not. The primary values are morally necessary because they are required for the satisfaction of these basic needs. Reasonable societies, therefore, must be committed to protecting primary values. They do so by primary principles.

Take the primary value of life as an illustration. All reasonable societies must be committed to the protection of human lives, so they must have a principle prohibiting murder. But this leaves open whether murder can ever be justified, how far its prohibition extends, what the status is of suicide, abortion, capital punishment, war, euthanasia, revenge, feuds, infanticide, and the like, and what is recognized as a justification or an excuse. These difficult questions must be answered by all societies, and they answer them differently. But this does not alter the primary value of life and the necessity of the primary principle prohibiting murder. All reasonable societies must recognize that there is a difference between clear cases in which a primary principle is unambiguously violated and unclear cases that stand in need of interpretation. Murder for fun, pleasure, or profit are clear cases in which a primary principle is violated. It may be unclear whether an act constitutes murder, but if it does, and if it is motivated by fun, pleasure, or profit, then any reasonable society will prohibit it. Not everyone is reasonable and morally committed, of course, but that casts no more doubt on the clear requirements of morality than the actions of stupid people on the clear requirements of health.

There may be reasonable moral disagreements about primary values. People may agree that a homicide has occurred but disagree whether it constitutes murder and, if so, whether it is justifiable or excusable. These disagreements are not intractable since the opposing sides are committed to the primary value of life and to the primary principle that protects it, so the burden of proof can be assigned. If they believe that murder is prohibited but that this homicide is not an instance of it, then they owe an explanation of why the act in question is an exception. Good explanations excuse the act on the ground that it was accidental, done in ignorance, or justified because the alternatives to it were worse. Bad explanations lack convincing excuses or justifications. There are also explanations that are not clearly good or bad because it is difficult to weigh the reasons adduced in support of them. Be that as it may, unclear cases do not call into question that all societies are justified in enforcing primary principles because they protect minimum requirements of good lives. Within the universal aspect of morality, therefore, primary principles should be enforced and their violation should not be tolerated. No reasonable society could tolerate actions that destroy the necessary conditions of good lives. The question of whether in this context toleration should be passive or active does not arise, for any toleration would be contrary to morality.

The social aspect of morality is concerned with secondary values and the secondary principles that protect them. These values and principles are socially variable: different societies have many different secondary values and principles, and they vary over time even in the same society. But this does not mean that they are morally less important than primary values and principles. They are concerned with moral identity, which is as important to good lives as the satisfaction of basic needs. They are secondary because their importance emerges only after the basic needs are by and large satisfied. Although their satisfaction is a condition of good lives, it may take many different forms. Secondary values include these forms, and some secondary principles are concerned with maintaining them. There is a great plurality of secondary values both within a society and among different societies. But at any given period in a society there are some prevalent secondary values, and they define the moral identity of a people. Their identity is at once individual and shared by others because living according to some set of secondary values is an essential feature of what people are, but it is a feature that greatly or partially overlaps with those of other participants.

One main type of secondary values has to do with the particular ways in which the primary values are interpreted in a society. Consider, for instance, the basic needs for food, intimacy, and conflict resolution. The need for food must be met, for otherwise we die, but there are great differences among societies about how it is met. All societies reject some perfectly nutritious food, such as beef, pork, human flesh, insects, or bitter or malodorous plants; they all regard some as delicacies; and often what is rejected by one is a delicacy in another. In all societies there are customs about what is eaten, when, and with whom, what should be raw and what cooked, who prepares the food, and so forth. The same is true of intimacy. In all societies there are close relationships that alleviate loneliness; provide mutual aid, respect, trust, satisfaction; and enable people to cope with the inevitable adversities in their lives. Love, friendship, family, and sex exist everywhere, but there are great variations in whom it is thought proper to love, what friendship implies, who counts as a family member or as a proper sexual partner. Similarly, all societies must have ways of resolving conflicts among their people, but different societies have different ways. Some rely on the legal or political system, others on religious authorities or public assemblies, yet others on oracles, or bribery, or bargaining, or on trials of strength, rhetoric, or some other skill. Every society has acceptable and unacceptable ways of satisfying basic needs, and these ways constitute one type of secondary value.

Another type has to do with areas of life whose connection with primary values is more remote. It includes ethnicity, religious affiliation, ways of making a living, education, patriotism, sports, music, literature, science, hobbies, and so forth. It includes also the countless customs, rituals, and ceremonies of everyday life that mark significant occasions such as birth, marriage, and death; conventions about flirtation, competition, clothing, and housing; and the appropriate ways of expressing gratitude, regret, contempt, resentment, admiration, and the like. It includes as well what counts as politeness, tact, generosity, promise, insult, superficiality, and so on.

People living together in a society are familiar with both types of secondary values. They create expectations and leave their mark on the character of people who have lived there for a sufficiently long time. They give form to life in that society by constituting the social framework in which individuals exist. Their expectations, characters, and forms of life jointly constitute a significant part of their moral identity. As the satisfaction of basic needs is a minimum requirement of good lives in the universal aspect of morality, so moral identity is a minimum requirement in the social aspect.

The moral identity of a society does not eliminate deep differences in religious, political, philosophical, or moral views, but defines the acceptable range of differences. Possibilities that fall outside that range may or may not be regarded as morally wrong; they may be thought of as matters of indifference or oddities that exist in other societies. Dueling, hara-kiri, flogging as criminal punishment, female circumcision, sexual initiation by priests, primogeniture, the reverence of fakirs, the medicinal use of human excrement, the training of castrati as singers, the worship of some species of animals fall outside the range, given our contemporary moral identity. Moral identity is thus constituted by both exclusion and inclusion. It includes the range of secondary values from among which people living in that society can choose some to live by. They form the accumulated moral capital of a society. Members can draw on them in order to adapt some to their own characters and circumstances and to construct out of them their own conceptions of a good life.

These secondary values continually change in response to changing cultural, social, technological, demographic, and other conditions, and the prevailing moral identity changes with them. But that does not mean that it is not important for good lives. It is as important as the satisfaction of basic needs because without it people living in a society would not know how to satisfy their basic needs, how to relate to one another, and how to make the choices that are open to them. That knowledge, however, is as consistent with changes in moral identity as knowledge of one's language is with changes in usage. Just as speaking a language is to know how to say what one wants to say, so having a moral identity is to know how to do what one wants to do.

Reasonable societies, therefore, must protect secondary values by enforcing secondary principles, which are derived from the changing moral identity of a people on the social level of morality. The enforcement, however, is of the *system* of secondary values and principles, not of the changing specific constituents of it. It is the *having* of a moral identity that is a minimum requirement of good lives, not the temporarily prevailing forms that make it up. Reasonable societies must combine recognition of the necessity of moral identity with toleration that allows for changes in its constituents. But should the toleration be passive non-interference or active encouragement and the provision of resources? It is important to remember that what is being tolerated are morally wrong actions that violate secondary principles and thus the prevailing moral identity. Since moral identity is necessary for good lives, its violation should not be encouraged. But since it is continually changing in response to changing circumstances, the changes should not be interfered with. The tolerated morally wrong action may be a sign that the secondary principle that it has violated should be changed because it no longer protects a condition of good lives. The ready availability of contraception, for instance, has surely changed for us in this way the moral status of chastity. The fact remains, however, that it is often hard to judge whether a violation of the prevailing moral identity signals moral change or immorality. The reason for toleration in such cases is the importance of keeping moral identity open to change. Otherwise it becomes the rigid protector of conditions whose necessity for good lives no longer holds. In the context of the social aspect of morality, therefore, there should be passive, but not active, toleration. People should be allowed morally wrong actions that violate the prevailing moral identity, but its violation should not be encouraged.

The personal aspect of morality is concerned with individuals trying to make good lives for themselves. Good lives include personal projects, which may be artistic, scientific, athletic, erotic, commercial, religious, horticultural, and so forth; they may include collecting, traveling, solitude, connoisseurship, competition, public service, craft, scholarship, raising children, teaching, and so on. These projects are personal in the sense that they are meaningful for those who are engaged in them, but they are rarely their creations. They are usually chosen from among the multitude of secondary values that the moral identity of the society affords. Such personal projects are a necessary part of good lives.

Another, equally necessary part is the transformation of one's character. People have various conceptions of a good life, and they try to live according to them. But there are always external and internal obstacles that stand in the way. External obstacles may be caused by bad luck, injustice, poverty, lack of encouragement, illness, and so on. Internal obstacles are people's own shortcomings, contrary inclinations, and bad judgments. The transformation of character is needed to cope better with external obstacles and to remove internal ones. This requires the development of the traditional moral virtues and personal excellences, such as talents, discipline, energy, dedication, constancy, patience, and so on. The transformation of character, then, has to do with the cultivation of virtues and personal excellences. Temperance, courage, and justice are traditionally thought to be necessary for all reasonable conceptions of a good life. But there are numerous other moral and intellectual virtues, as well as personal excellences, which are required by some conceptions of a good life but not others. Many virtues and personal excellences are personal, then, in the sense that they characterize a particular way of life. Conceptions of a good life, personal projects, virtues, and personal excellences are also secondary values. It is convenient to refer to them collectively, so they will be called the secondary values of self-direction. As the social aspect is concerned with secondary values required for moral identity, so the personal aspect is concerned with secondary values required for self-direction. And just as secondary principles should be enforced to protect moral identity, so secondary principles should be enforced to protect self-direction.

Secondary principles protect self-direction by protecting the conditions that make self-direction possible. This involves the encouragement of conceptions of a good life, personal projects, and character traits that conform to the requirements of the satisfaction of basic needs and the maintenance of moral identity. These requirements should be enforced within the universal and social aspects of morality. But there are additional requirements within the personal aspect because the conditions of self-direction may be threatened even if the satisfaction of basic needs and the maintenance of moral identity are protected. The threat is that some conceptions of a good life, personal projects, or character traits may prevent others from living according to their conceptions, pursuing their projects, or developing their character traits. It is, therefore, necessary to enforce secondary principles that coordinate the self-direction of people living together in a society and discourage conceptions of a good life, personal projects, and character traits that seriously interfere with those of others. Self-direction, therefore, may be reasonably limited by the enforcement of primary and secondary principles if it interferes with the satisfaction of basic needs, endangers the prevailing system of moral identity, or prevents others from living self-directed lives that conform to these conditions.

It follows that there should be active toleration of lives and projects that conform to the primary and secondary principles of the three levels but seem morally wrong because they are viewed from the perspectives of existing forms of self-direction. It is in the interest of people living in a society to encourage the widest range of self-direction that conforms to these conditions, even if the forms it takes seem morally wrong on other grounds. For new forms of self-directed lives enrich the existing possibilities by adding to them or stand as warning of possibilities whose realization ruins lives. When Mill and his followers advocate toleration, they think of this aspect of morality. There is no reason to disagree with them, provided they do not suppose that what is true of toleration within the personal aspect of morality is also true within the universal and social aspects.

The minimum requirements of morality are, then, the satisfaction of basic needs, the maintenance of moral identity, and the protection of self-direction. All societies can be criticized, both externally and internally, if they fail to meet them. The typical source of external criticism is the comparison of two societies. It is a relatively uncomplicated matter to point out that one society does significantly better in providing some requirement than another. Life expectancy in France is much higher than in Russia, so in that respect Russia is doing something wrong. The Canadians cope better with their ethnic and religious differences than the Irish, so the Irish are reasonably faulted. In Turkey women have a greater choice of lifestyle than in Iran, so Iran suffers in comparison. The external criticism of a society, of course, may be ignored by those who live in it, but that does not make the criticism any the less justified.

The internal criticism of societies proceeds by pointing at some inconsistency between how things are and how members of the society think they ought to be. If every adult citizen ought to have the vote but some are disenfranchised by deliberately erected obstacles, then criticism is justified. Or there are principles that continue to be accepted in a society even though the conditions that warranted them have changed. Thrift was a virtue before Keynesian economics, but it has become a matter of personal preference. If people in a society fail to recognize that, they are mistaken. Or there may be principles in a society that are based on factual error. It is not true that children benefit from corporal punishment, that suffering makes one better, or that saving money by itself leads to financial security. Principles that reflect these false beliefs ought to be rejected. The reason for stressing the possibility of external and internal criticisms is to make clear that thinking of morality in terms of its three aspects in no way commits one to the perpetuation of the existing principles in a society. Criticism is possible and may be justified within each of the three aspects of morality.

We can now be clearer about when morality should be enforced and when toleration is justified. In the universal aspect of morality, primary principles should be enforced and their violation should not be tolerated, for otherwise basic needs are unsatisfied. In the social aspect of morality, the system of secondary principles should be enforced, but the violation of particular secondary principles should be passively tolerated. The reason for enforcement is to protect the prevailing moral identity, and the reason for the toleration is to allow for changes in response to changing conditions. In the personal aspect of morality, secondary principles should be generally enforced because they protect the conditions of self-direction. But there should be active toleration of actions that are thought to be morally wrong because they violate prevailing forms of self-direction. Such actions may reflect new possibilities of life from whose success or failure everyone can learn. Finally, the justification for satisfying basic needs, maintaining moral identity, and protecting self-direction is that they are necessary for living good lives. Unfortunately, this is not the end of the matter because there is a serious complication that must be recognized and accommodated.

11.5 Principled Wrongdoing

The complication is that actions that conform to the principles of one aspect of morality may violate the principles of another aspect. Since morality has different aspects, the possibility of conflicts between them must be recognized. As a result, an action that is morally right within one aspect may be morally wrong within another aspect. If this happens, the question of whether or not the action should be tolerated has no clear answer. What might be the reasonable response to such conflicts?

The simplest response is unsatisfactory, but understanding why it is so will point toward one that is better. This unsatisfactory response is that since the universal aspect of morality is more basic than the social, which in turn is more basic than the personal, in conflicts between them the universal should prevail over the social, and the social over the personal. The reason that may be given for this response is that the satisfaction of basic needs is more important for good lives than the maintenance of moral identity, and that the maintenance of moral identity is more important than the protection of self-direction. This order of importance, it may be said, reflects the fact that self-direction presupposes the secondary values that moral identity maintains, and moral identity presupposes that the basic needs are being satisfied.

This response fails because although it is true that the personal aspect presupposes the social, which presupposes the universal, it does not follow that the presupposed aspect is more important than the presupposing one. The three aspects are equally necessary and equally important for good lives because lives may be bad even if the basic needs are satisfied, and they may remain bad even if moral identity is maintained. Good lives also depend on having a conception of a good life, meaningful personal projects, and appropriate character traits that self-direction provides. People may reasonably regard themselves deprived of the possibility of a good life even if their basic needs are met and the moral identity of their society is maintained because they are forced to live in a way that is contrary to what their self-direction prompts. And a whole society may similarly be deprived of the possibility of good lives even if the basic needs of its members are satisfied because its system of moral identity has been destroyed by invaders or adverse conditions. The simple response to conflicts among different aspects of morality fails because it tries to resolve the conflicts by falsely regarding the values and principles of one aspect as always more important than those of the others.

A better response requires understanding that the reasons for resolving these conflicts may be good from the point of view of one aspect and bad from the point of view of another aspect. To make this concrete, consider two examples. In the Apocrypha we read: "Eleazar, one of the scribes in high position, a man advanced in age and of noble presence, was being forced to open his mouth to eat swine's flesh. But he, welcoming death with honour rather than life with pollution, went up to the rack of his own accord, spitting out flesh, as men ought to go who have the courage to refuse things that it is not right to taste, even for the natural love of life."[23] Eleazar's conflict was between the secondary value of his religious conception of a good life on the personal level and the primary value of life on the universal level. He resolved it in favor of the personal level.

The reason he might have given is that he regarded a life that involves acting contrary to his religious beliefs as not worth living. We can all envisage situations in which we would rather die than live on certain terms, even if the terms that we would find unacceptable were quite different from Eleazar's. On the other hand, Eleazar's belief that pork is somehow harmful is false. The belief has long endured, and its significance transcends questions of nutrition and spoiled food, but the fact remains that this aura of significance rests on a factual error. Eleazar sacrificed his life in the service of an error, and that is a waste. There are, then, good reasons on both sides. To decide between them we have to think further. We have to ask whether Eleazar's belief about pork was merely symbolic or whether he had supposed that the symbolism rested on a factual base. If the first, we can see that he had a good reason to die, even if we do not share his reason. If the second, we shall think that his reason was bad. The weight of reasons may fall one way or another, depending on further reasons about the respective importance of facts and symbols in Eleazar's conception of a good life. So the conflict can be resolved on the basis of reasons, but it need not be resolved in favor of the primary value of life, as the simple response supposes. There may be good reasons why secondary values should override primary values.

Take conscientious objection to war as another example. My country is fighting against unprovoked aggressors to defend its moral identity. I have believed long and consistently that the deliberate killing of human beings is wrong under all circumstances. So I refuse to serve when conscripted. My self-direction conflicts with the moral identity of my society. I must follow one or the other. I recognize that there are good reasons on both sides, but I believe that in this case the personal should override the social. This belief may or may not be supported by good reasons. If I know that my society is going to punish me for refusing to serve and I am willing to take the punishment; if I know that the war may be lost and the aggressors may destroy the moral identity of my society; and if I still believe that deliberate killing is wrong because human lives are more important than my freedom and the moral identity of my society, then I have a good reason for my belief. But there are good reasons also against it, the most important of which is that the form of self-direction that I opt for over the moral identity of my society is sustained by that moral identity. If the moral identity were destroyed, my self-directed life would soon wither, so in opting as I do, I in effect endanger what I opt for.

The weight of reasons may fall one way or another, depending on how dangerous is the threat presented by the aggressor, how well considered is my belief that there are no circumstances in which there would be good reasons for deliberate killing, how defensible is the prevailing moral identity, how likely it is that I can sustain my self-direction in adverse circumstances, and so on. The point is that the conflict, and conflicts like it, can be resolved on the basis of reasons, although there is no general way of deciding what particular reasons will be relevant in a particular context, what weight should be assigned to them, and consequently what the most reasonable resolution will be. Good reasons need not be general.

It may be thought that this view about conflicts is too sanguine. It does not take account of deep religious, philosophical, and moral conflicts that may occur in a society. That there are deep conflicts must of course be acknowledged. It must also be acknowledged that after everything has been said and done, the conflicts may persist. If many of them persist, the society is in danger of disintegration. This threatens the very possibility of good lives, a prospect that all reasonable people living in a society would want to avoid. They would then have a very powerful reason to contain somehow their conflicts, as we are doing about abortion, the preferential treatment of minorities, voluntary euthanasia, and similar issues.

A further consideration is that it makes a great difference whether or not the conflicts are based on reasonable disagreements; disagreements, that is, in which the opposing sides adhere to logic, take account of the relevant facts, and recognize the obligation to meet serious objections. In many deep conflicts one or both sides are strongly and sincerely committed to views that fail these simple tests. There is then a good reason to reject their views, even if they do not themselves accept this reason. If they act on their unreasonable views, their actions may be morally wrong, even if they strongly and sincerely believe otherwise. The proper response, then, is to enforce the reasonable resolution of the conflict and not to tolerate the unreasonable and morally wrong action.

The fact is, however, that even if unreasonable views are discounted, deep conflicts will remain among people who hold reasonable but incompatible views; conflicts between liberals and conservatives, populists and elitists, religious believers and atheists, relativists and objectivists, perfectionists and pluralists, optimists and pessimists about human nature, and so on. But reasonable people, holding reasonable views, and living together in a society will try to live with their conflicts by tolerating actions that reflect them because they realize that the alternative is far worse. This is not a clean solution; it is, indeed, not even a solution but merely a modus vivendi. It has the virtue, however, of being faithful to the facts of moral life.

11.6 Consequences

One consequence of thinking about enforcement and toleration in terms of the three aspects of morality is that the enforcement of the relevant principles is seen as a necessary condition of good lives in each of the three aspects, although the justifications of their enforcement differ. In the universal aspect, justification appeals to basic needs; in the social aspect, to moral identity; and in the personal aspect, to self-direction. The legal enforcement of morality, therefore, is necessary and justified, and the egalitarian opposition to it is mistaken.

Another consequence is that the enforcement of morality is compatible with toleration, but what should and should not be tolerated varies with the aspects of morality. Actions that violate the primary principles that protect the satisfaction of basic needs ought not to be tolerated. Actions that conform to primary principles but violate some particular secondary principle ought to be passively tolerated. Actions that conform to primary principles, to the system of secondary principles that protect moral identity, and to secondary principles that protect self-direction, but represent new forms of self-direction ought to be actively tolerated, even if they seem morally wrong from the point of view of the existing forms.

Enforcement and toleration thus need to be balanced against each other, and their balance shifts from the universal, to the social, to the personal aspect of morality. The more universal a moral principle is, the stronger is the case for enforcing it and the weaker for tolerating its violation. The more personal a moral principle is, the stronger is the case for tolerating its violation and the weaker for enforcing it. But apart from obvious universal principles, there is no general answer, no blueprint for settling the question of what the right balance is between enforcement and toleration, because principles vary with the moral identities and forms of self-direction that prevail in different societies. In each society reasonable and objective judgments can be made about how important some principle is for good lives, but these judgments vary with contexts because the prevailing economic, technological, demographic, political, historical, and other conditions differ. In this respect, there are many reasonable and objective moral judgments, but they must be particular and cannot be universal or impartial. This counts against consequentialist and deontological versions of egalitarianism which assume that moral judgments must be universal and impartial.

The final consequence that needs to be pointed out is just how very misleading is the egalitarian rhetoric about enforcement and toleration. The legal enforcement of morality need not force a choice on people between "frustration and persecution," as Dworkin suggests; it need not be "an unjustifiable extension of the scope of the criminal law," as Hart claims; it need not be "an overt rejection of rationality," as Hughes opines; and it need not be "totally irrationalist," as Wollheim asserts.[24] It can be, in fact, a requirement that everyone committed to reason and morality will accept. And of course, it is accepted—their rhetoric notwithstanding—by egalitarians themselves. Their quarrel is not about the legal enforcement of morality in general but about what particular moral claim should be enforced. Does this mean, then, that egalitarians could accept the account of enforcement and toleration that has just been completed?

They could accept it, but only at a cost they may not be prepared to pay. For it would require them to give up the idea that a society ought to be neutral about the conceptions of a good life that its members hold, as well as the idea that egalitarianism has a stronger claim to toleration than, say, a pluralistic form of conservatism; and they would have to abandon the claim that everyone should be treated with equal concern and supported with appropriate resources. For if morality should be legally enforced, then a reasonable society cannot be neutral between conceptions of a good life that violate the prevailing moral identity and conditions of self-direction, and it cannot treat with equal concern their protectors and violators.

The upshot of this chapter is that the illusion that egalitarianism is the ideology of toleration is untenable. Egalitarians certainly tolerate some practices, but equally certainly, they use the legal system to prohibit others. The real question is not whether toleration is good and enforcement bad but what, according to reason and morality, should be tolerated and what should be enforced. That question has been answered in terms of the requirements of the three levels of morality.

12/

The Politics of Fairy Tales

Most Anglo-American academic books and articles on moral philosophy have a fairy-tale quality because the realities of politics, both contemporary and past politics, are absent from them.

STUART HAMPSHIRE, *Innocence and Experience*

12.1 The Illusion

The egalitarian thinkers we have been discussing are dissatisfied with the prevailing political arrangements of their society. They deplore the alleged injustice and inequality, and the inadequate protection of what they take to be people's rights. One naturally expects them, therefore, to propose policies that would right what they regard as wrong. But this expectation is not met. They proceed rather by putting forward an ideal, which yet-to-be-proposed policies ought to realize. They readily concede that the ideal has never been realized, but they nevertheless think that it ought to be.

This raises a host of questions. Since the source of the ideal is not a past or present political arrangement, it must be produced by some person or persons. But why should a society heed the preference of some particular people? Why should people who prize different values, honor different principles, subscribe to different conceptions of a good life regard something contrary to their own as an ideal? But suppose it was so regarded. There are usually many different ideals available. Why should one rather than any of the others be generally accepted as a guide to policies? As if these questions were not difficult enough, there is the further one about what concrete policies should be followed. If some policies are actually proposed, then why is the ideal needed? And if no policy is proposed, then what good is the ideal? To say that the ideal is needed to choose between policies is not a satisfactory answer because it ignores that both the ideal and the policies it endorses are controversial. Is it not needlessly cumbersome to try to improve matters by introducing an ideal that is sure to be controversial and then derive from it equally controversial policies? Why not just propose the controversial policies, defend them on their own merit, and forget about the ideal? If dissatisfaction is as rampant as egalitarians say, policies that improve matters would be surely welcome, in which case the controversial ideal would be unnecessary.

Egalitarian advocates of this approach, of course, are aware of these questions and propose answers to them by formulating what has come to be called an *ideal theory*. These theories are criticized, revised, and developed by other egalitarian thinkers, giving the appearance of intellectual ferment, but what in fact happens is that political allies united by a shared ideal discuss details without asking fundamental questions. They write books about each other's books, and mostly articles about each other's articles, while agreeing about the supposed wrongs and the ideal that would eliminate them. All this busywork rests on the illusion that the way to improve bad political arrangements is to make them conform ever more closely to an ideal. This illusion is false; it gives rise to a dangerous utopian approach to politics; and the ideal theories that rest on it are historically uninformed, politically impractical, and morally unacceptable because they ignore the actual conditions of particular societies. They are fairy tales, but unlike those for children, unbenign.

12.2   Ideal Theory

Rawls's work has the virtue of making explicit much that is implicit in the writings of other egalitarian thinkers. This is true of his proposal of an ideal theory as well. Rawls writes: "The reason for beginning with ideal theory is that it provides ... the only basis for the systematic grasp of ... more pressing problems. ... I shall assume that a deeper understanding can be gained in no other way, and that the nature and aims of a perfectly just society is the fundamental part of the theory of justice." His theory is ideal, first, because it provides "a standard whereby the distributive aspects of the basic structure of society can be assessed," and second, because "everyone is presumed to act justly and to do his part in upholding just institutions."[1] When a society meets the first condition, Rawls calls it "well-ordered," and when it meets the second condition, Rawls says "strict compliance" prevails. The conditions of actual societies are acknowledged to be non-ideal because they are not well-ordered and there is no strict compliance. An ideal theory, then, "presents a conception of a just society that we are to achieve if we can. Existing institutions are to be judged in the light of this conception and held to be unjust to the extent that they depart from it without sufficient reason."[2]

Rawls's ideal theory is a fairy tale because he derives the principles of justice from a hypothetical situation that is the product of his imagination: the original position in which principles are chosen behind the veil of ignorance (see 4.3). Rawls is not alone in proceeding in this manner. Dworkin does the same, although his hypothetical situation has to do with imaginary people on a nonexistent island paying in clamshells for miraculously available resources and participating in a compulsory scheme that forces them to buy insurance against bad luck (see 5.3). Waldron appeals to a reformulated version of a hypothetical contract to which people would consent provided they were asked, they were reasonable, they had the option of saying no, and a number of other unrealizable conditions were met.[3] Scanlon advances a similar idea, which he explains in terms of a hypothetical situation in which fully reasonable hypothetical people consider whether they could reasonably reject some moral or political principle presented for their examination.[4] David Gauthier, Jürgen Habermas, R. M. Hare, Christine Korsgaard, and Donald Moon also favor their own versions of this approach.[5]

The appeal to an ideal theory has several noteworthy features. One is that it permits its defenders to ignore facts that appear to be contrary to the theory. That in real life societies are not well-ordered and there is no strict compliance in them is simply written off as precisely those characteristic features of non-ideal conditions that the ideal theory is meant to eliminate. There is, thus, no evidence derivable from the history of a society, the conduct of human beings, or the prevailing political arrangements that could count against the ideal theory. Contrary facts are treated as evidence that the conditions of a society are non-ideal; and facts that conform to the ideal are cited as evidence that the society is progressing toward the ideal.

This feature of non-ideal theories explains why egalitarians can ignore the existence of widespread evil, the commonly shared belief that just policies aim at people having what they deserve and not having what they do not deserve, the groundswell of indignation at depriving people of their legally acquired property in order to benefit those who have less without considering the responsibility of the recipients for having less, and the conduct of virtually everyone in opposition to the egalitarian demand to treat people with equal respect regardless of their moral standing. Egalitarians view these facts as predictable and lamentable features of non-ideal societies. They claim that under the conditions their ideal theory aims at, these facts would not exist. But arguing this way imposes on egalitarians the burden of explaining what the ideal theory is based on, if not on the facts of history, psychology, and politics. We shall see that their explanation is unsatisfactory.

The second feature of the appeal to an ideal theory is that it provides a standard with reference to which the political arrangements of a society are evaluated. The achievement, or at least the approximation, of the ideal is the aim, and everything political may be judged by how well it serves that aim in comparison with other possible ways of serving it. Standards, however, need to be justified, and egalitarians need to explain what justifies theirs. This is especially difficult because, as we shall see, there are formidable objections to applying standards derived from an ideal theory to a non-ideal society. The third feature that egalitarians claim ideal theories possess is that they are the only possible ways of evaluating the political arrangements of a society. This claim will also be shown to be false.

12.3 Being Reasonable

If the concrete historical, psychological, and political conditions that prevail in existing societies are irrelevant, then what are ideal theories based on? We shall consider Thomas Hill's answer, which is exceptional in struggling with some of the most fundamental questions about egalitarianism.[6] (Rawls does the same, but as we have seen in chapter 4, his struggle does not yield acceptable answers.)

Hill defends a general idea that "has affinities, not only with Kant, but with Rousseau's political ideal, John Rawls's theory of justice, Thomas Scanlon's idea of moral justification, and no doubt with other views as well" (98). This idea is that "we can appropriately think of moral principles as principles that all *reasonable* human beings would accept, as justifiable to themselves and others, under certain ideal conditions" (96). These principles "trump the policies that *otherwise* they [i.e., reasonable human beings] might adopt to satisfy their personal desires" (97). Hill says that reasonable people, under ideal conditions, "would converge on certain general principles ... [and] acknowledge those principles as the final, unconditional authority regarding what ends they should seek and what means they may, and may not, use" (98). But there is a variety of such general principles, and the question arises, "why should one expect all reasonable people, regardless of their particular differences, to find such specific, substantive principles authoritative for them?" Because, says Hill, there is "a most comprehensive principle behind the belief in particular duties ... [namely] to restrict one's personal acts and policies to those compatible with whatever general principles everyone would accept if 'legislating' from the moral perspective," that is, from the ideal perspective of fully reasonable people (100). This most comprehensive principle is a "formal prescription," an "abstract rule," that says in effect: " 'Govern yourself, constrain your desires and plans, according to what is reasonable'." And what is reasonable is to participate "in ongoing, mutually respectful deliberations in which everyone must try to justify proposed policies and principles to everyone else who is willing to reciprocate" (101).

Hill's answer, then, is that an ideal theory is based on reason, not facts. The most comprehensive moral principle is simply a formal and abstract requirement of being reasonable. Facts are irrelevant to it, and dissent from it is unreasonable. Fully reasonable people would accept and live by the principle, and those who do not are more or less unreasonable. This principle is what an ideal theory embodies. The way to make non-ideal societies better is to keep changing their political arrangements to approximate ever more closely the ideal. And the way human beings can make themselves better is to strive to become ever more reasonable by subordinating their desires and plans to the most comprehensive moral principle, whose purpose is to coordinate the general pursuit of desires and plans. "In this model," says Hill, "all moral agents are assumed to have *autonomy*, which means, in part, that no one is bound by demands . . . unless such demands are backed by more basic principles that all rational agents with autonomy would accept" (97).

This defense of ideal theory as a requirement of reason, if successful, would show that an ideal theory is applicable regardless of the historical, psychological, and political conditions of non-ideal societies. For all conditions would be improved by being made more reasonable. The defense would show also that an ideal theory is applicable in all non-ideal societies because the requirements of reason are the same everywhere. Societies are non-ideal precisely because they fail to meet its requirements. This defense, however, presupposes a mistaken view of reason.

Ever since Aristotle, it has been customary to distinguish between theoretical and practical reason. Theoretical reason aims at truth expressed by propositions that ought to be believed. Practical reason aims at success conceived in terms of imperatives that ought to be acted on. Theoretical and practical reason, therefore, are different because they have different aims (truth vs. success) and different subject matters (propositions vs. imperatives). But they also overlap because successful actions often depend on believing true propositions, believing a true proposition is an action, the pursuit of truth is an imperative, and successful actions often consist in finding the truth.

Alongside the distinction between theoretical and practical reason, there has been a tendency to regard the overlap between them as sufficiently large to assimilate practical to theoretical reason. The result of this tendency has been the claim that the imperatives of practical reason ought to conform to the same standards as the truths of theoretical reason. Since the truth is *universal*, that is, the same for everyone, always, everywhere; *objective*, that is, holds regardless of subjective preferences; and *impersonal*, that is, independent of who accepts or rejects it, imperatives ought to be the same. The most uncompromising representative of this tendency is Kant, and the view of reason presupposed by Rawls, Hill, and many other egalitarians is Kantian. Although the overlap between theoretical and practical reason must be acknowledged, substantial enough differences remain to make their assimilation impossible and the standards of theoretical reason inapplicable to practical reason.

One crucial difference is that the truths of theoretical reason are not directed at any particular individual, but imperatives are. Imperatives typically tell individuals what they ought to do. What that is, however, often depends on their history, character, relationships, and circumstances, which vary with individuals. There are, therefore, many imperatives that are not universal, objective, and impersonal, nor is it reasonable to suppose that they ought to be. This much is uncontroversial. What is controversial is the further claim that the most important type of imperative is moral, and it is and ought to be universal, objective, and impersonal. But why should it be supposed that in moral situations actions should conform to an imperative that is the same for everyone, always, everywhere; holds regardless of subjective preferences; and is independent of whom it is directed toward? Why should practical reason require individuals to obey a moral imperative that is the same for all individuals? That this requirement holds *sometimes* may be readily acknowledged. But the claim is the much stronger one that in moral situations it holds *always*. Why must moral actions conform to the standards of universality, objectivity, and impersonality?

The value of practical reason is that it points to the action that is reasonable to perform. But if the Kantian understanding of practical reason were correct, there would be many situations in which practical reason could not point to the reasonable action. Suppose a man is considering whether he should leave his wife and children. If his decision is to be reasonable, he must take into account the nature and history of his relationship with his wife, the extent to which the children are dependent on him, the seriousness of his dissatisfaction with their life together, the chances of his own happiness within and outside the marriage, financial considerations, his wife's well-being, his future access to the children, and so forth. Assume that he wants to do what is reasonable and morally justifiable but he is not sure what that is.

If he turns to the Kantian understanding of practical reason, he can derive from it the imperative that he should test the various options available to him by the standards of universality, objectivity, and impersonality. In other words, he should do what he thinks after serious reflection any other person in his situation should do. But how is that going to help him decide what is reasonable to do? There could be no other person in his situation because his situation consists of *his* relationship with *his* wife and children, *his* financial affairs, the prospect of *his* happiness, the extent of *his* dissatisfactions. To all these the characters of the people involved, the history of their relationships, and the particularities of their circumstances are crucially relevant. If anyone else were in his situation, the situation would be fundamentally different because the character, history, and circumstances of the person who was in his place would be different. So considering what any other person should do in his situation would not help this man decide what he should do.

This, of course, is *not* to deny that he can make a reasonable decision. It is to deny rather that the reasonable decision will be universal, since it will apply only to his family and himself; or objective, since the subjective preferences of the people involved are centrally relevant; or impersonal, since the identity, character, history, and circumstances of those affected by the decision are crucial.

Take a different situation. A woman has to decide what to do. Her difficulty, however, is not to decide what course of action open to her is morally justifiable. What she has to decide is whether it would be reasonable for her to act in a way she knows is morally unjustifiable in order to achieve a nonmoral goal that is essential to what she reasonably conceives as her well-being. Say that she is a highly talented but unrecognized young painter who lives in great poverty. She badly needs money to continue with her art. She is offered a lucrative position as a commercial artist, provided she promises to stay in the job permanently. She has no intention of staying longer than it takes to save some money so that she can continue painting. She knows that it is morally unjustifiable to make a false promise, but she also knows that her life would be ruined if she could not go on painting. And so she deliberates about what to do.

The Kantian understanding of practical reason assumes that doing what is morally justifiable is always the most reasonable course of action, so the woman ought not make a false promise. But why should one accept that? Why should it be that making a reasonable decision always requires that moral considerations should override conflicting aesthetic, religious, personal, or other considerations? Why could not breaking a not terribly important promise, telling a not very damaging lie, being disloyal to a cause that would not be seriously jeopardized by one's defection be more reasonable than compromising one's art, committing what one regards as sacrilege, or abandoning what gives meaning to one's life? How could it be an imperative of practical reason to subordinate what is essential to one's well-being to a much less important requirement of morality?

Hill's answer to the questions raised by the husband who contemplates leaving and the young painter who contemplates dishonesty is that these people are not sufficiently reasonable. And if we feel the force of these questions, we too are deficient in reason. A fully reasonable person would not be divided between moral and nonmoral alternatives, nor would such a person have great difficulty deciding which of conflicting moral requirements is more important. As Hill puts it, "If completely rational and reasonable . . . they must, then, be presupposing among their deep commitments, some general principle, or point of view, that would explain why they regard it as reasonable to judge that they ought, on particular occasions, to do the morally required things, whether they want to or not" (99). But why does being fully reasonable presuppose a general principle? Why could it not be fully reasonable to pursue successfully reasonable ends by reasonable means, even though both the ends and the means are reasonable only given the particular character and circumstances of that particular person, and would not be reasonable for a person with different character and circumstances? Hill does not say.

The answer, however, is that practical reason is supposed to be fully reasonable only if it were like theoretical reason. If, that is, the imperative to do something were like the truth of a proposition in being universal, objective, and impersonal. But imperatives are not like truths, and practical reason is not like theoretical reason because the former depend on the particularities of a person's character and circumstances whereas the latter do not. In that case, however, the view of reason ideal theories presuppose is mistaken, and the attempt to base ideal theories only on reason and ignore the facts of non-ideal societies is a failure.

12.4 Respecting Humanity

Egalitarians may respond to these criticisms of the Kantian view of practical reason by conceding their force and denying that they invalidate the appeal to an ideal theory. Even if practical reason need not *always* conform to the standards of universality, objectivity, and impersonality, it *sometimes* must conform to them, and an ideal theory is based on the employment of practical reason when it gives rise to universal, objective, and impersonal imperatives. It may be claimed further that it is precisely these uses of practical reason that are morally speaking the most important. For the use of practical reason in moral matters aims at human well-being, and although there are many reasonable conceptions of well-being, all of them must recognize that there are some conditions that must be met by every reasonable conception. Human well-being depends on the satisfaction of basic physiological, psychological, and social needs, and an ideal theory is based on the universal, objective, and impersonal imperative that these needs ought to be met. This imperative is reasonable regardless of the conditions that prevail in particular societies and of the characters and circumstances of particular individuals. In the Kantian language adopted by Rawls, Hill, and many others, the imperative is to respect the humanity of each individual human being.

Hill distinguishes between two kinds of respect. One is owed to people in recognition of their merit or excellence, but this is not the kind he wants to discuss. The other is owed to people "*as human beings . . .* for *humanity* (or being human) is itself a moral status or position that calls for respectful recognition. . . . We can coherently respect even viciously immoral people *as human beings,* even though, as individuals, they fall far short of how human beings should conduct themselves" (90). Hill defends this second type of respect. He explains that "granting everyone due respect is a basic moral requirement not derivative from the desirability of promoting other good consequences. . . . Kantians take the principle of respect for humanity as . . . serving as a limit to what we may legitimately do in our efforts to promote the general welfare" (93). Hill recognizes that "self-protection, punishment, and moral censure" (114) are reasonable measures when facing "viciously immoral people" (90), but he denies that these measures need to show disrespect: "since just and respectful punishment and moral censure are available to express appropriate moral attitudes and protect legitimate interests, there is no good reason to set aside our initial presumption that all human beings have . . . a respectworthy status that need not be earned and cannot be forfeited" (117).

Hill's conclusion is certainly right: morality sets limits to what can be permissibly done to even the worst people. One can accept this, however, without accepting Hill's reason for it. The reason why we should not transgress moral limits need not be the absurd respect of "viciously immoral people" but that we do not want to become the kind of people who inflict extreme forms of pain, humiliation, deprivation, or terror even on evildoers who deserve it. One does not have to be a Kantian to recognize that there are reasonable moral limits. But this is a side issue. The serious objection is that when Hill attempts to justify his view of how morality requires people to treat each other, he appeals to an understanding of respect that is quite different from the one that involves setting limits. And that other understanding is contrary to reason.

Hill says: "The Kantian moral perspective implicitly contains within it an important, though relatively formal, requirement of respect. In accepting moral constraints as what, ideally, all human beings would agree upon in reasonable, joint deliberations, we are, in a sense, respecting each person as a potential co-legislator of the basic principles we must all live by. The aim is to see that our conduct can be justified to others who are able and willing to take up the moral point of view" (101). Now this requirement of respect goes far beyond the earlier one of "serving as a limit to what we may legitimately do in our efforts to promote the general welfare" (93). The new requirement includes that we "must *listen* to one another . . . be *sincere* . . . and *non-manipulative . . . convince* others . . . *broaden one's knowledge . . . see issues from others' point of view . . . invite criticism . . . acknowledge . . . fallibility*" (104). These requirements of respect impose positive obligations on all reasonable people to do much more than refrain from treating immoral people in inhuman ways. Hill acknowledges that this "is an ideal," but he says that it "makes vivid and brings together important aspects of what moral deliberation may be thought, at its best, to be" (104). This ideal rests on an implicit assumption. Once it is made explicit, it will be seen as untenable, and the absurdity of the ideal will become undeniable.

As a start, let us note that the ideal cannot be achieved. According to Hill, "this ideal 'moral legislation' . . . is supposed to be guided by legislators' mutual commitment to essential features of . . . constitutive aspects of the ideal of living in community with other free, equal, and reasonable moral agents who constrain their personal pursuits by mutually agreed standards" (97). Hill makes clear that "all human beings . . . [are] potential co-legislators" (103) and that the ideal that the *"humanity* of each person is treated by others as an 'end in itself', at least in the 'thin' sense that the 'reasonable will' of each person, along with every other, is what counts as the final authority" (97). One reason why this ideal cannot be achieved is that it is physically impossible for billions of people to come together and listen to one another in the recommended manner.

Let us suppose, then, that what Hill has in mind is not an actual meeting but merely an imagined one that serves as a thought experiment. Suppose that the participants in this thought experiment are thoughtful and articulate and include a Maoist, a shaman, a Shiite, an orthodox Jew, an Eskimo, a Zen master, an Australian Aborigine, and a Sudanese slave-trader. Let us further suppose, what is extremely unlikely, that all these people actually agree that the satisfaction of basic physiological, psychological, and social needs must be guaranteed for all human beings. Their task is to arrive at "mutually agreed standards" that would guide their policies. Who could reasonably suppose that they would come to an agreement? Who could even suppose that they would listen to one another, see the issues from the others' point of view, invite criticism of their own, acknowledge fallibility, and generally proceed in the manner Hill's ideal prescribes?

Hill may say that these people are unlikely to follow the prescriptions of the ideal because the cultural divide between them is too great. Let us, then, suppose instead that the co-legislators are reasonable people from our society: a conservative anti-egalitarian, a Kantian egalitarian, a Protestant fundamentalist, a radical feminist, a libertarian anarchist, a Trotskyite, a Black Muslim, and an animal liberationist. Suppose further that they are willing to deliberate in the ideal manner. Does it now look any the less absurd that they will reach agreement about the standards that should constrain their personal pursuits and guide their policies?

It cries out for an explanation how Hill could think that the outcome of his thought experiment will be that "ideally, all human beings would agree . . . in reasonable, joint deliberations" on the requirement of "respecting each person as a potential co-legislator of the basic principles we must all live by" (101). People who are divided by serious disagreements about basic moral matters may listen to one another, but what they hear will be morally unacceptable to them; they may make an effort to see the issues from the others' point of view, but they will deplore how wrongheaded these others can be; they may invite criticism of their own position, but they will easily meet it; they may acknowledge their own fallibility, but they will see no reason for actual doubt. Hill simply fails to recognize that people with deep and reasonable moral convictions often have basic disagreements with one another. These disagreements are *moral*, so that the parties to them are bound to see one another as advocating what is morally wrong. They will see one another as living and acting in morally objectionable ways, and if they take the trouble to understand the others' point of view, their disagreements will only deepen.

But the reasons for the absurdity of the ideal are even stronger than these. For we have so far considered only moral disagreements that make the ideal so obviously unattainable. People disagree with one another not only about the right moral outlook but also about how important any moral outlook is. Hill assumes that reasonable people assign overriding importance to moral considerations. But many people do not do that. They believe, and have reasons for believing, that their own or their family's well-being, or their cause, or their creative ventures, or their culture, or their country is more important than moral considerations. They believe that it is reasonable that nonmoral considerations should often override moral considerations if they come into conflict. Evil is widespread partly because there are many such people. Hill's ideal will have no appeal to them. And, it must be stressed, they may have reasons for their beliefs and they may be as articulate about them as those who are committed to morality.

These disagreements within and about morality are commonplaces of social life. They falsify Hill's ideal in obvious ways. One cannot help wondering, therefore, how thoughtful people, such as Hill and his fellow Kantians, can accept such a flawed ideal. The answer is that they regard disagreements with the ideal as showing that people are less than fully reasonable. The ideal postulates that the co-legislators must be fully reasonable. If they are, defenders of the ideal assume, they will proceed as the ideal requires. If this assumption were true, the ideal would not be absurd. We must, therefore, consider whether it is true.

12.5   The Optimistic Faith

The assumption in question is the optimistic faith, which holds that human beings are basically inclined toward the good, and only bad political arrangements deter them from living and acting accordingly. This is the assumption presupposed by ideal theories. For what makes a theory ideal is that it constructs some kind of a hypothetical situation that makes it possible to imagine bad political arrangements out of the way. According to ideal theories, if a society is "well-ordered," that is, its political arrangements are good, then there will be "strict compliance," that is, the basic goodness of human nature will shine forth as autonomous people live according to their own conception of the good and do not interfere with others doing likewise. If human beings were basically inclined toward the good, then fully reasonable people would act as ideal theories claim, and if they did not, it would have to be because they were prevented from being fully reasonable by non-ideal conditions.

Rawls, as usual, makes this more explicit than most of his fellow egalitarians. He says that "no race or recognized group of human beings" lacks "the capacity for moral personality," and people who have that capacity "are distinguished by two features: first they are capable of having (and are assumed to have) a conception of their good (as expressed by a rational plan of life); and second they are capable of having (and are assumed to acquire) a sense of justice, a normally effective desire to apply and to act upon the principles of justice." Thus each person has a "fundamental preference . . . for conditions that enable him to frame a mode of life that expresses his nature as a free and equal rational being."[7]

Hill, describing the Kantian view, says something quite similar. "Kant's argument assumes that all 'human beings', or persons with 'humanity', have, at least potentially, the capacity and predisposition to deliberate from a moral perspective and to act accordingly, and Kant apparently had faith that virtually all the (adult) people we are likely to meet, perhaps outside institutions for the insane, in fact have the essential attributes of 'humanity.'" Thus "Kant . . . seemed to accept without much question the predisposition to morality as a basic feature of human nature. He granted that human beings have, in addition, an innate tendency to evil, but even that, as Kant interpreted it, was just a tendency, under temptation, to refuse to follow a moral law that in our hearts we acknowledged as authoritative for us" (106). Hill then asks, "Are there, despite Kant's faith, functioning adult members of our biological species who do not have, even potentially, the capacity for morality?" (107). And his answer is that there is "a strong . . . presumption that, until *proved* otherwise, virtually all the cognitively able and functioning people we meet have at least the *potential* capacity and disposition to engage with others in mutually respectful, reciprocal moral relations" (108). So Hill shares what he calls "Kant's faith" and what we have been calling "the optimistic faith."

The optimistic faith, however, is a fairy tale. There is indeed a strong presumption connected with it, but it is one for rejecting it. For there are excellent reasons against the optimistic faith and no reason for it. To begin with the obvious, the claim that "virtually all the (adult) people we are likely to meet" have "the capacity and predisposition to deliberate from a moral perspective and to act accordingly" (106) is evidence for the sheltered life Kant and his egalitarian followers have lived or are living. They are indeed fortunate if they are unlikely to meet the tens of thousands of Communist and Nazi concentration camp guards and torturers who murdered millions of innocent people; the Red Guards whom Mao set loose upon his unfortunate country; the soldiers of Pol Pot who murdered, often in unspeakably cruel ways, about a quarter of Cambodia's population; the terrorists who deliberately murder, maim, and kidnap innocent people in order to destabilize regimes or get rid of opponents; the drug lords of Central Asia and South America who make immense profit out of ruining the lives of countless people, often children; the dictators and their henchmen in countries such as Iraq, Iran, Uganda, Yugoslavia, Chile, Rwanda, and numerous other places; and similar evildoers. The egalitarians who hold this faith must be oblivious to the history of the twentieth century.

Now it may be claimed in defense of the optimistic faith that although all these people are immoral, they still have "the capacity and predisposition to deliberate from a moral perspective and to act accordingly." But this claim is totally unconvincing for several reasons. First, there is no evidence available for it, and the available evidence—the evil actions of these people—indicates the opposite.

Second, even if the claim were true, it would be insufficient as a defense of the optimistic faith. For it would show merely that there is a predisposition to act morally, but evil actions show that there is also a predisposition to act immorally. These predispositions prompt incompatible actions, and the evil actions show that the predisposition to act immorally is often stronger than the predisposition to act morally. The optimistic faith assumes that the reverse is true.

Third, the optimistic faith also assumes that it is predispositions that are morally important. But why should one think that? Surely, it is much more important what people make of their predispositions. After all, the purpose of political arrangements is to enable people to live together. The actions they perform are much more important from that point of view than their predispositions, which may be undeveloped, poorly developed, developed and misused, incompatible with other capacities, and so forth. The optimistic faith needs to show that under ideal conditions people will act in morally good ways. To show that people have certain predispositions is not enough to show that they actually act on them.

Fourth, what predispositions people have must be inferred from their actions. If morally good actions are counted as evidence for a moral predisposition, then morally evil actions must be counted as evidence for an immoral predisposition. But this is not how defenders of the optimistic faith count them. They count them as evidence for "a tendency, under temptation, to refuse to follow a moral law that in our hearts we acknowledge as authoritative for us" (106). How do defenders of the optimistic faith know what evildoers acknowledge in their hearts? Why not count morally good actions as evidence for a tendency, under temptation, to refuse to follow an immoral law that in our hearts we acknowledge as authoritative for us?

The reasonable interpretation of the evidence, of course, is not that people are dominated by their predisposition to act immorally. What the evidence indicates is that people have both moral and immoral predispositions, and sometimes one, sometimes the other is dominant. People are neither basically good nor basically bad, but basically ambivalent. In that case, however, the assumption that would save ideal theories from absurdity is false. For ideal theories, then, could not take for granted that if people were fully reasonable, they would act in strict compliance with the principles of a well-ordered society. Fully reasonable people may be immoral, if their predisposition to act immorally is dominant. They may just place higher value on their own or their loved ones' well-being, or on their personal projects, or on creating or protecting great works of art, or on the glory of their religion, country, or cause than on "respecting each person as a potential co-legislator of the basic principles we must all live by" (101). Ideal theories fail to recognize this, and that is why they are fairy tales. And the reason why they are unbenign is that they are prevented by this failure from taking seriously the danger that widespread evil presents.

There is one last consideration Hill offers in favor of the optimistic faith. He points out, rightly, that thinking of some people as having no or diminished predisposition for morality has led to horrendous abuses and to causing evil as great as it was meant to condemn. Holy wars, inquisitions, crusades, heresies, witch hunts, and similar horrors were often justified by the supposed moral incapacity of their unfortunate victims. Surely, however, the way to avoid these undeniable evils is not to cultivate the unreasonable optimistic faith but to face evil and do what we reasonably can to oppose it.

12.6 Realistic Politics

The argument has aimed to show that the attempt to derive reasonable policies from an ideal theory rests on an illusion. Reasonable policies must take into account the facts of history, psychology, and politics that characterize particular societies. When practical reason is used to improve the political arrangements of a society, it cannot rely merely on universal, objective, and impersonal considerations; it must rely also on the particularities of the context to which it is applied. Since these particularities vary, there cannot be an ideal theory that would hold for all societies. An ideal theory is impossible even if it aims at the most general level and calls for all human beings merely to respect one another as co-legislators of the political arrangements under which they wish to live. For that aim could be achieved only if the optimistic faith were acceptable and the co-legislators were motivated predominantly by morality. The optimistic faith, however, is unacceptable and dangerous. Unacceptable, because widespread evil and perennial disagreements both within and about morality invalidate it. And dangerous, because it falsely supposes that putting forward an ideal will cope with widespread evil. A reasonable approach to politics must do more than describe what would be good and then hope that it will be sufficient to convert evildoers to morality. It is not sufficient, as history amply shows.

These criticisms of ideal theories notwithstanding, it is thought by many egalitarians that the formulation of an ideal theory is necessary because the improvement of bad political arrangements is impossible without it. They think that both the identification of a political arrangement as bad and the proposal of policies that would make it better presuppose a universal standard that defines what is bad and what would be better. This standard is an ideal theory, and political thought supposedly cannot do without it. As Rawls puts it: "The reason for beginning with ideal theory is that it provides, I believe, the only basis for the systematic grasp of . . . more pressing problems. . . . I shall assume that a deeper understanding can be gained in no other way, and that the nature and aims of a perfectly just society is the fundamental part of the theory of justice."[8] Furthermore, "viewing the theory of justice as a whole, the ideal part presents a conception of a just society that we are to achieve if we can. Existing institutions are to be judged in the light of this conception and held to be unjust to the extent that they depart from it without sufficient reason."[9] This belief is false. Political arrangements can be criticized and improved without reliance on a universal standard and an ideal theory.

It is true that there is a universal consideration that all reasonable policies must take into account: the need to satisfy basic physiological, psychological, and social needs that are the same for all human beings. This, however, is only a minimum requirement. Most political problems concern matters far above the satisfaction of basic needs; choices among policies that satisfy basic needs must be made on other grounds; and coping with serious problems may be important enough to justify ignoring some basic needs. The existence of minimum requirements of human well-being, therefore, cannot be the universal requirement with reference to which the different policies of different societies aiming to cope with different problems could be evaluated.

In closing we shall sketch an alternative to ideal theories and provide reasons for preferring it. The alternative is to begin with where we are, "we" being the members of a society, usually the citizens of a state. The society, like all societies, faces a variety of problems. Substantial numbers of people are dissatisfied with some existing political arrangement; hostile neighbors threaten; scarce resources have to be distributed among competing interests; religious, political, ethnic, regional, economic, and other conflicts need to be adjudicated; the crime rate has to be reduced; the infrastucture must be maintained; present requirements must be balanced against planning for the future; and so forth.

There are usually many possible ways of coping with each problem, but not all are live options because the moral, political, religious, and aesthetic traditions and customs of a society rule out some possibilities as unacceptable to many people. Realistic politics is motivated by the need to cope with the problems a society faces. Its aim is to find a generally acceptable way of coping. And the task of realistic political thought is to weigh the respective importance of the problems and the feasibility of the various ways of coping. But this approach cannot merely focus on the particular problems at hand. It must take into account the overall effect of a policy—of ignoring a problem or coping with it in a certain way—on other problems, on the available resources, on the prevailing traditions and customs, in other words, on the society as a whole.

Realistic politics has a standard for evaluating policies: success in coping with the problems in a way that members of the society find generally acceptable. The proper use of practical reason in such political contexts is to deliberate about and arrive at successful policies. This use of practical reason must be particular because the problems and the acceptable policies are particular. It is the exception, not the rule, that the successful policies of one society can be carried over to another. There is no universal moral ideal, beyond the basic minimum, which would determine for all societies what successful policies would have to be. But that does not mean that in any particular society practical reason could not be used to find and evaluate various policies.

This sketch of realistic politics, in conjunction with the foregoing arguments in this chapter, shows that realistic politics is preferable to the illusion of ideal theories. For realistic politics is reasonable, and ideal theories are not. Furthermore, an ideal theory must eventually prompt policies, and the formulation and evaluation of these policies is possible only by realistic political thinking. Ideal theories, therefore, presuppose realistic politics. If realistic politics is successful, ideal theories are not needed. And if realistic politics is unsuccessful, ideal theories are of no help.

13/

The Illusions of Egalitarianism
vs. the Realities of Politics:
Conclusion

My hope is to . . . [have written] a book that will be useful, at least to those who read it intelligently, and so I thought it sensible to . . . discuss . . . how things are in real life. . . . Many authors have constructed imaginary republics . . . that have never existed and never could; for the gap between how people actually behave and how they ought to behave is so great that anyone who ignores everyday reality in order to live up to an ideal will soon discover he has been taught to destroy himself.

NICCOLÒ MACHIAVELLI, *The Prince*

The criticisms are now complete. They were meant to show that egalitarian liberalism rests on illusions and an unfounded optimistic faith in the basic goodness of human beings. The illusions and the faith symbiotically reinforce each other. They are widely enough held to make egalitarianism the dominant ideology in the West, and at many places elsewhere. Its popularity is due to the moral vision that egalitarian rhetoric has articulated and made attractive with remarkable success. It is a vision of a society in which good and reasonable people cooperate to design and maintain political arrangements that provide equal freedom, rights, and resources, and thereby enable everyone to live according to a wide plurality of different conceptions of a good life. Existing societies, then, are criticized for having unequal political arrangements. The aim of egalitarian politics is to improve these arrangements by making freedom, rights, and resources more equal.

This appears to be an attractive moral vision, partly because it flatters humanity by stressing the human propensity for the good and blaming the evils of history and contemporary life on political arrangements that corrupt human beings against their goodwill and efforts to be reasonable. Who indeed would not want this to be true? But wanting it does not make it so, the flattery is humbug, and the moral vision is the product of wishful thinking that refuses to face the multitude of facts contrary to it. The vision is dangerous because it is meant to be a practical guide to politics, but the policies it prompts ignore crucially relevant facts, and that makes it impossible to cope with the concrete problems that threaten the stability of society. As a result, the problems fester, the danger grows, and realistic policies are decried because they are at odds with the flattering vision.

It is hidden from no one that egalitarian policies in education, welfare, criminal justice, foreign aid, immigration, drugs, and taxation do not work. In America elementary and high schools produce graduates who lack the most basic knowledge and skills. Colleges and universities have largely abandoned the time-honored goal of teaching the classic works that embody the accumulated wisdom of the ages. They pursue instead the political agenda of transforming society in accordance with a radicalized version of the egalitarian vision. The welfare system has produced a dependent underclass that perpetuates itself at an increasing rate. Violent crime and theft are among the highest in the world, but law enforcement is handicapped by rules that protect criminals at the expense of their victims. Billions spent on foreign aid enrich corrupt politicians in distant lands, lead them to demand it as a right while scorning its source, and leave poverty much as it was. Illegal immigrants are allowed to flood the country, become a further drain on the failed systems of education and welfare, and remain ignorant of the language and political life of the surrounding society. Drug addiction is rampant and gives rise to a vast alternative, criminal economy. The tax system is incomprehensible to all but experts, full of loopholes, resented by taxpayers, and designed to penalize the productive and the successful. Yet egalitarians do not acknowledge that the responsibility for this dismal state of affairs lies with failed policies that have been pursued now for several generations. Instead, they attribute their failure to not being egalitarian enough. They propose as a remedy to spend even more in support of the discredited efforts and to get it by taxing even higher those who produce the resources that are wasted by chasing the doomed egalitarian vision.

The way out of this dismal state of affairs is to recognize the illusions for what they are, abandon the optimistic faith, and face the realities of politics. It is suicidal to suppose that the widespread evils that threaten society can be avoided by a policy that aims to provide equal freedom, rights, and resources to good and bad, prudent and imprudent, law-abiding and criminal people. The fact is that the propensity for both good and evil is implicit in human nature, and a society must have policies that encourage the good and curb the evil.

It endangers the possibility of civilized life to hold people responsible for their habitual patterns of evil actions only if they are intentional. The fact is that most evil is non-intentional and a society must protect itself against it by condemning and punishing those who cause it. That they cause it non-intentionally may extenuate the degree of responsibility, condemnation, and punishment to which they are liable, but it is a destructive folly to suppose that it exempts them.

It corrupts justice to use it as an instrument for depriving people who have more of legally acquired property in order to benefit those who have less. The fact is that justice is essentially connected with policies that aim to ensure that people have what they deserve and do not have what they do not deserve.

The claim that the government ought to treat all citizens with equal consideration perverts the elementary requirement of morality to treat good and bad people differently. The fact is that a society cannot long endure unless it rewards and protects its productive members and punishes and curbs depredators, cheaters, and free-riders.

No reasonable person can continue to accept the myth that all human beings have equal worth in light of the great differences in innate capacities and lifelong patterns of action. The fact is that the worth of human beings depends on whether they act on their capacities, whether the capacities they act on are good or evil, and whether their patterns of actions over time contribute to or detract from the betterment of the human condition.

The sentimentality that regards compassion as the basis of morality is indefensible. It demeans its recipients, fails to recognize people's merits and demerits, ignores their individuality in dishing out indiscriminate compassion, and obscures the fundamental difference between those who brought misfortune on themselves and those who suffer through no fault of their own. The fact is that morality often requires treating people justly, as they deserve; blaming them for not doing their jobs or for violating the contracts they have made; and criticizing their culpable failures rather than responding to them with compassion. Compassion is fine when it is morally appropriate, but it often is not, so it cannot be the basis of morality.

The intrusive meddling that endeavors to lay guilt on people because they have comforts when others in faraway countries live in poverty is nothing but rampant moralizing. It gives a bad name to morality and turns people away from it. The fact is that moral responsibility begins with one's family, friends, work, neighbors, and fellow citizens. As connections become more tenuous, so responsibility weakens. The more remote people are, the harder it is know whether their plight is their own making and whether one's help would be wasted. It is far more realistic, therefore, to discharge one's clear and well-understood responsibilities close to home.

The attempt to privilege equal freedom as the value that should override any other value that conflicts with it shares the fatal defect of all ideologies. They all hold that some one or few values should always take precedence, but they take for granted that a great many other values are already in place. The fact is that all values presuppose other values. Values form a system of interdependent and mutually reinforcing parts. It is a symptom of narrow understanding and lack of perspective to focus on one element in this complex system and inflate its importance at the expense of others. Realistic politics recognizes that the system of values must be defended as a whole. If in a particular period, place, and context its defense requires favoring one value over others, realistic politics will not make the mistake of supposing that this will continue to be reasonable in another period, place, and context. Freedom is certainly valuable, but so is peace, prosperity, order, security, civility, and so forth. All ideologies are committed to the irremediably bad judgment of stressing one or a few values and forgetting about the rest.

To attempt to combine political impartiality toward all conceptions of the good with personal commitment to a particular conception is to chase a psychological impossibility. Conceptions of the good cannot be compartmentalized in this way. Those who try to do it are driven to chronic double-mindedness in which they still have to act, but whatever they end up doing will compromise their integrity and wholeheartedness. The fact is that realistic politics must be committed to some substantive conception of the good and cannot remain impartial to all conceptions. What is important is that the commitments be made to a reasonable conception that can count on the allegiance of many people living in a particular society.

The question of what conception is reasonable leads directly to the question of what is within and outside the limits of toleration. The rhetoric of egalitarian liberalism has systematically claimed for itself the honor of being the paragon of toleration, but this is no more than a hypocritical pretense. Egalitarians favor toleration of a very wide range of sexual practices because they regard them as harmless, but they do not favor toleration of a similarly wide range of attitudes toward religion, the economy, morality, or indeed sexual practices, which are basically at odds with their own. Anyone can claim to be the paragon of this kind of toleration. Realistic politics must provide a principled way of deciding what should and should not be tolerated. Violation of the conventions that protect the universal conditions of all good lives should not be tolerated. Nor should there be toleration of attempts to destroy the system of values that gives moral identity to a society, although attempts to change parts of the system should not only be tolerated but welcomed. The widest scope of toleration should be provided in the personal realm that exists within the limits set by the universal requirements of all good lives and the social requirement of protecting the system of values that constitutes moral identity.

Finally, the supposition that the political problems of a society require solutions derived from an ideal theory must be seen as useless and dangerous. For an ideal theory by its very nature ignores the concrete circumstances of particular societies and aims to impose on them a set of abstract principles said to be warranted by the very nature of reason. But the practical use of reason cannot be abstract, and attention to the particular is necessary for a reasonable approach to political problems. Realistic politics, therefore, will start with the problems a society faces and endeavor to cope with them in ways that have proved successful in the past, given the history, traditions, and customs of a particular society.

The motivation for holding these illusions and ignoring political realities is the equally flawed optimistic faith in the basic goodness of human beings. The facts are ignored because the faith implies that they are superficial appearances that mislead about the fundamental realities of politics. The illusions are sustained because the faith implies that only halfhearted commitment to egalitarian policies prevents them from succeeding. The failure of the policies is thus always blamed on the failures of individuals to pursue them with sufficient determination.

The source of this optimistic faith is a complex emotion that combines the wish for human well-being, pity for suffering, and hope for a better world. The emotion can be a force for the good, but egalitarians have encouraged it to grow into a ruling passion, and they have based on it an ideology that systematically falsifies the facts. Its deepest flaw is the doomed effort to make the world conform to how egalitarians feel about it rather than, as reason dictates, make their feelings conform to how the world is.

The aim of the argument has been to expose the falseness of the illusions and the unreasonableness of the faith on which egalitarianism rests. This aim has been critical, not the constructive proposal of an alternative. But in the course of the argument there have emerged some considerations that should guide the formulation of alternative policies. By way of a conclusion, stated briefly without supporting arguments and qualifications, here they are:

(1) Curbing evil is a means to pursuing the good and has priority over it.

(2) People's primary responsibility is for their actions, not intentions. The lack of intention may lessen condemnation and punishment but does not provide exemption from responsibility.

(3) Justice consists in people getting what they deserve and not getting what they do not deserve.

(4) Moral worth depends on moral merit, and both are possessed unequally.

(5) Responsibility toward others weakens as connections become more remote.

(6) Reasonable politics is particular, context-sensitive, and not impartial.

(7) There is no value that is always more important than any other value that conflicts with it.

(8) Protection of what is necessary for the stability of society must be combined with toleration of transgressions against what is not.

(9) The aim of politics is to cope with specific problems, not to realize an ideal.

Notes

1. The Politics of Illusions: Introduction

1. Jean-Jacques Rousseau, *Letter to Beaumont*, in *Oeuvres complètes*, 5 vols. (Paris: Gallimard, 1959–95), 935. The translation is Timothy O'Hagan's in *Rousseau* (London: Routledge, 1999), 15.

2. Immanuel Kant, *Religion within the Bounds of Reason Alone*, trans. Theodore M. Greene and Hoyt H. Hudson (New York: Harper & Row, 1960), 39, 31.

3. John Stuart Mill, *Utilitarianism* (Indianapolis: Hackett, 1979), chap. 3, 31–32.

4. John Rawls, *A Theory of Justice* (Cambridge: Harvard University Press, 1971), 506.

5. Ibid., 561.

6. Ibid., 476.

7. Ibid., 245.

8. John Maynard Keynes, *Two Memoirs* (New York: Augustus M. Kelley, 1949), 99–103.

9. John Kekes, *A Case for Conservatism* (Ithaca: Cornell University Press, 1998).

2. The Inconsistency of Aims

1. See, e.g., Maurice Cranston, "Liberalism," in *The Encyclopedia of Philosophy*, 8 vols., ed. Paul Edwards (New York: Macmillan, 1967), 4:461; Ronald Dworkin, *A Matter of Principle* (Cambridge: Harvard University Press, 1985), 183; Richard E. Flathman, *Toward a Liberalism* (Ithaca: Cornell University Press, 1989), 2; Joseph Raz, *The Morality of Freedom* (Oxford: Clarendon Press, 1986), 1; Alan Ryan, "Liberalism," in *A Companion to Contemporary Political Philosophy*, ed. Robert E. Goodin and Phillip Pettit (Oxford: Blackwell, 1993), 291; and Jeremy Waldron, "The Theoretical Foundations of Liberalism," *Philosophical Quarterly* 37 (1987): 127.

2. Isaiah Berlin, "Two Concepts of Liberty," in *Four Essays on Liberty* (Oxford: Oxford University Press, 1969), 131.

3. In what is perhaps the dominant contemporary version of liberal egalitarianism, this conception of good life is thought of in terms of autonomy. "The core of this tradition is an insistence that the forms of social life be rooted in the self-conscious value affirmations of autonomous individuals." Bruce A. Ackerman, *Social Justice and the Liberal State* (New Haven: Yale University Press, 1980), 196. "The most important task for which autonomy has been harnessed in contemporary political philosophy is to argue for a certain ideal of the liberal state. . . . The root idea is that the state must recognize and acknowledge the autonomy of persons." Gerald Dworkin, "Autonomy," in *A Companion to Contemporary Political Philosophy*, 361. "The liberal individual

is fully rational, where rationality embraces both autonomy and the capacity to choose among possible actions on the basis of one's conception of the good as determined by one's reflective preferences. . . . As an autonomous being, the liberal individual is aware of the reflective process by which her later selves emerge from her present self, so that her preferences are modified, not in a random or uncontrolled way, but in the light of her own experiences and understanding." David Gauthier, *Morals by Agreement* (Oxford: Clarendon Press, 1986), 346. "Acting autonomously is acting from principles that we would consent to as free and equal rational beings. . . . They are the principles that we would want everyone (including ourselves) to follow were we to take up together the appropriate general point of view. The original position defines this perspective." John Rawls, *A Theory of Justice* (Cambridge: Harvard University Press, 1971), 516; see also Rawls's *Political Liberalism* (New York: Columbia University Press, 1993), 72. "One common strand in liberal thought regards the promotion and protection of personal autonomy as the core of the liberal concern." Raz, *Morality of Freedom*, 203. "The essence [of liberalism] is that individuals are self-creating, that no single good defines successful self-creation, and that taking responsibility for one's life and making of it what one can is itself part of the good life." Ryan, "Liberalism," 304.

For detailed accounts of autonomy, see John Christman, ed., *The Inner Citadel* (New York: Oxford University Press, 1992); Gerald Dworkin, *The Theory and Practice of Autonomy* (Cambridge: Cambridge University Press, 1988); and Lawrence Haworth, *Autonomy* (New Haven: Yale University Press, 1986).

4. Rawls, *Theory of Justice*, 245.

5. Ibid., 252.

6. Ronald Dworkin, "Liberalism," in *Matter of Principle*, and *Sovereign Virtue: The Theory and Practice of Equality* (Cambridge: Harvard University Press, 2000).

7. Cranston, "Liberalism"; Richard E. Flathman, "Liberalism," in *Encyclopedia of Ethics*, 2d ed., ed. Lawrence C. Becker and Charlotte B. Becker (New York: Routledge, 2001); Ryan, "Liberalism"; Waldron, "Theoretical Foundations of Liberalism."

8. E.g., Thomas Nagel, *Mortal Questions* (New York: Cambridge University Press, 1979) and *Equality and Partiality* (New York: Oxford University Press, 1991).

9. Rawls, *Theory of Justice*, 439.

10. Raz, *Morality of Freedom*, e.g., 380–84.

11. Stuart Hampshire, *Innocence and Experience* (London: Allen Lane, 1989), 67, 77.

12. Ibid., 67.

13. Ibid., 77.

14. Annette Baier, "Secular Faith," in *Postures of Mind* (Minneapolis: University of Minnesota Press, 1985).

15. David Hume, *A Treatise of Human Nature* (Oxford: Clarendon Press, 1960), 535.

16. Baier, "Secular Faith," 293–95.

17. Ibid., 307. Emphasis in original.

18. Jonathan Glover, *Humanity: A Moral History of the Twentieth Century* (New Haven: Yale University Press, 2000). Quotations from this work are cited directly in the text by page number.

19. Stuart Hampshire, *Justice Is Conflict* (Princeton: Princeton University Press, 2000), ix.

20. Hampshire, *Innocence and Experience*, 8.

21. Ibid., 90.

22. Ibid., 107.

23. Ibid., 186.

24. Judith Shklar, "The Liberalism of Fear," in *Liberalism and the Moral Life*, ed. Nancy Rosenbaum (Cambridge: Harvard University Press, 1989), 21.

25. Ibid., 29, 30.

26. See notes 6–10 above.

3. The Denial of Responsibility

1. Albert Hofstadter, *Reflections on Evil* (Lawrence: University Press of Kansas, 1973), 17.

2. Ibid., 5–6, 8, 9, 20, 7.

3. Stanley Benn, "Wickedness," *Ethics* 95 (1985): 796.

4. Ibid., 803, 798, 799.

5. Gary Watson, "Responsibility and the Limits of Evil," in *Responsibility, Character, and the Emotions*, ed. Ferdinand Schoeman (Cambridge: Cambridge University Press, 1987), 275.

6. Ibid., 276.

7. Susan Wolf, "Asymmetrical Freedom" in *Moral Responsibility*, ed. John M. Fischer (Ithaca: Cornell University Press, 1986), 233.

8. Susan Wolf, *Freedom within Reason* (New York: Oxford University Press, 1991), 79.

9. Ibid., 43.

4. The Corruption of Justice

1. John Rawls, *A Theory of Justice* (Cambridge: Harvard University Press, 1971) and *Political Liberalism* (New York: Columbia University Press, 1993). The second book introduces changes to the version presented in the first book, but for present purposes these changes are irrelevant. Some of Rawls's critics are John Charvet, *A Critique of Freedom and Equality* (Cambridge: Cambridge University Press, 1981); Antony Flew, *The Politics of Procrustes* (Buffalo: Prometheus Books, 1981); Harry G. Frankfurt, "Equality as a Moral Ideal," in *The Importance of What We Care About* (Cambridge: Cambridge University Press, 1988), and "Equality and Respect," in *Necessity, Volition, and Love* (Cambridge: Cambridge University Press, 1999); Friedrich A. Hayek, *The Mirage of Social Justice* (Chicago: University of Chicago Press, 1976); John Kekes, *Against Liberalism* (Ithaca: Cornell University Press, 1997); J. R. Lucas, "Against Equality," *Philosophy* 40 (1965): 296–307, and "Against Equality Again," *Philosophy* 42 (1967): 255–80; Wallace Matson, "What Rawls Calls Justice," *Occasional Review* 89 (1979): 45–57, and "Justice: A Funeral Oration," *Social Philosophy and Policy* 1 (1983): 94–113; David Miller, *Principles of Social Justice* (Cambridge: Harvard University Press, 1999); Margaret Moore, *Foundations of Liberalism* (Oxford: Clarendon Press, 1993); Jan Narveson, *Respecting Persons in Theory and Practice* (Lanham, Md.: Rowman & Littlefield, 2002); Robert Nozick, *Anarchy, State, and Utopia* (New York: Basic Books, 1974); Louis Pojman, "A Critique of Contemporary Egalitarianism," *Faith and Philosophy* 8 (1991): 481–504; and Joseph Raz, *The Morality of Freedom* (Oxford: Clarendon Press, 1986).

2. Aristotle, *Nicomachean Ethics*, trans. W. D. Ross, rev. J. O. Urmson, in *The Complete Works of Aristotle*, ed. Jonathan Barnes (Princeton: Princeton University Press, 1984), especially 1131a10–25.

3. Rawls, *Theory of Justice*, 310. Further quotations from this work are cited directly in the text by page number.

4. Ronald Dworkin, *Sovereign Virtue: The Theory and Practice of Equality* (Cambridge: Harvard University Press, 2000), 5.

5. Miller, *Principles of Social Justice*, chap. 4.

6. Ibid., 81.

7. The results have been collected and summarized in Norman Frohlich and Joseph Oppenheimer, *Choosing Justice: An Experimental Approach to Ethical Theory* (Berkeley: University of California Press, 1992).

8. The analysis is indebted to Joel Feinberg, "Justice and Personal Desert," in *Nomos VI: Justice* (New York: Atherton Press, 1963); William A. Galston, *Justice and the Human Good* (Chicago: University of Chicago Press, 1980); David Miller, *Social Justice* (Oxford: Clarendon Press, 1976); and especially George Sher, *Desert* (Princeton: Princeton University Press, 1987).

9. See Rawls, *Theory of Justice*, 3, and Nozick, *Anarchy, State, and Utopia*, 228.

10. Rawls, *Theory of Justice*, 504–12.

11. Friedrich A. Hayek, *The Constitution of Liberty* (Chicago: University of Chicago Press, 1960), chap. 6.

5. The Groundlessness of Egalitarianism

1. "Every nation of the world is divided into haves and have-nots. . . . The gap . . . is enormous. Confronting these disparities, the egalitarian holds that it would be a morally better state of affairs if everyone enjoyed the same level of social and economic benefits." Richard J. Arneson, "Equality," in *A Companion to Contemporary Political Philosophy*, ed. Robert Goodin and Phillip Pettit (Oxford: Blackwell, 1993), 489. "From the standpoint of politics, the interests of the members of the community matter, and matter equally." Ronald Dworkin, "In Defense of Equality," *Social Philosophy and Policy* 1 (1983): 24. "Everyone matters just as much as everyone else. It is appalling that the most effective social systems we have been able to devise permit . . . material inequalities." Thomas Nagel, *Equality and Partiality* (New York: Oxford University Press, 1991), 64. "Being egalitarian in some significant way relates to the need to have equal concern, at some level, for all persons involved." Amartya Sen, *Inequality Reexamined* (Cambridge: Harvard University Press, 1992), ix. "A basic principle of equality [is] the principle of equal consideration of interests. The essence of the principle of equal consideration of interests is that we give equal weight in our moral deliberations to the like interests of all those affected by our actions." Peter Singer, *Practical Ethics*, 2d ed. (Cambridge: Cambridge University Press, 1993), 21. "We want equalization of benefits . . . [because] in all cases where human beings are capable of enjoying the same goods, we feel that the intrinsic value of the enjoyment is the same. . . . We hold that . . . *one man's well-being is as valuable as any other's.*" Gregory Vlastos, "Justice and Equality," in *Social Justice*, ed. Richard B. Brandt (Englewood Cliffs, N.J.: Prentice-Hall, 1962), 50–51.

2. The Institute for Research on Poverty at the University of Wisconsin-Madison, designated a National Poverty Research Center by the U.S. Department of Health and Human Services, reports that in 1998 12.7 percent of the U.S. population lived in poverty.

3. "What makes a system egalitarian is the priority it gives to the claims of those . . . at the bottom. . . . Each individual with a more urgent claim has priority . . . over each individual with a less urgent claim." Thomas Nagel, "Equality," in *Mortal Questions* (Cambridge: Cambridge University Press, 1979), 118. "We can express a more general principle as follows: . . . first, maximize the welfare of the worst off . . . second, for equal welfare of the second worst-off . . . and so on until . . . the equal welfare of all the preceding." John Rawls, *A Theory of Justice* (Cambridge: Harvard University Press, 1971), 82–83.

4. The passages are from Ronald Dworkin, *Sovereign Virtue: The Theory and Practice of Equality* (Cambridge: Harvard University Press, 2000), 1; Will Kymlicka, *Contemporary Political Philosophy* (Oxford: Clarendon Press, 1990), 5; Singer, *Practical Ethics*, 16; Vlastos, "Justice and Equality," 51; Bernard Williams, "Philosophy as a Humanistic Discipline," *Philosophy* 75 (2000): 492.

5. A partial list of such critics is John Charvet, *A Critique of Freedom and Equality* (Cambridge: Cambridge University Press, 1981); Antony Flew, *The Politics of Procrustes* (Buffalo: Prometheus Books, 1981); Harry G. Frankfurt, "Equality as a Moral Ideal," in *The Importance of What We Care About* (Cambridge: Cambridge University Press, 1988), and "Equality and Respect," in *Necessity, Volition, and Love* (Cambridge: Cambridge University Press, 1999); Friedrich A. Hayek, *The Constitution of Liberty* (Chicago: University of Chicago Press, 1960); John Kekes, *Against Liberalism* (Ithaca: Cornell University Press, 1997); J. R. Lucas, "Against Equality," *Philosophy* 40 (1965): 296–307, and "Against Equality Again," *Philosophy* 42 (1967): 255–80; Alasdair MacIntyre, *After Virtue* (Notre

Dame: University of Notre Dame Press, 1984); Wallace Matson, "What Rawls Calls Justice," *Occasional Review* 89 (1978): 45–57, and "Justice: A Funeral Oration," *Social Philosophy and Policy* 1 (1983): 94–113; Jan Narveson, *Respecting Persons in Theory and Practice* (Lanham, Md.: Rowman & Littlefield, 2002); Louis P. Pojman, "A Critique of Contemporary Egalitarianism," *Faith and Philosophy* 8 (1991): 481–504; and George Sher, *Desert* (Princeton: Princeton University Press, 1987).

6. Richard J. Arneson, "What, If Anything, Renders All Humans Morally Equal?" in *Singer and His Critics*, ed. Dale Jamieson (Oxford: Blackwell, 1999), 103.

7. Dworkin, *Sovereign Virtue*, 130.

8. Ronald Dworkin, "Equality—An Exchange," *TLS* (December 1, 2000), 16.

9. Will Kymlicka, *Liberalism, Community, and Culture* (Oxford: Clarendon Press, 1989), 40.

10. Nagel, *Equality and Partiality*, 20.

11. Arneson, "All Humans Morally Equal?" 126

12. Brian Barry, "Equality," in *Encyclopedia of Ethics*, ed. Lawrence C. Becker and Charlotte B. Becker (New York: Garland, 1992), 324.

13. Isaiah Berlin, "Equality," in *Concepts and Categories*, ed. Henry Hardy (London: Hogarth, 1978), 102.

14. Joel Feinberg, *Social Philosophy* (Englewood Cliffs, N.J.: Prentice-Hall, 1973), 94.

15. Will Kymlicka, *Contemporary Political Philosophy* (Oxford: Clarendon Press, 1990), 4–5.

16. Nagel, *Mortal Questions*, 108.

17. Ibid., 112.

18. Nagel, *Equality and Partiality*, 5.

19. Rawls, *Theory of Justice*, 507 and 509.

20. Larry Temkin, *Inequality* (Oxford: Oxford University Press, 1993), 5–6.

21. John Stuart Mill, *On Liberty* (Indianapolis: Hackett, 1978), 51.

22. Dworkin, *Sovereign Virtue*, 117–18. Further quotations from this work are cited directly in the text by page number.

23. Rawls, *Theory of Justice*, 311–12.

24. Ibid., 312.

25. Rawls, *Theory of Justice*, 3.

26. Ronald Dworkin, "Rights and Justice," in *Taking Rights Seriously* (Cambridge: Harvard University Press, 1977), 182; Kymlicka, *Contemporary Political Theory*, 5; Nagel, *Equality and Partiality*, 64–65.

27. Frankfurt, "Equality as a Moral Ideal," 134–35.

28. Nagel, *Equality and Partiality*, 28.

6. The Myth of Equality

1. John Stuart Mill, *The Subjection of Women* (Arlington Heights, Ill.: AHM, 1980), 1.

2. For a dissenting egalitarian argument, see Gerald A. Cohen, *If You're an Egalitarian, How Come You're So Rich?* (Cambridge: Harvard University Press, 2000), chap. 9.

3. Ronald Dworkin, *Sovereign Virtue: The Theory and Practice of Equality* (Cambridge: Harvard University Press, 2000), 11.

4. Gregory Vlastos, "Justice and Equality," in *Social Justice*, ed. Richard B. Brandt (Englewood Cliffs, N.J.: Prentice-Hall, 1962), 45. Further quotations from this work are cited directly in the text by page number.

5. Elliott Mossman, ed. and trans., *The Correspondence of Boris Pasternak and Olga Friedenberg, 1910–1954* (New York: Harcourt, 1982), 303–4.

6. David Hume, *A Treatise of Human Nature* (Oxford: Clarendon Press, 1960), 535.

7. John Rawls, *A Theory of Justice* (Cambridge: Harvard University Press, 1971), 505.

8. See Richard J. Arneson, "What, if Anything, Renders All Humans Morally Equal?" in *Singer and His Critics*, ed. Dale Jamieson (Oxford: Blackwell, 1999), 103–28.

9. Ibid., 126.

10. Rawls, *Theory of Justice*, 104, 102.

11. Ibid., 504, 505, 506, 507.

12. Rawls, *Theory of Justice*, 507.

13. Thomas E. Hill, Jr., in "Must Respect Be Earned?" in *Respect, Pluralism, and Justice* (New York: Oxford University Press, 2000), offers a Kantian defense of equal worth. Of the four objections to equal worth, the last three apply to Hill's argument, which will be considered further in chap. 12.

7. The Tyranny of Do-Gooders

1. Lawrence A. Blum, "Compassion," in *Moral Perception and Particularity* (New York: Cambridge University Press, 1994), 181.

2. Some others who share this view are Lawrence A. Blum in *Friendship, Altruism, and Morality* (London: Routledge, 1980) and *Moral Perception and Particularity;* Michael Slote in *Morals from Motives* (New York: Oxford University Press, 2001); and Laurence Thomas in *Living Morally* (Philadelphia: Temple University Press, 1989); as well as various feminists advocating what has come to be called a morality of caring.

3. Martha Nussbaum, *Upheavals of Thought* (Cambridge: Cambridge University Press, 2001), 309.

4. Martha Nussbaum, "Aristotelian Social Democracy," in *Liberalism and the Good*, ed. R. Bruce Douglass, Gerald M. Mara, and Henry S. Richardson (New York: Routledge, 1990), 203–52; see 240–42.

5. Ibid., 217.

6. Ibid., 206.

7. Nussbaum, *Upheavals of Thought*, 416. Further quotations from this work are cited directly in the text by page number.

8. Nussbaum, "Aristotelian Social Democracy," 226.

9. Ibid., 227.

10. Ibid., 238.

11. Ibid.

12. Nussbaum, "Aristotelian Social Democracy," 214.

13. John Stuart Mill, *On Liberty* (Indianapolis: Bobbs-Merrill, 1956), 16–17.

14. Ibid., 93.

15. Aristotle, *Nicomachean Ethics*, trans. W. D. Ross, rev. J. O. Urmson, in *The Complete Works of Aristotle*, ed. Jonathan Barnes (Princeton: Princeton University Press, 1984), 1109b23–29, 1106b29–35.

16. See *Upheavals of Thought*, 392, 403, and 401.

17. Nussbaum, "Aristotelian Social Democracy," 216.

8. The Menace of Moralism

1. Peter Singer, *Practical Ethics* (Cambridge: Cambridge University Press, 1993), 2d ed., 232.

2. According to the Institute for Research on Poverty, in 1998 12.7 percent of the U.S. population lived in poverty.

3. Singer, *Practical Ethics*, 222.

4. Ibid.

5. Ibid.

6. Ibid., 224.

7. Peter Singer, *Writings on an Ethical Life* (New York: HarperCollins, 2000), 110.

8. Ibid., 111.

9. Singer, *Practical Ethics*, 229, 230.

10. Ibid., 229.

11. Ibid., 21.

12. Ibid., 24.

13. See Harry G. Frankfurt, "Equality as a Moral Ideal," in *The Importance of What We Care About* (New York: Cambridge University Press, 1988).

14. Singer, *Practical Ethics*, 11, 12.

15. Ibid., 12, 13, 14.

16. Singer, *Writings on an Ethical Life*, 242.

17. Ibid., 243.

18. Ibid., 270.

19. Ibid., 271.

20. John Stuart Mill, *On Liberty* (Indianapolis: Hackett, 1978), 5–6.

21. Singer, *Practical Ethics*, 235.

22. Singer, *Writings on an Ethical Life*, 115.

23. Ibid.

24. Singer, *Practical Ethics*, 241.

25. Ibid., 238.

26. Ibid., 241.

27. "About 62 percent of the budget . . . was allocated to social spending in fiscal 1996. Among the programs funded are Social Security, Medicare, Medicaid, various other health programs, education and training, social services, veterans' programs, unemployment insurance, and welfare." Bruce Wetterau, *Desk Reference on the Federal Budget* (Washington, D.C.: Congressional Quarterly, 1998), 117.

9. The Ideology of Freedom

1. See Judith Shklar, "The Liberalism of Fear," in *Liberalism and the Moral Life*, ed. Nancy L. Rosenbaum (Cambridge: Harvard University Press, 1989); Robert Nozick, *Anarchy, State, and Utopia* (New York: Basic Books, 1974); and Joseph Raz, *The Morality of Freedom* (Oxford: Clarendon Press, 1986).

2. Shklar, "Liberalism of Fear," 21.

3. Raz, *Morality of Freedom*, 2. Further quotations from this work are cited directly in the text by page number.

4. John L. Mackie, "Can There Be a Right-Based Moral Theory?" *Midwest Studies in Philosophy* 3 (1978): 355.

5. John Rawls, *A Theory of Justice* (Cambridge: Harvard University Press, 1971), 3.

6. Ronald Dworkin, *Sovereign Virtue: The Theory and Practice of Equality* (Cambridge: Harvard University Press, 2000), 1.

7. Peter Singer, *Writings on an Ethical Life* (New York: HarperCollins, 2000), 16.

8. Martha Nussbaum, *Upheavals of Thought* (Cambridge: Cambridge University Press, 2001), 392.

9. E.g., by Michael Oakeshott in *Rationalism in Politics*, ed. Timothy Fuller (Indianapolis: Liberty Press, 1991); Karl R. Popper, *The Open Society and Its Enemies* (London: Routledge, 1945); and Edward Shils, *The Virtue of Civility*, ed. Steven Grosby (Indianapolis: Liberty Press, 1997). Oakeshott, Popper, and Shils continue a tradition of thought in which some of their predecessors are Montaigne, Hume, Tocqueville, and Max Weber.

10. Ronald Dworkin, *Taking Rights Seriously* (Cambridge: Harvard University Press, 1977), 171.

11. For such an account, see John Kekes, *The Morality of Pluralism* (Princeton: Princeton University Press, 1993) and *A Case for Conservatism* (Ithaca: Cornell University Press, 1998).

10. The Burden of Double-Mindedness

1. See, for instance, Bruce Ackerman, *Social Justice and the Liberal State* (New Haven: Yale University Press, 1980); Ronald Dworkin, "Liberalism," in *A Matter of*

Principle (Cambridge: Harvard University Press, 1985); and John Rawls, *A Theory of Justice* (Cambridge: Harvard University Press, 1971).

2. Jeremy Waldron, "Theoretical Foundations of Liberalism," *Philosophical Quarterly* 37 (1987): 127–50.

3. Thomas M. Scanlon, *What We Owe to Each Other* (Cambridge: Harvard University Press, 1998).

4. Ronald Dworkin, "In Defense of Equality," *Social Philosophy and Policy* 1 (1983): 24; Thomas Nagel, "Equality," in *Mortal Questions* (Cambridge: Cambridge University Press, 1979), 112; Gregory Vlastos, "Justice and Equality," in *Social Justice,* ed. Richard B. Brandt (Englewood Cliffs: Prentice-Hall, 1962), 43.

5. Nonperfectionist egalitarianism has been criticized on moral and political grounds by many people. See, e.g., Joseph Raz, *The Morality of Freedom* (Oxford: Clarendon Press, 1986), and George Sher, *Beyond Neutrality* (Cambridge: Cambridge University Press, 1997). The present criticism rests on psychological grounds. It aims to show that in a nonperfectionist society there would be unavoidable psychological obstacles to good lives.

6. Thomas Nagel, *Equality and Partiality* (New York: Oxford University Press, 1991), 11.

7. Dworkin, "In Defense of Equality," 24; Nagel, "Equality," 112; Vlastos, "Justice and Equality," 43.

8. Nagel, "Equality," 112.

9. Rawls, *Theory of Justice*, 587.

10. Nagel, *Equality and Partiality*, 14. For a suggestive criticism of Nagel's view from the left, see Gerald A. Cohen, *If You're an Egalitarian, How Come You're So Rich?* (Cambridge: Harvard University Press, 2000).

11. Thomas Nagel, *The View from Nowhere* (New York: Oxford University Press, 1986), 197.

12. Ibid., 199.

13. Ibid.

14. This account is based on Nagel, *View from Nowhere*, chap. 10.

15. Nagel, *View from Nowhere*, 203.

16. Nagel, "Equality," 108.

17. Nagel, "Moral Conflict and Political Legitimacy," *Philosophy and Public Affairs* 16 (1987): 229.

18. Nagel, *Equality and Partiality*, 163 n. 49.

19. Nagel, *View from Nowhere*, 3, 8, 10, 12, 205.

20. Nagel, *Equality and Partiality*, 5.

11. The Rhetoric of Toleration

1. Ronald Dworkin, *Sovereign Virtue: The Theory and Practice of Equality* (Cambridge: Harvard University Press, 2000), 211.

2. Charles Larmore, *Patterns of Moral Complexity* (New York: Cambridge University Press, 1987), 23.

3. John Rawls, *Political Liberalism* (New York: Columbia University Press, 1993), xxv.

4. Patrick Devlin, "Morals and the Criminal Law," in *The Enforcement of Morals* (London: Oxford University Press, 1968).

5. Ibid., 13.

6. Ronald Dworkin, "Liberty and Moralism," in *Taking Rights Seriously* (Cambridge: Harvard University Press, 1977), 246.

7. Herbert L. A. Hart, "Social Solidarity and the Enforcement of Morality," *University of Chicago Law Review* 55 (1967): 2.

8. Herbert L. A. Hart, *The Morality of the Criminal Law* (London: Oxford University Press, 1965), 41.

9. Graham Hughes, "Morals and the Criminal Law," *Yale Law Journal* 71 (1961–62): 662.

10. Richard Wollheim, "Crime, Sin, and Mr. Justice Devlin," *Encounter* (November 1959): 39.

11. See Basil Mitchell, *Law, Morality, and Religion in a Secular Society* (Oxford: Oxford University Press, 1968); Simon Lee, *Law and Morals* (Oxford: Oxford University Press, 1986); and Robert P. George, *Making Men Moral* (Oxford: Clarendon Press, 1993), chap. 2.

12. Ronald Dworkin, "Liberalism," in *A Matter of Principle* (Cambridge: Harvard University Press, 1985), 187.

13. Dworkin, *Sovereign Virtue*, 1, 3.

14. Thomas Nagel, *Equality and Partiality* (New York: Oxford University Press, 1991), 74, 64, 20.

15. John Rawls, *A Theory of Justice* (Cambridge: Harvard University Press, 1971), 3, 246.

16. John Rawls, *The Law of Peoples* (Cambridge: Harvard University Press, 1999), 106.

17. Susan Mendus, "Toleration," in *Encyclopedia of Ethics*, 2d ed., ed. Lawrence C. Becker and Charlotte B. Becker (New York: Routledge, 2001).

18. Maurice Cranston, "Toleration," in *Encyclopedia of Philosophy*, ed. Paul Edwards (New York: Macmillan, 1967).

19. Rawls, *Political Liberalism*, xviii.

20. Dworkin, *Sovereign Virtue*, 1, 3.

21. Nagel, *Equality and Partiality*, 11.

22. Rawls, *Political Liberalism*, 5.

23. Apocrypha, Maccabees 2, 6:18.

24. As cited in notes 6, 7, 9, and 10.

12. The Politics of Fairy Tales

1. John Rawls, *A Theory of Justice* (Cambridge: Harvard University Press, 1971), 9, 8.

2. Ibid., 246.

3. Jeremy Waldron, "Theoretical Foundations of Liberalism," *Philosophical Quarterly* 37 (1987): 127–50.

4. Thomas M. Scanlon, *What We Owe to Each Other* (Cambridge: Harvard University Press, 1998).

5. David Gauthier, *Morals by Agreement* (Oxford: Clarendon Press, 1986); Jürgen Habermas, *The Theory of Communicative Action* 2 vols., trans. Thomas McCarthy (Boston: Beacon Press, 1984, 1987); R. M. Hare, *Freedom and Reason* (Oxford: Clarendon Press, 1963) and *Moral Thinking* (Oxford: Clarendon Press, 1981); Christine M. Korsgaard, *Creating the Kingdom of Ends* (Cambridge: Cambridge University Press, 1996); and J. Donald Moon, *Constructing Community* (Princeton: Princeton University Press, 1993).

6. Thomas E. Hill, Jr., "Must Respect Be Earned?" in *Respect, Pluralism, and Justice* (New York: Oxford University Press, 2000), 87–118. Quotations from this work are cited directly in the text by page number; all emphasis is original.

7. Rawls, *Theory of Justice*, 506, 505, 561.

8. Rawls, *Theory of Justice*, 9.

9. Ibid., 246.

Works Cited

Ackerman, Bruce. *Social Justice and the Liberal State*. New Haven: Yale University Press, 1980.

Aristotle. *Nicomachean Ethics*. Translated by W. D. Ross, revised by J. O. Urmson. In *The Complete Works of Aristotle*, edited by Jonathan Barnes. Princeton: Princeton University Press, 1984.

Arneson, Richard J. "Equality." In *A Companion to Contemporary Political Philosophy*, edited by Robert Goodin and Phillip Pettit. Oxford: Blackwell, 1993.

——. "What, If Anything, Renders All Humans Morally Equal?" In *Singer and His Critics*, edited by Dale Jamieson. Oxford: Blackwell, 1999.

Baier, Annette. *Postures of Mind*. Minneapolis: University of Minnesota Press, 1985.

Barry, Brian. "Equality." In *Encyclopedia of Ethics*, edited by Lawrence C. Becker and Charlotte B. Becker. New York: Garland, 1992.

Benn, Stanley. "Wickedness." *Ethics* 95 (1985): 795–810.

Berlin, Isaiah. *Four Essays on Liberty*. Oxford: Oxford University Press, 1969.

——. *Concepts and Categories*, edited by Henry Hardy. London: Hogarth, 1978.

Blum, Lawrence A. *Friendship, Altruism, and Morality*. London: Routledge, 1980.

——. *Moral Perception and Particularity*. New York: Cambridge University Press, 1994.

Charvet, John. *A Critique of Freedom and Equality*. Cambridge: Cambridge University Press, 1981.

Christman, John, ed. *The Inner Citadel*. New York: Oxford University Press, 1992.

Cohen, Gerald A. *If You're an Egalitarian, How Come You're So Rich?* Cambridge: Harvard University Press, 2000.

Cranston, Maurice. "Liberalism." In *Encyclopedia of Philosophy*, edited by Paul Edwards. New York: Macmillan, 1967.

——. "Toleration." In *Encyclopedia of Philosophy*, edited by Paul Edwards. New York: Macmillan, 1967.

Devlin, Patrick. *The Enforcement of Morals*. London: Oxford University Press, 1968.
Dworkin, Gerald. *The Theory and Practice of Autonomy*. Cambridge: Cambridge University Press, 1988.
———. "Autonomy." In *A Companion to Contemporary Political Philosophy*, edited by Robert E. Goodin and Phillip Pettit. Oxford: Blackwell, 1993.
Dworkin, Ronald. *Taking Rights Seriously*. Cambridge: Harvard University Press, 1977.
———. "In Defense of Equality." *Social Philosophy and Policy* 1 (1983): 24–40.
———. *A Matter of Principle*. Cambridge: Harvard University Press, 1985.
———. *Sovereign Virtue: The Theory and Practice of Equality*. Cambridge: Harvard University Press, 2000.
———. "Equality—An Exchange." *TLS*, December 1, 2000.
Feinberg, Joel. "Justice and Personal Desert." In *Nomos VI: Justice*. New York: Atherton Press, 1963.
———. *Social Philosophy*. Englewood Cliffs, N.J.: Prentice-Hall, 1973.
Flathman, Richard E. *Toward a Liberalism*. Ithaca: Cornell University Press, 1989.
———. "Liberalism." In *Encyclopedia of Ethics*, 2d edition, edited by Lawrence C. Becker and Charlotte B. Becker. New York: Routledge, 2001.
Flew, Antony. *The Politics of Procrustes*. Buffalo: Prometheus Books, 1981.
Frankfurt, Harry G. *The Importance of What We Care About*. New York: Cambridge University Press, 1988.
———. *Necessity, Volition, and Love*. New York: Cambridge University Press, 1999.
Frohlich, Norman, and Joseph Oppenheimer. *Choosing Justice: An Experimental Approach to Ethical Theory*. Berkeley: University of California Press, 1992.
Galston, William A. *Justice and the Human Good*. Chicago: University of Chicago Press, 1980.
Gauthier, David. *Morals by Agreement*. Oxford: Clarendon Press, 1986.
George, Robert P. *Making Men Moral*. Oxford: Clarendon Press, 1993.
Glover, Jonathan. *Humanity: A Moral History of the Twentieth Century*. New Haven: Yale University Press, 2000.
Habermas, Jürgen. *The Theory of Communicative Action*. 2 vols. Translated by Thomas McCarthy. Boston: Beacon Press, 1984, 1987.
Hampshire, Stuart. *Innocence and Experience*. London: Allen Lane, 1989.
———. *Justice Is Conflict*. Princeton: Princeton University Press, 2000.
Hare, Richard M. *Freedom and Reason*. Oxford: Clarendon Press, 1963.
———. *Moral Thinking*. Oxford: Clarendon Press, 1981.
Hart, Herbert L. A. *The Morality of the Criminal Law*. London: Oxford University Press, 1965.
———. "Social Solidarity and the Enforcement of Morality." *University of Chicago Law Review* 55 (1967): 1–13.
Haworth, Lawrence. *Autonomy*. New Haven: Yale University Press, 1986.
Hayek, Friedrich A. *The Constitution of Liberty*. Chicago: University of Chicago Press, 1960.

———. *The Mirage of Social Justice.* Chicago: University of Chicago Press, 1976.

Hill, Thomas E., Jr. *Respect, Pluralism, and Justice.* New York: Oxford University Press, 2000.

Hofstadter, Albert. *Reflections on Evil.* Lawrence: University Press of Kansas, 1973.

Hughes, Graham. "Morals and the Criminal Law." *Yale Law Journal* 71 (1961–62): 662–83.

Hume, David. *A Treatise of Human Nature.* Oxford: Clarendon Press, 1960.

Kant, Immanuel. *Religion within the Bounds of Reason Alone.* Translated by Theodore M. Greene and Hoyt H. Hudson. New York: Harper & Row, 1960.

Kekes, John. *The Morality of Pluralism.* Princeton: Princeton University Press, 1993.

———. *Against Liberalism.* Ithaca: Cornell University Press, 1997.

———. *A Case for Conservatism.* Ithaca: Cornell University Press, 1998.

Keynes, John Maynard. *Two Memoirs.* New York: Augustus M. Kelley, 1949.

Korsgaard, Christine M. *Creating the Kingdom of Ends.* Cambridge: Cambridge University Press, 1996.

Kymlicka, Will. *Liberalism, Community, and Culture.* Oxford: Clarendon Press, 1989.

———. *Contemporary Political Philosophy.* Oxford: Clarendon Press, 1990.

Larmore, Charles. *Patterns of Moral Complexity.* New York: Cambridge University Press, 1987.

Lee, Simon. *Law and Morals.* Oxford: Oxford University Press, 1986.

Lucas, J. R. "Against Equality." *Philosophy* 40 (1965): 296–307.

———. "Against Equality Again." *Philosophy* 42 (1967): 255–80.

MacIntyre, Alasdair. *After Virtue.* Notre Dame: University of Notre Dame Press, 1984.

Matson, Wallace. "What Rawls Calls Justice." *Occasional Review* 89 (1978): 45–57.

———. "Justice: A Funeral Oration." *Social Philosophy and Policy* 1 (1983): 94–113.

Mendus, Susan. "Toleration." In *Encyclopedia of Ethics* 2d edition, edited by Lawrence C. Becker and Charlotte B. Becker. New York: Routledge, 2001.

Mill, John Stuart. *On Liberty.* Indianapolis: Hackett, 1978.

———. *Utilitarianism.* Indianapolis: Hackett, 1979.

———. *The Subjection of Women.* Arlington Heights, Ill.: AHM Publishing, 1980.

Miller, David. *Social Justice.* Oxford: Clarendon Press, 1976.

———. *Principles of Social Justice.* Cambridge: Harvard University Press, 1999.

Mitchell, Basil. *Law, Morality, and Religion in a Secular Society.* Oxford: Oxford University Press, 1968.

Moon, J. Donald. *Constructing Community.* Princeton: Princeton University Press, 1993.

Moore, Margaret. *Foundations of Liberalism.* Oxford: Clarendon Press, 1993.

Mossman, Elliott, ed. and trans. *The Correspondence of Boris Pasternak and Olga Friedenberg, 1910–1954.* New York: Harcourt, 1982.

Nagel, Thomas. *Mortal Questions*. Cambridge: Cambridge University Press, 1979.

——. *The View from Nowhere*. New York: Oxford University Press, 1986.

——. "Moral Conflict and Political Legitimacy." *Philosophy and Public Affairs* 16 (1987): 215–40.

——. *Equality and Partiality*. New York: Oxford University Press, 1991.

Narveson, Jan. *Respecting Persons in Theory and Practice*. Lanham, Md.: Rowman & Littlefield, 2002.

Nozick, Robert. *Anarchy, State, and Utopia*. New York: Basic Books, 1974.

Nussbaum, Martha. "Aristotelian Social Democracy." In *Liberalism and the Good*, edited by R. Bruce Douglass, Gerald, M. Mara, and Henry S. Richardson. New York: Routledge, 1990.

——. *Upheavals of Thought*. Cambridge: Cambridge University Press, 2001.

Oakeshott, Michael. *Rationalism in Politics*. Edited by Timothy Fuller. Indianapolis: Liberty Press, 1991.

O'Hagan, Timothy. *Rousseau*. London: Routledge, 1999.

Pojman, Louis. "A Critique of Contemporary Egalitarianism." *Faith and Philosophy* 8 (1991): 481–504.

Popper, Karl R. *The Open Society and Its Enemies*. London: Routledge, 1945.

Rawls, John. *A Theory of Justice*. Cambridge: Harvard University Press, 1971.

——. *Political Liberalism*. New York: Columbia University Press, 1993.

——. *The Law of Peoples*. Cambridge: Harvard University Press, 1999.

Raz, Joseph. *The Morality of Freedom*. Oxford: Clarendon Press, 1986.

Rousseau, Jean-Jacques. *Letter to Beaumont*. In *Oeuvres complètes*, 5 vols. Paris: Gallimard, 1959–95.

Ryan, Alan. "Liberalism." In *A Companion to Contemporary Political Philosophy*, edited by Robert E. Goodin and Phillip Pettit. Oxford: Blackwell, 1993.

Scanlon, Thomas M. *What We Owe to Each Other*. Cambridge: Harvard University Press, 1998.

Sen, Amartya. *Inequality Reexamined*. Cambridge: Harvard University Press, 1992.

Sher, George. *Desert*. Princeton: Princeton University Press, 1987.

——. *Beyond Neutrality*. Cambridge: Cambridge University Press, 1997.

Shils, Edward. *The Virtue of Civility*. Edited by Steven Grosby. Indianapolis: Liberty Press, 1997.

Shklar, Judith. *Liberalism and the Moral Life*. Edited by Nancy Rosenbaum. Cambridge: Harvard University Press, 1989.

Singer, Peter. *Practical Ethics*. 2d edition. Cambridge: Cambridge University Press, 1993.

——. *Writings on an Ethical Life*. New York: HarperCollins, 2000.

Slote, Michael. *Morals from Motives*. New York: Oxford University Press, 2001.

Temkin, Larry. *Inequality*. Oxford: Oxford University Press, 1993.

Thomas, Laurence. *Living Morally*. Philadelphia: Temple University Press, 1989.

Vlastos, Gregory. "Justice and Equality." In *Social Justice*, edited by Richard B. Brandt. Englewood Cliffs, N.J.: Prentice-Hall, 1962.

Waldron, Jeremy. "The Theoretical Foundations of Liberalism." *Philosophical Quarterly* 37 (1987): 127–50.

Watson, Gary. "Responsibility and the Limits of Evil." In *Responsibility, Character, and the Emotions,* edited by Ferdinand Schoeman. Cambridge: Cambridge University Press, 1987.

Wetterau, Bruce. *Desk Reference on the Federal Budget.* Washington, D.C.: Congressional Quarterly, 1998.

Williams, Bernard. "Philosophy as a Humanistic Discipline." *Philosophy* 75 (2000): 477–96.

Wolf, Susan. "Asymmetrical Freedom." In *Moral Responsibility,* edited by John M. Fischer. Ithaca: Cornell University Press, 1986.

———. *Freedom within Reason.* New York: Oxford University Press, 1991.

Wollheim, Richard. "Crime, Sin, and Mr. Justice Devlin." *Encounter* (November 1959): 34–40.

Index